Problems of Cooperation for Development

Problems of Cooperation for Development

Gerald M. Meier
Professor of International Economics
Stanford University

New York
OXFORD UNIVERSITY PRESS
London   1974   Toronto

For all four

Preface

This book explores the ways by which governments, international organizations, and multinational enterprises can cooperate in reorienting development strategy toward more effective "outward-looking policies" and policies of "redistribution through growth." The potential is examined in the three policy-areas of foreign aid, private overseas investment, and international trade.

Aid, investment, and trade—these are still the dominant problems in the relationship between rich and poor countries. But the international community must find new forms of cooperation to ease these problems. Disenchantment with aid, the prominence of the multinational corporation in foreign investment, and the issues of export-substitution are casting a new light on the old problems. The approach to the Policy Problems in this book is therefore from the standpoint of new strategies of aid diplomacy (Problem I), resources diplomacy (Problem II), and commercial diplomacy (Problem III).

This is the third of three volumes on problems in international political economy, and is designed as a self-contained study of international development problems. It is also the culmination of the first volume on trade policy and the second volume on international monetary policy.[1]

* * * * *

1. Volume one is *Problems of Trade Policy* (1973); volume two is *Problems of a World Monetary Order* (1974).

I have written this book with the same purposes in mind that I expressed in the first volume's introductory words to the student:

From a study of the policy problems in this book I want you to appreciate that economics is still concerned with social betterment; that economic problems cannot be solved in a political vacuum; that qualitative appraisals may be as important as quantitative calculations; and that in public policy formulation, the formal economic principle must usually give way at some point to a value judgment.

These problems do not allow a technocratic approach to policy-making. On the contrary, they emphasize that most policy problems have no natural boundaries and that decision-making is an art as well as a science. Long ago, Keynes observed economics does not constitute a body of knowledge immediately applicable to policy. Notwithstanding all the advances in the "science" of decision-making, few—if any—economists would yet deny Keynes's dictum. And all who have experienced the complexities of actual decision-making in international economic affairs will appreciate that technical analysis must sooner or later yield to judgment—or to the qualities of imagination and intuition which Keynes believed to be as much a part of economics as logic and fact.

A word on organization. This book begins with a general background to the problems of international inequality and development that should be relevant for each Policy Problem. The materials for each Policy Problem are then set forth in a way that I thought would best reveal the sequence of events and the execution of policy decisions. I have tried to unfold the "biography" of each policy situation by presenting an analytical narrative and a set of source materials, so that you might gain a sense of the crucial issues in each situation, the types of international conflict involved, and the modes of resolution and cooperation effected. This normally involves placing the problem in its larger context (Section A), followed by the development of the factual situation and the presentation of the actual decision (Section B). To allow you to discover the major policy issues in the problem, I have tried to use to advantage, documents, reports, and other source materials—while providing continuity with a narrative. Some "seasoning" has been added by giving the observations of actors, observers, or commentators of the time. Finally, I have provided some questions designed to aid you in analyzing and evaluating the specific policy decisions (Section C), and suggestions for additional readings (Section D).

This method of presenting Policy Problems is intended to encourage your own thinking about these problems. While materials are offered to illuminate the particular Policy Problem, it is up to you to identify and analyze the major issues; and you must be prepared to adopt and defend your own policy position with respect to the problem's resolution. You need not worry about a "correct" answer to the problem, but you should be very much concerned about the quality of the reasoning behind your own answer—about the "why" of your conclusion. Your specific recommendations are not as important as your understanding of the complexity of the Policy Problem and your clarity on criteria for judging the merits of alternatives. Each problem has two objectives: to extend your capacity to evaluate the quality of public policy-making and to suggest ways of improving the process in international economic affairs.

In considering each problem, you will therefore have to exercise your own judgment on a set of questions: What were the crucial policy issues in the problem? How were they resolved? Would another course of action have been preferable? What do you now conclude about the desirable future course of action?

* * * * *

Mrs. Kay Agnew and David Depue generously provided invaluable assistance. Grateful acknowledgment is also made to the Center for Research in International Studies at Stanford University and to the International Legal Center for course development and research support. Above all, I am again indebted to my students at Stanford for enduring early drafts of these Policy Problems, and for stimulating their final revision.

February 1974 G.M.M.
Stanford, California

Contents

Problems of Cooperation
for Development

Background:
International Poverty
and Development Policy

1. REORIENTATION OF DEVELOPMENT POLICY

New policy measures in support of economic development are now very much a matter of international debate. The Policy Problems in this book ask whether the rules of conduct embodied over the past quarter-century in the Bretton Woods system should now be modified and new policy options offered to the less-developed countries (LDCs). Should there be a new boldness in foreign aid programs? New approaches to private foreign investment? More favorable treatment for exports from LDCs?

The world economy has been undergoing a process of international economic integration for more than four centuries, but only in the last quarter-century has the international community recognized the special problems of the poor countries. This post-World War II era has also been distinguished from earlier periods by the emergence of a number of genuinely international economic institutions—the IMF, IBRD, GATT, OECD, FAO, UNCTAD, and UNIDO, among others.[1]

1. In order: the International Monetary Fund (IMF), International Bank for Reconstruction and Development (IBRD or World Bank), General Agreement on Tariffs and

Although the concerted effort to accelerate economic development is a new phenomenon—almost an international novelty (the 1970's constitute only the "Second Development Decade")—nonetheless, disenchantment and disillusionment have already set in. Few of the poor countries have been able to achieve the major objectives of their development plans: a rapid increase in per capita income, a high level of employment, a reduction of inequalities in income distribution, the avoidance of marked disparities in the growth of different regions within the country. On the contrary, the amount of unemployment has increased; the distribution of income has become more unequal in many countries; and there has been a growing schism between the traditional rural sector and the modern urban industrial sector.

The number of success stories is indeed small. At the same time, the appeal for an expanded program of foreign economic assistance receives an unfavorable reception in the rich countries: aid has become a wearisome topic. And yet the problems of international poverty will not disappear; the challenge of social and economic betterment for "one hundred nations and two billion people" will persist.

In discussing this challenge, the President of the World Bank has emphasized that "the state of development in most of the developing world today is unacceptable—and growing more so." [2] It is a disconcerting fact that the rate of growth in per capita real product was about 3.8 per cent for developed market economies during the 1960's (compared with about 2.4 per cent during the 1950's), but below 2 per cent a year for the LDCs during the 1960's (compared with about 2.4 per cent a year in the 1950's). Even worse, in the poorest countries, with 67 per cent of the population in the developing countries, per capita income grew at only 1.5 per cent annually during the

Trade (GATT), Organization for Economic Cooperation and Development (OECD), Food and Agriculture Organization (FAO), United Nations Conference on Trade and Development (UNCTAD), United Nations Industrial Development Organization (UNIDO).

2. Robert S. McNamara, Address to the United Nations Conference on Trade and Development, Santiago, April 14, 1972. For a statistical review, see this Address and also *United Nations Yearbook of National Accounts*, annual.

1960's. The absolute gap in per capita income has accordingly widened. Even if the LDCs were to enjoy a much higher rate of growth in per capita income than the rate in the rich countries, the gap in absolute levels of per capita income would still tend to widen—unless the LDCs were to have an incredibly high rate of growth. In actuality, the annual growth of per capita income at the beginning of the 1970's was less than 2 per cent in Latin America, only about 2 per cent in East Asia, merely 1 per cent in Africa, and only about one-half per cent in South Asia. At these rates, the doubling of per capita income in East Asia would require nearly 35 years, in Latin America more than 40 years, in Africa almost 70 years, and in South Asia, nearly a century and a half.

Of even more concern than the "widening gap" between rich and poor countries—the relative poverty—is the absolute poverty suffered by hundreds of millions in the developing countries—a condition of life that denies its victims basic human necessities. Again, in the words of the President of the World Bank:

"Despite a decade of unprecedented increase in the gross national product of the developing countries, the poorest segments of the population have received relatively little benefit. Nearly 800 million individuals—40 per cent out of a total of two billion—survive on incomes estimated (in U.S. purchasing power) at 30 cents a day in conditions of malnutrition, illiteracy, and squalor. They are suffering poverty in the absolute sense.

"Although the collection of statistics on income distribution in the developing world is a relatively recent effort, and is still quite incomplete, the data point to what is happening. Among 40 developing countries for which data are available, the upper 20 per cent of the population received 55 per cent of national income in the typical country, while the lowest 20 per cent of the population receives 5 per cent. That is a very severe degree of inequality—considerably greater than in most of the advanced countries." [3]

As we analyze the problems in this book, we must be mind-

3. Robert S. McNamara, Address to the Board of Governors, Nairobi, September 24, 1973, p. 10.

ful of the impact of international policies on this increasingly acute problem of the domestic distribution of income. Issues of distributive justice and equity are inherent in the development process; and even though questions regarding distribution are not always asked explicitly, they are nonetheless being answered in reality. In cooperating for development, national governments and international institutions will in the future have to show explicit concern for a more equitable distribution of the benefits of development policy.

Given that the desired rate of development has been rarely achieved, and that absolute poverty persists, there is need for a world-wide reappraisal of postwar development experience. A major part of this reappraisal must center upon the interdependence between international capital movements, international trade, and development programs—and the policy implications for aid reform, investment reform, and trade reform. The Policy Problems in this book examine some of these implications by asking: How can the quality of the aid relationship be improved? How can managerial and technical knowledge be more effectively transferred to poor countries? How can trading relationships between poor and rich countries contribute more to development?

2. REFORM OF INTERNATIONAL INSTITUTIONS

These problem-areas overlap. Instead of the ad hoc and piece-meal policy-making of the past, new approaches are sought for joint policy integration by the developed countries, less-developed countries, and international organizations alike. The problems raise policy issues that entail for the postwar group of international economic institutions either adaptation to their changing environment and the new demands being made upon them, or a more radical change in the whole framework of international economic organizations.

Following World War II, the IBRD, IMF, and GATT were established to provide a more adequate framework for a liberalized trade and payments system in an expanding world economy. While the World Bank was designed to provide official development assistance, the IMF was intended to repair the prewar disintegration of the international monetary system, and GATT was expected to reverse the protectionist and discriminatory trade practices that had multiplied during the depression years of the 1930's.

The World Bank initially, however, was more concerned with postwar reconstruction of Western Europe than with the development of the newly emergent countries of Africa and Asia. The amount of assistance that the Bank in its early years of operation could offer to the LDCs was modest in total and supplied on commercial terms. While the amount has subsequently increased, and terms have been "softened," nonetheless the LDCs still complain that the amount of assistance is inadequate; the Bank remains too conservative and cautious in its operations; loans are made mainly for specific projects rather than development programs; inadequate support is given to social investment in education, housing, health; the International Development Association (IDA), the "soft loan" affiliate of the Bank, lacks sufficient financial support; and the "least developed" countries that are most in need of aid have been the most neglected. The LDCs have persistently sought a quantitative increase and qualitative changes in the Bank's program.

In their conception, the IMF and GATT were designed mainly to meet the monetary and trade problems of the advanced industrial countries. To an ever increasing extent during the postwar period, the problems raised by the emergence of newly developing countries have been superimposed upon the Fund and GATT. Both institutions have made efforts to adapt to the new set of development problems, but the LDCs remain unsatisfied and economic development lags.

Developing countries contend that the Fund does not provide sufficient international liquidity, is concerned more with the international monetary problems of the major industrial nations than with those of the poor primary-producing countries, and is too orthodox in its advocacy of domestic stabilization programs at the expense of economic growth in the LDCs. These complaints have culminated recently in the insistence that international monetary reform be linked to development assistance through the creation of additional Special Drawing Rights that would initially be allocated to the LDCs.[4]

Nations in UNCTAD also claim that GATT imposes too heavy a burden of commitments on the poor countries. GATT, it is said, has exercised more of a negative role in preventing discrimination than a positive role in permitting or promoting the kind of compensatory discrimination to which the LDCs feel entitled—usually called preferences. A particular grievance is that the liberalization of trade achieved by GATT has been mainly to the advantage of the industrial countries, and perhaps even at the expense of the developing countries. It is argued that GATT has not benefited the LDCs because it is based on the "classic concept that the free play of international economic forces by itself leads to the optimum expansion of trade and the most efficient utilization of the world's productive resources; rules and principles are therefore established to guarantee this free play . . . The free play concept is admissible in relations between countries that are strictly similar, but not between those whose structures are altogether different as are those of the industrially advanced and the developing countries."[5]

Once it is recognized that all nations are not equal and that the LDCs are in a special situation, then there is a need for "different attitudes from those prevailing in the past, and these attitudes should converge towards a new trade policy for development."[6]

UNCTAD demands extensive reforms in the system of international trading arrangements and international monetary arrangements in order to confer more benefits upon the developing countries. Integral to all the Policy Problems in this book is the question whether the solutions to these problems can best be accommodated within the existing international economic order, or whether new rules of conduct and new international economic institutions are necessary, either as advocated by UNCTAD or in some other form. In analyzing the

4. See G. M. Meier, *Problems of a World Monetary Order* (1974), pp. 224–35.

5. *Towards a New Trade Policy for Development*, Report by the Secretary-General of UNCTAD (Raúl Prebisch), United Nations, 1964, p. 27.

6. *Ibid.*, p. 107.

process of policy-making with respect to international development issues, we shall have to study international organizations not simply as the institutional context for these policy decisions, but more significantly in terms of the choice of public policies. And these policies run the gamut of the total international development effort—official development assistance, private overseas investment, and trading relationships. Recognizing the complaints of the LDCs, we shall have to give full attention to the various ways by which a reform of international economic institutions and a change in the "international rules of the game" might accelerate international development.

3. THE NEW ORTHODOXY OF DEVELOPMENT

There are fashions in development programming, and alternating periods of optimism and pessimism regarding development prospects. In the early postwar period when concerted attention was first given to the problems of emerging countries, development strategy focused on three essential ingredients: a comprehensive development plan, a strategy of industrialization via import substitution, and the receipt of foreign aid. The widespread conviction was that government must be the primary agent in producing economic modernization, and that developmental efforts must be coordinated within a national development plan. Given the criticisms of the price system, the intermixture of a desire for social reform along with development, and the character of the persistent and pervasive obstacles to development, it is understandable why central planning was more attractive to the governments of poor countries than was ever true in the historical experience of the presently economically advanced Western nations.

Governments of newly developing countries commonly turned to the adoption of a national development plan as if this were itself a precondition for development. But although the case for planning was *prima facie* strong, the experience with planning has been disappointing. While the formulation of development plans improved markedly with the experience of the second or third five-year plan, nonetheless the record of development planning reveals that the ability to implement a

domestic plan has not improved in step with the ability to
formulate a plan. Many development plans have met the tests
of a good plan on paper, only to fail in practice. The assessment is now widespread that comprehensive development
planning has been premature for most of the LDCs. For a variety of reasons, their plans have not met with practical implementation: among these reasons, we might cite the over-
reaching for the highest level of theory in preparing the
development plan, the undersupplying of the plan with
needed data, the underemphasizing of the pattern of sequen-
tial decision-making, and the overtaxing of administrative competence and managerial capacity.[7]

The import-substitution strategy has also proved costly.
Rarely has this actually succeeded in relaxing the foreign exchange constraint, easing the labor absorption problem, or
furthering industrialization by proceeding from the finishing
assembly-stage down through the intermediate and basic production processes. At the same time as import-substitution
policies have subsidized the urban industrial sector, they have
in effect imposed a penalty on agriculture and exports.[8]

Recognizing the limitations of the import-replacement strategy, UNCTAD I (Geneva, 1964) was notable for its admission
that import-substitution possibilities have become exhausted
and that export promotion must instead be emphasized. If a
comprehensive national development plan and import substitution were the main components of an inward-looking policy
of development, more reliance on the market mechanism and
export promotion are the essentials of the new emphasis on
outward-looking policies of development. Foreign aid is now
considered not simply as a means of filling the savings gap and
foreign exchange gap, but also as a means of underwriting
trade liberalization and policy reform measures.

After the strains that have been placed on the Bretton Woods

7. For a more extensive critique, see Albert Waterston, *Development Planning: Les-
sons of Experience* (1965); Benjamin Cohen and Gustav Ranis, *Government and Economic Development* (1971); M. Faber and Dudley Seers (eds.), *The Crisis in Planning:
The Issues and the Experience* (1972).

8. The limitations to import substitution are discussed further in Policy Problem
III, below.

system, the developed and less-developed countries alike are seeking the establishment of a new international economic order. As part of the new order, there must be attention to the "second-generation" problems of development—the realization of the potential of the green revolution and rural development, the promotion of industrialization via export substitution, and the reduction of unemployment by somehow enabling low-skilled surplus labor to become economically relevant in a world economy that ranges from preindustrial to postindustrial societies.

Outward-looking policies are normally advocated to secure the gains from trade, the intertemporal gains of export-led development, and the relaxation of the savings and foreign exchange constraints through the inflow of foreign capital. Although these objectives are worthy in their own right, it is now even more important that the outward-looking policies be shaped to the solution of the second-generation problems of development.

The Policy Problems in this book are therefore related to how cooperation in outward-looking policies by nations, international institutions, and multinational enterprises might contribute to the total international development effort. The first Policy Problem examines how official development assistance might be improved in quantity and quality. The second Problem considers how a recipient developing country might assess the benefits and costs of private foreign investment and adopt policies that might raise the social net benefit in the recipient country. The third Problem investigates how trade policy—namely, the granting of preferential treatment to developing countries—might secure a transfer of resources from rich to poor countries and ameliorate the labor absorption problem.

4. TRADE AND AID NEEDS

The foreign exchange bottleneck is a common element in all the Policy Problems. With high requirements for imports to support their development objectives, it is not surprising that LDCs have confronted a persistent shortage of foreign exchange. The foreign exchange constraint can be expressed in terms of balance of payments pressure, or a widening "trade gap," as in much of the UNCTAD literature. According to UNCTAD, the poor countries are faced with a potential "trade gap," the size of which has been estimated on various assumptions regarding world market prospects and domestic growth rates. As a reflection of the excess of the domestic use of resources over the domestic supply of resources, the "trade gap" includes the excess of projected imports of goods and services over the corresponding projection of export earnings plus the payments that must be made for interest, profits, and dividends falling due on past loans and investments. Even if the lowest of UNCTAD's projections of the trade gap are used, it is clear that the needs exceed the available resources, and that major policy adjustments will be necessary if the trade gap is to be filled. When import requirements exceed export potential, methods must be found for bridging the gap to make possible the assumed rates of development. If a developing country's demand for imports were uncontrolled, the value of its imported goods would exceed the level that it could support by export revenue alone. At the same time, the flow of foreign capital from developed countries to LDCs has leveled off and the external debt-servicing problem has intensified, as will be emphasized in Problem I. The import surplus supported by foreign capital has therefore fallen markedly in recent years, and the net transfer of resources beyond imports based on exports has become relatively insignificant for the majority of LDCs. If the foreign exchange constraint is not removed, and the LDC can not fulfill the import requirements of its development program, the LDC must then pursue policies that will relax the foreign exchange constraint by accomplishing one or a combination of the following: import replacement, export expansion, terms of trade improvement, a larger inflow of foreign capital—or else the LDC will be forced to abandon the primary objective and reduce its rate of development. As illustrated by the Policy Problems in this volume—whether it be by an increase in public foreign capital inflow, private foreign investment, or an expansion of exports of manufactures—the common objective is to relax the foreign exchange constraint so that the attainable rate of development might be higher, and absolute poverty diminished.

5. THE WIDER PROBLEMS

For their effective solution, the policy issues raised in this book should be treated as part of the wider problems of harmonization of policies between rich and poor countries, harmonization of policies among the poor countries themselves, and reform of international economic institutions.

An important influence on the future course of the LDCs is the fact that rich and poor countries now coexist, and the income differential between rich and poor countries is now greater than in earlier periods of Western development. The existence of advanced industrial societies ahead of them makes a number of important differences to the development prospects of the emergent societies when they embark on development. On the one side, the coexistence of rich and poor countries now has a number of drawbacks for the LDCs. A partial list might include such influences as the following: the advanced state of medical knowledge that can be borrowed from rich countries makes it possible now to reduce deaths cheaply and rapidly, without contributing to an equivalent reduction in births; the transfer of labor-saving technology to LDCs which is encouraged by attitudes toward modernization and the prestige of Western technology tends to aggravate the underutilization of labor in the LDCs; the knowledge of organizations and institutions that prevail in the advanced countries may be ill-adapted to the needs of LDCs—for example, the trade union structure may be inappropriate for conditions of labor surplus, or public expenditure on social welfare services developed in advanced industrial welfare states may be premature for LDCs, or large-scale business enterprises may be undesirable in lesser-developed economies.[9]

As Professor Simon Kuznets observes, "[I]t may well be that, despite the tremendous accumulation of material and social technology, the stock of innovations most suitable to the needs of the less developed countries is not too abundant. . . . [T]he material technology evolved in the developed countries may not supply the needed innovations. Nor is the social tech-

9. For a full discussion of the effects of the coexistence of rich and poor countries, see Paul P. Streeten, "The Frontiers of Development Studies: Some Issues of Development Policy," *Journal of Development Studies*, October 1967, pp. 2–24.

nology that evolved in the developed countries likely to provide models of institutions or arrangements suitable to the diverse institutional and population-size backgrounds of many less developed countries . . . [A] substantial economic advance in the less developed countries may require modifications in the available stock of material technology, and probably even greater innovations in political and social structure." [10]

On the other side, however, this coexistence may now make the problems of development less difficult for the emergent nations. Some advantages may accrue to presently poor countries from their position of being latecomers to development and being able to draw selectively upon some of the accumulated stock of knowledge in countries that have already developed. The very existence of advanced countries should also ease the development of poor countries by providing a flow of resources from the rich to the poor countries. Harmonization of policies between the rich and the poor countries will, however, be necessary if the difficult decisions that must be made to accelerate development are to be effectively realized.

International development problems also have to be mitigated by a lessening of competitive policies among the LDCs themselves. The attempts of many poor countries to develop simultaneously may intensify the task for any one of them: policies adopted by one developing country may hinder the development of another. For example, the poor countries compete among themselves in attempting to attract private capital and managerial services, in trying to foster industrialization by import-substitution policies, in imposing other restructive nationalistic policies that have "beggar-my-neighbor" (usually poor neighbor) effects, and in competing among themselves in their attempt to increase their exports. Not only are complementary efforts by poor and rich countries needed; so too should there be harmonization of policies among the poor countries themselves.

10. S. Kuznets, "Modern Economic Growth: Findings and Reflections," *American Economic Review*, June 1973, p. 256.

A more appropriate institutional mix is also necessary for problems of development. At present, GATT looks after commercial policy, while the World Bank is concerned with long-term lending, and the IMF concentrates on balance-of-payments problems and exchange rates. Yet these problems overlap, and the desirability of more cooperation by GATT, the Bank and the IMF is clearly warranted. Economic development problems cannot be so easily separated into the jurisdictions of these three international economic institutions. A joint consideration of foreign aid problems, foreign investment problems, and trade problems is often desirable.

In large part, the international saving-investment nexus is at the center of the international development process. But the world has yet to solve this problem. If domestic policy has finally become effective in coping with the saving-investment problem, the same is not yet true for international policy. Lagging exports and the discipline of the balance of payments have exercised under the gold-exchange standard a balance-of-payments drag on international expansion, just as lagging investment and the discipline of a balanced budget once exercised a fiscal drag on domestic expansion. In the decade of the Great Depression of the 1930's, we had to rid ourselves of misconceptions about "fiscal deficits"; now in the Second Development Decade we also have to do so for "balance of payments deficits"—especially when the "deficit" is for a reserve-currency country such as the United States. For accelerated development, more elasticity in the international monetary system may be necessary so that capital outflows and a deficit in the balance of payments of a reserve-currency country can be more readily tolerated.

The international saving-investment problem may also be eased by having the World Bank assume an expanded role in foreign assistance. Instead of bilateral aid, many would argue for an increase in the subscribed "capital" of the World Bank and its subsidiaries, and for the Bank's enlarging and liberalizing its lending activities in the fields of agriculture, industry, education, and the general support of development programs.

At the UNCTAD conferences, a major contention has been that GATT should grant more exceptions to the LDCs: special preferences should be allowed on their exports of semi-manufactures and manufactures; LDCs should be enabled to extend tariff preferences to each other without being bound to offer such preferences to other GATT members; they should not be required to bind their tariffs; and subsidies on their exports should be allowed. In advocating these changes in GATT rules, the LDCs are challenging the values of full reciprocity of bargaining and nondiscrimination when development is taken as a primary objective of international policy. GATT's new chapter on trade and development still does not squarely meet this issue. The challenge remains, and the rules of GATT, along with those of the IMF and World Bank, will continue under pressure as new standards of international conduct are advocated to meet the external needs of national development planning.

Perhaps the ultimate question is whether development plans can be fulfilled without the supportive existence of an international public sector. An advanced country's public sector has essentially three tasks: to maintain full employment, redistribute income, and provide remedies for market failure. But what is the international analogue? Where is the international deficit spending in the international system? The redistribution of income from rich to poor countries? The remedial policies that offset "disequalizing" market forces, or that correct for inappropriate transfers of goods, technology, and institutions from the rich countries?

In the last analysis, the diminution of absolute poverty and the narrowing of international inequality may have to depend on substitute arrangements for an international public sector. Whatever the specific content of these arrangements, they will require cooperation among the rich countries in transferring resources to poorer countries, cooperation between multinational corporations and host countries in raising the net benefit from foreign investment, and cooperation between rich and poor nations in facilitating outward-looking policies of development.

The following Policy Problems relate to the search for these new cooperative arrangements.

Problem I
Official Development Assistance: Reorienting Aid Strategy

A. THE CONTEXT

Economists should have by now written themselves out on the question of foreign aid. True, there is fatigue with foreign aid—but it has strangely not resulted in a diminution—but rather an increase—in the outpouring of literature on aid. If there has been disillusionment with previous assistance programs, there is still the hope for improved policies in the future. If, as the United Nations Committee for Development Planning states, the International Development Strategy remains "much more a wish than a policy," there are still proposals for new approaches to aid. Several group Reports have recently been issued, all seeking to identify the objectives and policy instruments for a more effective international assistance program.

This Policy Problem involves a critical assessment of these Reports. It asks how can the programs of official development assistance (ODA) be upgraded—in amount and in uses—so that their effect on development will be improved.

Answers may depend on such technical concepts and quantitative calculations as "the grant equivalent of a capital flow" or "statistical indicators of growth performance." But beyond

17

the economist's usual concern with foreign-exchange constraints, savings gaps, shadow prices, project feasibility studies, and the intricacies of decision analysis and programming
models—beyond all these technicalities lie moral considerations and political dimensions that are not captured in pure
economic analysis. "Development" is itself a value term, and a
country's development process has an inescapable political
quality. Economic, moral, and political considerations are all
intrinsic to the shaping of an assistance program—and, as is
common to most issues in international political economy, it is
this mixture which makes this Policy Problem complex.

1. THE MEANING OF "AID"

At the outset, it is necessary to be clear on what is meant by
"foreign aid." Aid has the effect of transferring real resources
from developed countries to the LDCs. The transfer occurs
through explicit capital movements or through nonmonetary
transfers of technical assistance. This Problem focuses on the
capital transfers, but it should be recognized that only a part of
the total capital flow to LDCs can be considered as "aid." To
qualify as "aid" the capital flow should meet two criteria: (1) it
should be offered on "concessional" terms, i.e., the rate of interest, amortization, and maturity on a loan should be "softer"
than the commercial terms of a normal market transaction; and
(2) the objective of the capital flow should be noncommercial,
devoted solely to the objective of the recipient country's development. "Pure aid" would therefore be a grant (no interest,
no repayment) to be used as the recipient wishes. In reality,
capital transfers include both official and private capital flows.
The private capital flow should not be considered as aid when
it represents a normal, commercial, market transaction. If the
official capital flow is a loan, only that part of the loan that is
concessional—i.e., the "grant equivalent"—should be considered as aid. If the official capital flow does have some commercial motivation (to promote exports), it should not be considered as aid; but it is difficult to strain out such motivations in
the aggregate statistics, and all official grants and loans are
conventionally included in statistics of the "aid program." Military aid is, however, conventionally excluded from measure-

ments of foreign aid flows. Also, this Problem gives no consideration to the disguised forms of aid—such as aid through a trade policy of tariff preferences (discussed in Problem III, below), or aid through international monetary reform.[1]

Thus, as stated in another study,[2] "the concept of foreign aid which we shall use, and which is increasingly accepted, will embrace official grants and concessional loans, in currency or in kind, which are broadly aimed at transferring resources from the DC's to the LDC's on developmental and/or income-distributional grounds. In adopting this definition, we note that: (1) the administrators of foreign aid programs may, and often will, claim that 'security,' 'commercial' and other such advantages will accrue to the donor country; and (2) a net balance-sheet of the true 'gain' or 'loss' to the LDC's *and* to the DC's, would involve a complex analysis extending not merely to military aid and private capital flows, but also to international trade and other aspects."

The face value of official capital flows does not denote the "real cost" of aid to the donor country—that is, the sacrifices made by the capital exporting country. This is because there is a return flow of amortization and interest payments on aid-loans, and some of the aid may be tied by requiring the recipient country to import from the aid-giving country. To approximate the real cost, the nominal flow of aid-loans must therefore first be converted to its "grant-equivalent." This procedure is explained in the next extract.

ALTERNATIVE MEASURES OF RESOURCE FLOWS *

How large is the financial contribution that rich countries make to poor ones? The question seems simple, but there is no single answer or, more exactly, the answer depends on the definition adopted.

In theory, the flow of financial resources can be defined in the following different ways:

* UNCTAD, *Costs and Benefits of Aid: An Empirical Analysis*, Report by John Pincus, TD/7/Supp. 10 (October 26, 1967), pp. 2–4.

1. See G. M. Meier, *Problems of a World Monetary Order* (1973), Problem III, section 3.

2. Jagdish N. Bhagwati, "Amount and Sharing of Aid," in *Assisting Developing Countries*, Overseas Development Council Studies, 1 (1972), p. 74.

a. gross, without subtracting return flows of interest, amortization, dividends, capital repayment and capital exports;

b. net, to subtract some or all of these items and reinvested earnings of foreign enterprises;

c. to include or exclude private investment;

d. in so-called "real cost" terms, designed to measure the sacrifices made by donors;

e. in "real benefit" terms, designed to measure the benefit to the recipient;

f. in balance-of-payments terms, designed to show the direct and indirect effects of flows of financial resources on the foreign exchange position of both exporters and importers of capital.

This analysis is concerned with items (d) and (e) in the foregoing list—real cost and real benefit. What is the meaning of "real costs" or "real benefits" in this connection? The real cost of capital flows for a capital exporter is the income he forgoes as a result of the outflow of capital in the light of alternative possible uses of the same funds. For a capital importer the real benefit is measured by the net increment in income made possible by investing the capital inflow received, as compared with making the same investment with capital from other sources. Both real costs and real benefits can be measured approximately using existing data sources, although precise estimates would require a more comprehensive research effort than has yet been undertaken.

In order to explain the method, it is necessary to introduce the concept of a grant equivalent as a method of measuring capital flows. It is clear that for many purposes it would be a mistake to give equal weight to each dollar of capital outflow. A grant of one dollar costs the donor more than a ten-year interest-free loan of the same amount. The loan, in turn, costs him more than a credit, payable in one year, bearing 6 per cent interest. Therefore, the problem is how to find a method that will give each form of capital outflow its appropriate weight.

The answer is found by referring to a table of annuity values. Banks, insurance companies and other financial institutions are often faced with the need to put a present valuation on future cash flows. For example, a customer might ask an insurance company how much he would have to pay today in order to be assured of an annuity income of $1,000 annually starting at age 60, twenty years from now, the income to continue for his normal life expectancy of twelve years thereafter. If the insurance company assumes that it can invest the customer's payment now at an interest rate of 5 per cent (over and above administrative costs, profits, etc.), then it can answer his question by referring to a table that shows the amount of money that one must invest today at 5 per cent return in order to produce the required sum of money from twenty to thirty-two years hence. Thus, to produce $1,000 twenty years from now it is necessary to invest $358.94 today at 5 per cent. Adding up this series of terms for the twelve-year period starting twenty years from now produces a sum amounting to $3,507.49. This is the sum of money that the customer would have to invest today at 5 per cent (excluding charges for the insurance company's costs and profits) in order to receive $1,000 per year for twelve years, starting twenty years from now and ending twelve years thereafter.

We can look at the same numbers a little differently and say that the present value of an annual income of $1,000 from 1987 to 1998 is $3,507.49, when discounted at an interest rate of 5 per cent. In other words, that future flow of income is worth $3,507.49 today.

The same analysis can be applied to the international flow of resources. Country A lends $1 million to country B at 3 per cent interest, to be repaid over twenty years in equal annual instalments, after an initial five-year grace period and annual payments of $67,215.71 for twenty years thereafter. What is the present value to the lender of this future flow of repayments? The answer depends on the rate at which the lender could invest the funds if they were not lent to country B. If the funds are raised by taxation, then the alternative is the long-term rate of safe return that private investors could earn, which is approximated in most capital-exporting countries by the going rate for real estate mortgages. If the rate were 3 per cent, the same rate as the actual loan, then the present value of the repayment flow would be $1 million. If the rate were higher, say, 6 per cent, then the present value of the repayment flow to the lender would be less than $1 million, because he could have invested the money at a 6 per cent return instead of a 3 per cent return. In the example cited here, the present value would be $702,487. In other words, with long-term domestic investments yielding 6 per cent, country A incurs a cost of $297,513 (equal to $1 million minus the present value of $702,487), when lending $1 million to country B at an interest rate of 3 per cent, repayable over twenty years with a five-year grace period.

This cost of $297,513 (amounting to nearly 30 per cent of the face value of the loan in this example) is called the "grant equivalent" of that particular loan, because it represents the present value of the foregone return on capital. It arises from the difference between market rates of return on investment (assuming that market rates reflect the social return to capital) and the lower return forthcoming from the actual loan made to country B. The grant equivalent will be a higher proportion of the face value of the loan, (a) as the market rate of interest diverges more from the interest rate of the loan; and (b) the longer the grace period and the amortization period.

If the market rate of interest is equal to the loan rate, then the present value equals the amount of the loan and the grant equivalent is zero. If the market rate of interest is lower than the loan rate, then the "subsidy" to the borrower is negative, from the lender's viewpoint.

There can, of course, be considerable range in the rate of discount selected (ideally, the marginal social rate of return for capital at equilibrium exchange rates), so that the resulting estimates of "adjusted" aid flows are imprecise. Notwithstanding this imprecision, a number of estimates made by different economists of the extent to which bilateral, official loan aid in the 1960's overstated the nominal figures indicate that nominal loan figures should be reduced by about 20 to 30 per cent of the nominal amounts. Further, the tying of aid reduces the real cost of aid to the donor because the excess cost of the imports from the tied source, as compared with cheaper sources of supply, represents an export subsidy which the recipient country pays to the donor country's exporters to secure the aid-financed contracts. Aid-tying saves the aid-giving country the costs of the export subsidy. Professor Bhagwati concludes that "the saving in the real cost of aid to the donor countries, arising from aid-tying by source, can thus be put down safely at a *minimum* of 10 per cent and is likely to be more in the range of 20–25 per cent of the total, bilateral aid flows.

"Thus, if we adjust for these two important factors of loans and aid-tying, we are left with the striking conclusion that no more than half of the nominal aid flows constitute a draft on the real resources of the donor countries." [3]

Similarly, the real worth of aid to the recipients is less than the nominal value to the extent that aid-tying reduces the real worth, and loans are less valuable than grants. The real worth is, however, not fully symmetrical with the real cost for a number of reasons, as explained below.

RECIPIENTS' BENEFIT APPROACH *

The same real-cost analysis for capital flows can be applied from the viewpoint of recipients' benefit. The values will normally di-

* UNCTAD, *Costs and Benefits of Aid: An Empirical Analysis*, Report by John Pincus, TD/7/Supp. 10 (October 26, 1967), pp. 26–27.

3. *Ibid.*, pp. 90–91.

verge from those shown under the donors' cost definition, for several reasons.

Firstly, the interest rate for discounting will usually be different in donor and recipient countries. The higher the long-term real rate of interest in the recipient country, the larger the grant equivalent of a loan. Thus, for the $1 million loan cited above, offered at an interest rate of 3 per cent for twenty years, with a five-year grace period and a donor's discount rate of 6 per cent, the donor's grant equivalent was $297,513. For a recipient who would have to pay 8 per cent in order to raise capital domestically, the grant equivalent of the same loan would be $437,780. Naturally, if the recipient's discount rate is lower than the donor's, the grant equivalent to recipients will be less than those to donors.

Secondly, in cases where foreign-exchange controls are practised, one appropriate rate for discounting is that which the recipient would have to pay on the international securities market, as measured for example by bond rates (including flotation costs) for countries that are able to float international market loans (for example, Mexico, Jamaica, Israel); or by the effective rates for suppliers' credit in other cases.

Thirdly, from the viewpoint of aid recipients, tied aid may reduce the grant equivalent of aid if the prices charged for goods by the supplier exceed the world price. Thus the calculation of effective rates of interest charged for suppliers' credits, as discussed in the preceding paragraph, should include an adjustment of effective interest rates to allow for the difference, if any, between suppliers' prices and world prices. The appropriate adjustment for over-pricing of tied aid is very difficult to calculate because of the differences in the quality and specifications of goods supplied by different exporters. Relatively accurate estimates of the costs of tied aid are possible only for standardized commodities such as agricultural products, raw materials, and semi-finished bulk goods. For many consumer goods, machinery and other forms of capital equipment, problems of non-comparability arise to impede the price comparisons. Despite the many difficulties that arise in estimating the excess costs to recipients involved in tied aid, some indications are available. One study of the costs of tied aid to Pakistan concluded that the aid actually received by that country in recent years could have been purchased for 12 per cent less if all aid were untied. It has been estimated that purchasing all United States aid-financed commodities in the United States resulted in a 17 per cent excess cost, as compared to world market prices, for the year of 1965.

A fourth difference between the donors' cost and recipients' benefit estimates concerns the "grant equivalent" of private investment. From the viewpoint of the national economy, the grant equivalent is the difference between the discounted value of foreign investors' future return on investment (where the percentage return on investment is used as the rate of discount) and the host country's own discount rate for capital. If the investor's rate of return is higher than the host country's borrowing rate for foreign capital of the same maturity, then the "grant equivalent" is negative.

In practice, the only way to measure foreign investors' discount rates of return on equity investment is to make three simplifying assumptions: (i) new investment will earn the same average rate of return as existing investment; (ii) future rates of return will be the same as current rates; (iii) foreign investors will reinvest depreciation allowances, so the income stream arising from the investment stream can be assumed to continue indefinitely.

This type of calculation necessarily abstracts from certain technical assistance and technology transfer elements inherent in much private investment, unless these accrue to the investor in the form of higher rates of return. Both of these effects (training and "know-how") add to the recipient's benefit and thus, in effect, raise his rate of discount and hence also the grant-equivalent ratio of each unit of private capital inflow. However, the practical difficulties of measurement are so great that it is best treated as a qualitative consideration.

It has been estimated that during the 1960's, the real worth of any nominal aid flows, on the average, was likely to have declined by 15 to 20 per cent due to aid-tying and by 20 to 25 per cent because of price increases on imports into the recipient countries.[4]

2. TERMS OF AID

Along with the quantum of official development assistance (ODA) the terms of aid are most important in determining the net flow of resources. The "harder" the terms of a loan, the less is the net flow of resources. This will, in turn, extend the time needed to transfer a given amount of resources for the development effort, and will also increase the amount of aid required to bring about the given amount of transfer of resources. This is illustrated in Figures 1 and 2. These figures compare the effects of making loans on different terms—ranging from the softest terms of the International Development Association (IDA), an affiliate of the World Bank, on through harder terms.

4. *Ibid.*, p. 92.

In particular, the following terms are compared to illustrate the approximate range of magnitudes involved:

1. IDA soft terms: interest free except for 0.75 per cent service charge, 50 years maturity, 10-year grace period before repayments of principal begin;

2. United States Agency for International Development (AID) minimum terms: 2½ per cent interest, 40 years maturity, 10-year grace period with 1 per cent interest;

3. AID medium terms: 3½ per cent interest, 20 years maturity, 8-year grace period;

4. World Bank (IBRD) hard terms: 5½ per cent interest, 13 years maturity, 3-year grace period.[5]

As Figure 1 shows, the net flow of resources will decline more rapidly, the harder are the terms of the loan. Even if the lending rate is maintained at a rate of $100 per annum, when the loan is made on hard terms the annual debt service charges exceed the $100 inflow after the eighth year.

Figure 2 illustrates how the gross quantum of aid must increase, as the terms harden, in order to maintain a given net flow of $100 per year. If there is still to be a net flow of $100 in the tenth year, there must be a gross flow of $109 in the tenth year on the softest IDA terms, and as much as $270 on the hard terms specified.

3. ALLOCATION OF AID

It would be convenient if a set of unambiguous criteria could be established for evaluating the allocation of aid among recipient countries. This is, however, seeking the unattainable when the objectives of an aid-allocation system are multiple and ill-defined. Perhaps the clearest approach to a set of criteria for increasing the effectiveness of aid has been based on the principle that the allocation system should provide an incentive to improved performance by the recipient. This idea of "incentive programming" based on performance criteria has been explained in these terms:

> Since the amount of aid required to achieve any given developmental objective depends largely on the use that a

5. At the end of 1973, the World Bank's typical loan was 20 to 25 years maturity with 7.25 per cent interest.

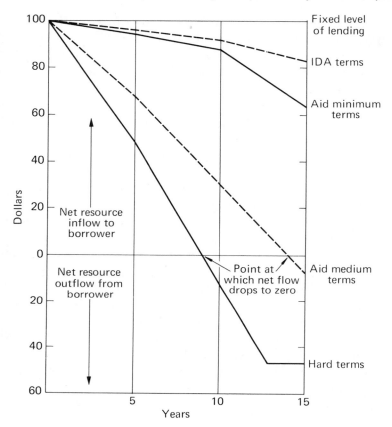

Fig. 1
Decline in net flow of resources if gross lending is maintained at a fixed level of $100 per year
(Harder terms mean less real impact for each dollar of assistance)

country makes of its added output, aid allocation should be designed to improve the indirect effects of growth and not concentrate only on the efficient use of aid-financed commodities. To vary aid with performance, it is necessary to carry out an overall analysis of the economy. . . .

The potential effects of an incentive programming system can only be determined after the major donors have made it clear that better performance will lead to more aid when it is warranted rather than to cutting down assistance . . . The control mechanism should be redesigned with the economic development of the recipient country as its primary objec-

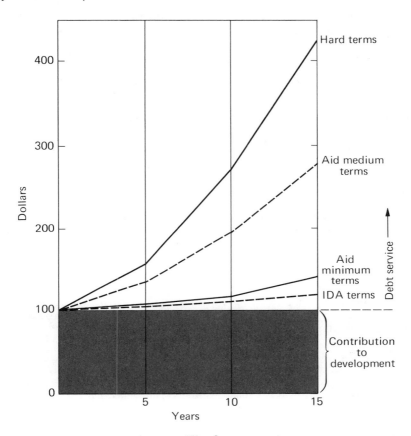

Fig. 2
Gross lending per year required to maintain an annual net flow of $100
(Harder terms mean that more aid is needed to do the same job)

tive. As information on performance improves, it should be possible to shift increasingly from project control to a programme type of control. . . .

With growing information, it should be possible to establish usable measures of savings, investment, and balance of payments performance that would provide an adequate basis for control. For example, a country which has been performing well—investing productively and saving 20–25 per cent of the resulting increase in national income—could be safely provided whatever assistance it needed to achieve growth rates of up to perhaps 7 per cent. So long as this performance was maintained, additional aid could only accelerate the rate of growth and reduce the total amount of assistance ultimately needed to attain self-sustaining growth.[6]

The United Sates AID program early acknowledged the principle of performance criteria when it proclaimed that "self-help" was to be the dominant theme of the United States assistance efforts. This was enunciated in the 1966 AID program, in the following terms.

EMPHASIS ON SELF-HELP *

Foreign assistance can add an important margin of resources and skills to the self-help efforts of other countries. But it cannot spare others the need to make the major effort themselves.

Self-help was formally made a criterion for aid in the Foreign Assistance Act of 1961. Since then, AID has led the way among free world donors in relating assistance to sound self-help measures.

At the simplest level, this means cost-sharing in any AID-assisted project, with the U.S. contribution of exports or American commodities related to the host government's carrying its share of local costs.

In Thailand in 1964, for example, the Thai Government contributed more to the cost of AID-assisted development projects than we did. AID's contribution for American exports and commodities totaled $6.9 million, and the Thais contributed the equivalent of $7 million for local costs: labor, materials, support services, and the like.

Performance in development, however, is more than a matter of sharing project costs. It involves every major aspect of a country's development effort: tax policies, budgeting, exchange controls, government actions that affect the climate for private initiative, the relative emphasis being given to agriculture, industry, education, health, and the like.

In countries to which the United States is giving substantial development assistance, self-help and the measurement of satisfactory performance is a complex matter. Overall country performance must be thoroughly reviewed and taken into account. In some instances, assistance agreements are entered into which contain specific provisions as to what an aid recipient will or will not do. For example:

* Agency for International Development, *Proposed Mutual Defense and Development Programs for FY 1966* (1965), pp. 6–7.

6. Hollis B. Chenery, "The Effectiveness of Foreign Assistance," in *International Co-operation in Aid*, edited by Ronald Robinson (1967), pp. 74–75.

Disbursement of a large program loan to a Latin American country was explicitly tied to action on measures to slow a sharp rise in living costs, including specific limits on government surpluses, reform of foreign exchange rate policy and fixed limits to the expansion of bank credit. The conditions were met and the loan was disbursed on schedule.

In an Asian country an increased commodity loan to finance essential U.S. imports for the private sector was linked to elimination of controls that slowed the import of needed raw materials, stifled private sector growth and invited corruption. The country removed import licensing requirements, introduced an excise tax to discourage speculation, and the loan was authorized.

The U.S. assistance program for another Latin American country was tied to performances on a stated series of reforms including reduction of the government's cash deficit, tax reform, tighter money control and the adoption of measures to eliminate operating deficits in public enterprises. U.S. assistance was to be released in stages, based on performance. On the basis of performance at the time, the bulk of the assistance was withheld.

In measuring self-help, AID is concerned with performance that directly affects economic growth and social development. Assistance is not tied to political conformity or the way a country chooses to vote in the United Nations.

But when countries divert their scarce resources into arms in order to mount political adventures against their neighbors, they waste substance badly needed for the welfare of their own people.

The United States cannot afford to provide major assistance to countries that choose to make their own development a minor concern.

The minimum appropriations requests for both fiscal years 1965 and 1966 reflect AID's determination to limit assistance to those making the best use of it.

An important element of this Problem is to determine to what extent the United States assistance program and the programs of other countries and multilateral agencies have followed "performance criteria" in their allocation systems. Many students of aid would contend that it is difficult to establish a significant correlation between variation in aid and performance.

The major progress in improving the quality of assistance has been in moving from overly narrow project appraisals to the more comprehensive program approach. Although a program will incorporate a set of projects, a development program is more than this, and even the single project cannot be evaluated independently of the program in which it is embedded. The need for a program approach is emphasized in the next extract.

COUNTRY AID PROGRAMMING *

Most donors now take their aid allocation decisions against the background of the overall development situation of the aid recipients rather than purely on an individual project basis. There are obviously considerable differences in the practices of various donors as regards the scope of the preparatory fact-finding and analysis and the specificity and firmness of the resultant planning. However, a country aid programme usually incorporates the following essential elements:

i. It is based on an assessment of the development situation, priorities and prospects of the recipient country as a whole.

ii. It is drawn up for the whole, or at least the essential part, of the aid activities of the donor in a given country.

iii. It includes some quantitative indications of the overall level of aid to be given and its broad sectoral composition.

iv. It places the aid activities of the donor in a longer perspective than one year.

The consideration of the whole of the various aid activities of a given donor in a given recipient country and especially the resultant integration of capital and technical assistance, is expected to contribute to the more effective use of aid. In donor countries where a number of agencies are involved, country programming may facilitate the necessary co-ordination among them and strengthen the hand of the central aid agency. Even within aid agencies, once the programme and administrative structures have reached a certain size and complexity, country aid programming is an important instrument to ensure internal co-ordination and consistency of policy.

The increased awareness of the overall development needs and problems at the level of individual developing countries can also provide useful feedback for the shaping of donors' overall aid policies, including such matters as the geographical distribution of aid, the relative emphasis on project and programme aid, sectoral specialisation and the need for local cost financing. Greater knowledge of developing countries' needs may perhaps even influence decisions on the aggregate level of aid. The studies underlying country programming may also provide useful information on problems and opportunities arising in the field of private capital flows, including export credits, and may point to constraints stemming from trade and other policies of donor countries.

It is important for several reasons that recipients have at least a general idea of the size and nature of aid they can expect from their main donors over several years in the future. The pluri-annual character of most donor country programmes has a special value for aid recipients. An unduly short time-horizon for the planning of development can lead to wrong decisions

* OECD, *Development Co-operation, 1973 Review*, Report by Edwin M. Martin (November 1973), pp. 55–56.

in the allocation of resources and inadequate approaches to long-term problems. The desire to achieve wide-spread results in too short a time often leads to a diffusion of resources. Deep-seated structural problems, such as those faced in agriculture and rural development, in education and vocational training, for example, can only be solved through patient and systematic approaches with long-term planning horizons. It is evident also that advance indications of future aid levels will facilitate investment planning and the spacing of development projects over time. Broad agreement between donors and recipient on the kind of projects that are to be financed will make possible and encourage more careful project preparation.

The ultimate goal of development assistance, even if each individual donor's aid is small in relation to total resources and needs, should be the promotion of the economic and social development of the country as a whole, rather than the construction of individual capital projects or the rendering of specific technical assistance services. The proper selection of sectors and projects is, therefore, at least as important for the effective use of resources as the detailed appraisal of individual projects. Country aid programming is precisely intended to help:

a. the donor identify those priority sectors and projects to which he can best make a contribution and which the recipient has not chosen to handle from other sources, and

b. the recipient identify those priority sectors and projects for which he wants help from that particular donor.

The country-framework should also make possible a better understanding of the institutional bottlenecks and thus provide a better basis for technical assistance, institution-building activities and policy advice.

A radically different approach to aid allocation was enunciated by the President of the World Bank in 1973. The emphasis was now to be given to the effects of aid on the distribution of income and the contribution of external assistance to a policy of "redistribution through growth."

REORIENTING DEVELOPMENT POLICY *

The need to reorient development policies in order to provide a more equitable distribution of the benefits of economic growth is beginning to be widely discussed. But very few countries have actually made serious moves in this direction. And I should stress that unless national governments redirect their policies toward better distribution, there is very little that inter-

* Address to the Board of Governors of the World Bank Group, by Robert S. McNamara (September 24, 1973), pp. 11–12.

national agencies such as the World Bank can do to accomplish this objective.

Without intruding into matters that are the proper concern of individual governments, I would like to discuss an important first step that could lead to a more rapid acceptance of the required policy changes. This step would be to redefine the objectives and measurement of development in more operational terms. While most countries have broadened the statements of their development goals to include references to reducing unemployment and increasing the income of the poor—as well as emphasizing traditional growth in output—they still measure progress toward these complex objectives with a single measuring rod: the growth of GNP.

But the fact is that we can no more measure the achievement of multiple development objectives by the GNP alone than we can describe the quality of life in a city exclusively by its size. The Gross National Product is an index of the total value of goods and services produced by an economy; it was never intended to be a measure of their distribution.

It is important to remember that indices of the increase in gross national product implicitly weight the growth of each income group according to its existing share of total national income. Since in the developing countries the upper 40% of the population typically receive 75% of all income, the growth of GNP is essentially an index of the welfare of these upper income groups. It is quite insensitive to what happens to the poorest 40%, who collectively receive only 10–15% of the total national income.

Were we to fashion a new index which gave at least the same weight to a 1% increase in the incomes of the poorest groups in society as it gave to a 1% increase in the incomes of the well-to-do, we would get a much different picture of development in the past decade. The growth of total income in several of the largest countries in Latin America and Asia, for example, would be significantly lower than the growth as measured by the GNP.

But, in a number of cases—including for instance, Sri Lanka and Colombia—the opposite would be true. In these countries, giving equal weight to the growth of income of each citizen, regardless of his income level, would result in a more accurate assessment of development performance than does GNP because it would give credit for some redistribution of the benefits of growth toward the lower income groups.

Adopting this kind of a socially oriented measure of economic performance would be an important step in the redesign of development policies. It would require governments, and their planning and finance ministries, to look at the allocation of resources in a much more comprehensive way. For they would have to consider not only the total output of an investment but also how the benefits would be distributed. This would give practical, operational significance to the rhetorical statements of social objects now embodied in most development plans. And it would insure that important questions of equity became an integral part of project evaluation procedures both within the developing countries and the lending agencies. We are, in fact, beginning to develop this approach in the World Bank.

This proposed reorientation of development strategy rests on a philosophy of aid quite different from statistical indicators of performance in the more conventional sense of growth and resource mobilization phenomena. If it dethrones GNP and looks to the quality of the development process, it raises at the same time some disconcerting questions about possible trade-offs between maximum current output and maximum employment, and between growth and more equitable distribution.[7] It also raises problems of how to incorporate distributional effects into benefit/cost analysis of a project.[8]

4. THE RECENT RECORD

After examining the performance of the "development partnership"—multilateral institutions, bilateral donors, and recipients—during the period 1967–72, the Chairman of the Development Assistance Committee (DAC) of the Organization for Economic Cooperation and Development (OECD) concluded:

"In a sentence, one might sum up the situation as one in which on the whole the overall donors' record has been poor with respect to the volume of aid, but good in improving its quality, while recipients have a good record on the volume of their growth, but a poor one with respect to its quality in terms of the impact on all elements of their populations." [9]

In the multilateral assistance program, a leading role has been assumed by the United Nations Development Program (UNDP) in the programing of technical cooperation and by the World Bank group. The expansion in the volume and geographical coverage of lending by the World Bank is summarized below.

7. Paul Streeten, *The Frontiers of Development Studies* (1972), chapter 19.
8. John H. Adler, "Development and Income Distribution," *Finance and Development* (September 1973), pp. 2–5.
9. OECD, *Development Co-operation, 1973 Review*, p. 121. The DAC comprises 16 advanced industrial nations of the OECD.

IBRD ACTIVITY *

This expansion on the part of the IBRD was largely financed by a rise in borrowings on the world capital markets from $1.5 billion in the 1966–68 period to $3.1 billion in that of 1970–72.

The marked increase in IDA lending depended largely on an increase in the resources made available to the Association from a level of $250 million a year in the first replenishment period 1964–67 to $400 million a year in the second replenishment period 1968–70, and to $800 million a year in the third replenishment period 1971–73. This continuing upward trend is reflected also in the recent decision by contributing members to recommend the fourth replenishment at the rate of $1.5 billion a year for the 3-year period 1974–76.

At the end of 1972, undisbursed funds were 34 per cent of total commitments outstanding while they were only 28 per cent at the end of 1968. In 1971 the Bank undertook a staff study of the reasons underlying the lengthening interval between IBRD commitments and disbursements since FY 1964, and in 1972 extended the study to cover IDA loans as well. The find-

Table I. Summary of Lending Operations by the World Bank Group, 1966/1968 and 1970/1972

$ *Million.*

		1966/1967–1967/1968 (Fiscal years)	1970/1971–1971/1972 (Fiscal years)
IBRD	Commitments	1,624	3,887
	Number of countries	50	53
	Disbursements	1,562	2,097
	Number of countries	61	64
IDA	Commitments	460	1,584
	Number of countries	22	47
	Disbursements	661	496
	Number of countries	34	50
IFC	Commitments	100	217
	Number of countries	18	23
	Disbursements	58	133
	Number of countries	24	30
Total	Commitments	2,184	5,688
	Number of countries	55	79
	Disbursements	2,281	2,726
	Number of countries	79	89

* OECD, *Development Co-operation, 1973 Review,* Report by Edwin M. Martin (November 1973), pp. 128–31.

ings of the study revealed that the problem resulted mainly from factors inherent in the changing pattern of the Bank's lending, e.g. the shift from developed to developing countries, changes in the sector composition of loans with more emphasis on projects such as education and water supply which tend to be slow disbursing; tighter policy against retroactive financing; and increases in the average size and complexity of projects.

There were no changes in the terms of IDA credits, but the interest rate on IBRD loans was increased in 1971 from 6 per cent in 1967 to 7¼ per cent. Programme loans increased as a percentage of total commitments from zero in 1970–72. Some increase in the use of funds to cover local costs was also permitted.

An analysis of trends in the geographical distribution of IBRD and IDA lending in the period 1970–72 as compared with 1966–68 shows that the emphasis of IBRD lending has continued to be on Central and South America, rising from 40 per cent in 1966–68 to 42 per cent in 1970–72. There was a shift away from Asia, the percentage declining from 39 per cent to 20 per cent, and a corresponding increase in loans to Europe from 10 per cent to 20 per cent. IDA lending focused mainly on Africa and Asia during both periods, but shifted slightly in 1970–72 away from the former in favour of the latter, the percentage to Africa declining from 36 per cent to 28 per cent, while the proportion going to Asia rose from 58 to 65 per cent.

More important over the long run than these changes were the steps taken in this period to diversify the purposes of lending away, though slowly, from a heavy concentration on the basic infrastructure needed to support GNP growth, largely in the modern sector, to a variety of sectors whose progress is now deemed essential to balanced development, thus reflecting the newer concepts of the Pearson Commission Report and the DD-II Strategy.

In this respect the major emphasis was on agriculture and education, the former rising from 12 per cent of total commitments in 1966–68 to 15 per cent in 1970–72, and the latter from 4 per cent to 5 per cent.

But it is also important to note that in this period the first loans were made for family planning, nutrition, scientific research, urban development, including housing, and tourism. Work was also started on projects for public health and for integrated rural development on a more specific basis than previously.

In the same spirit, staff provision has been made in recent years to ensure that appropriate attention can be directed to such special features of project appraisal as employment aspects and environmental effects.

Outside the lending field, there were several significant expansions of Bank activity and one important innovation. In 1967 there were 11 aid coordination groups sponsored by the Bank and 8 meetings of them took place that year. By 1972 the number had risen to 16 and 11 meetings were held.

The Bank now prepares economic reports on a much expanded basis, covering 60–70 countries each year. The frequency of these reports varies from annual to triennial, depending on the country: every country will be covered at least once every three years. Basic economic reports, taking a long-term perspective on development prospects and problems of the economy, are to be prepared for about 15 countries each year. Normally, one will be prepared for each country every five years or so.

The scope of country economic reports has been greatly broadened to include social development, as well as economic, aspects—e.g. employment, income distribution, population growth and education. Staff of other organisations in the UN system and outside consultants are often associated with the Bank's missions.

The performance of bilateral donors can be inferred from the next extract which summarizes the flow of official development assistance (ODA) from major countries.

BILATERAL DONORS *

Flow of Resources from DAC Countries

Looking at the ODA volume performance of DAC countries over the period 1967 to 1972, it appears that net disbursements, expressed in current US dollars, rose by 32 per cent. Increases were registered by all DAC countries, except Italy and the United States. However, the significance of these nominal increases as regards the real value of aid varies greatly, owing to price rises and variations in exchange rates. Since the GNP of all DAC countries combined rose by 63 per cent over the period, ODA disbursements expressed as a proportion of GNP fell from 0.42 per cent in 1967 to 0.34 per cent in 1972. It has remained approximately at that level since 1970, after an almost steady decline during the sixties.

This table gives rise to mixed feelings. It is encouraging to note that the majority of DAC countries increased—in some cases substantially—the share of their GNP devoted to official development assistance. In five countries (Belgium, Denmark, the Netherlands, Norway and Sweden) improved performance reflects policy decisions taken in the late sixties to set aid volume targets expressed in terms of national accounts aggregates, accompanied by medium-term plans for aid appropriations, and calling for substantial increases in aid flows. According to the present plans, aid appropriations are to be increased:

—by Belgium to 0.7 per cent of GNP in 1975;

—by Denmark to 0.66 per cent in 1977–78;

—by the Netherlands to at least 1 per cent of net national product (NNP), or 0.8 per cent of GNP, as regards ODA appropriations, and to 1.5 per cent of NNP in 1976 as regards gross aid appropriations;

* OECD, *Development Co-operation, 1973 Review*, Report by Edwin M. Martin, (November 1973), pp. 136–44.

Table II. ODA as a Percentage of GNP

Country	1967	1972
Australia	0.60	0.61
Austria	0.14	0.09
Belgium	0.45	0.55
Canada	0.32	0.47
Denmark	0.21	0.45
France	0.71	0.67
Germany	0.41	0.31
Italy	0.22	0.08
Japan	0.31	0.21
Netherlands	0.49	0.67
Norway	0.17	0.41
Portugal	0.54	1.91
Sweden	0.25	0.48
Switzerland	0.08	0.22
United Kingdom	0.44	0.40
United States	0.43	0.29
Total DAC countries	0.42	0.34

—by Norway to 1 per cent of GNP in 1978;
—by Sweden to 1 per cent of GNP in 1974–75.
These five countries together provided 10 per cent of DAC ODA in 1972 (5 per cent in 1967). Four of them (Belgium, Netherlands, Norway and Sweden) have accepted the 0.7 per cent of GNP target for ODA net disbursements for 1975.

Unfortunately, the largest country (United States) and some other relatively large ones (in particular Germany and Japan) let their assistance efforts, measured in percentage of GNP, decline and this brought the DAC average down.

Terms and Conditions of ODA

For DAC donors taken together the average terms of ODA remained unchanged between 1967 and 1972 at the high level of 84 per cent grant element. For individual donors, however, the five-year period witnessed significant changes. Austria, Germany and Italy showed a significant improvement in their financial terms between 1967 and 1972 whereas for the United States there was some hardening over this period.

The *untying* of development assistance is an issue which has particularly preoccupied the DAC and other international fora, especially UNCTAD, during the period under review; it also occupies a prominent place in the Strategy for the Second UN Development Decade. Preparations in the DAC for a General Agreement on Untying of multilateral contributions and bilateral development assistance loans were interrupted in the summer of 1971. Some Member countries, however, have taken a number of steps towards untying a larger proportion of their development assistance or allowing procurement in developing countries, and mitigating possibly harmful effects of tied aid.

In 1969, the United States authorized procurement with AID loans in all Latin American countries (except Cuba) and at the same time increased the permissible foreign content of commodities procured with its assistance. In 1970, these relaxations of regulations were extended to include most developing countries. Also in 1970, Canada decided that up to 20 per cent of its bilateral aid allocations could be used for either procurement in developing countries or to meet local costs. At the same time Canadian aid funds became available for shipping costs on non-Canadian vessels. Potentially more far-reaching were the decisions taken by Japan in late 1972 which, on the one hand, removed all legal obstacles to the extension of untied bilateral aid, and on the other, announced its readiness to allow procurement in developing countries for its official loans.

Other donors have either eliminated specific restrictions on some of their programmes (i.e. Germany: untied capital project aid and, since 1970, technical assistance equipment), or eased them (such as Australia's decision in 1972 to reduce the tied share of its contributions to some United Nations programmes).

Finally, most countries have gradually taken a number of technical measures, such as advance bidding, more extensive "shopping lists," internal competitive bidding, technical advice to importers, price and quality checks, and more liberal rules for subcontracting in third countries to mitigate the potentially harmful effects of tying.

In addition, the DAC, following the initiative of some of its Members, has recently sought to achieve progress on aid untying, pending the conclusion of a general agreement. At the High-Level Meeting on 18th and 19th October, DAC Member countries agreed that, consistent with existing general practices, they shall extend their official financial development assistance contributions pledged henceforth to multilateral institutions free for procurement at least in those countries that are members or associate members of those institutions or are recognised by the insitutions concerned as significant contributors. A majority of DAC countries declared themselves ready to join in an agreement on the untying of their bilateral development loans in favour of procurement in developing countries in accordance with agreed rules for determining eligibility to participate in procurement, hoping that other DAC countries would soon adhere to this agreement. The High-Level Meeting agreed that the DAC should pursue the issue of untying actively and should contribute to the preparation of texts, when necessary, to give effect to agreements reached among Member countries concerned on this issue.

Composition of ODA

The most striking change in the composition of DAC countries' ODA over the period was the rapid increase in their multilateral contributions. These rose as a proportion of their combined GNP from 0.05 per cent in 1967 to 0.08 per cent in 1972 and their share in total net ODA disbursements doubled.

In all but one country multilateral ODA contributions increased in current dollars over the period. In the case of two of the three countries where the share of multilateral ODA in the total declined, Norway and Sweden, these decreases reflect the modesty of their bilateral programmes in 1967 rather than a lack of growth since in both countries the share of GNP devoted to multilateral ODA increased substantially over the period.

The nature of the statistical data makes it difficult to quantify the changes in emphasis that have taken place in the *sectoral distribution* of DAC countries' ODA over the years 1967–72. There has been a growing awareness among all donors of the need to assist agriculture, and more recently of the necessity to alleviate the effects of unemployment, but this has not been reflected in the statistics. On the other hand, available data illustrate the rapid growth of population programmes during the period under review. In 1967, only two countries, Sweden and the United States, extended this type of assistance and their bilateral ODA disbursements totalled approximately $7 million. By 1972, more than half the DAC countries assisted population programmes through a variety of channels (bilateral, multilateral and through subsidies given to private organisations) and ODA disbursements were in the vicinity of $160 million. Although Sweden and in particular the United States—whose programmes increased ten-fold over the period to $125 million—continue to dominate this area, the resources devoted by the other DAC donors in 1972 exceed by far the combined efforts of 1967.

DAC countries' *food aid* (net disbursements) has fluctuated around the $1.2 billion level for most of the period and its share in total ODA has gradually declined to about 15 per cent in 1972. It has consistently played a significant part (about one-quarter of net ODA) in the programmes of two donors, Canada and the United States, who between them supply about three-quarters of it, and briefly in that of Japan. However, in the last three years of the period, the programmes of the EEC (to which five DAC countries contributed) have more than doubled and in 1972 overtook those of Canada. In the 1970's a tendency towards diversification in the composition of the commodities supplied became noticeable. Although wheat and wheat flour continue to be the largest single item, there has been an increase in the share of dairy products (in particular as concerns the EEC), and on the part of the United States in the importance of blended products such as CSM and WSB developed specifically to provide high-protein foods.

Geographic Distribution of ODA

It is not enough to make available an adequate amount of aid on sufficiently concessional terms to the economic sectors most important to the overall development of each country. In addition the resources provided must be distributed by donors among the developing countries in such a way as to contribute best to their progress, with some special attention to bringing the poorest among them up to minimum levels of living.

DAC data do not yet permit more than a tentative and limited analysis of how well donors have been doing in these respects over the past five years. Trend data are only available for 1969–72 and even for that period cannot be shown separately for the different types of aid such as food aid, technical assistance, programme aid, etc. Nor can any but the most general conclusions be drawn about progress in adjusting terms to the needs of the various groups of countries.

In addition, it must be kept in mind throughout that the data are in varying degrees incomplete because they focus on bilateral flows from DAC donors. The volume both from multilateral sources and from non-DAC bilateral sources is increasing and for some countries now provides a major portion of concessional aid. Therefore this analysis can only treat donor distribution policies with a broad brush.

Data in previous Reports in this series have made clear the wide difference in treatment accorded by most donors to recipients with which they have "Special Links, compared with that given to other countries." Subsequent analysis will therefore distinguish nearly always between these recipients and a group of 91 Selected Countries without "Special Links."

The data now available emphasise further how unique are the criteria used by donors in handling aid to these "Special Link" areas, and how little it has changed in recent years. For example, average per capita gross receipts from bilateral DAC donors were four times as great for "Special Link" recipients as for the others in 1969–1971, though the difference was much less for percentage of imports. Between 1969 and 1972, the preferential treatment of the "Special Link" group increased on all bases: by 1972, their receipts per capita were almost six times those of the countries without Special Links.

Within each of these two groups the point of greatest interest is how well recent United Nations injunctions to give preferential treatment to the poorest countries are being observed. Since there is still an inadequate growth in the total volume of aid, it is also important to know to what extent funds have been released, or are still available for release, by reducing flows to the richer and less needy developing countries in each group.

Between 1969 and 1972 the distribution of aid among the income groups of the 91 Selected Countries improved materially. On all three bases, per capita, percentage of GNP, and percentage of imports, the greatest increases were received by the least-developed countries, and declines were registered for each of the two highest income groups. This is encouraging.

There was no such pattern for "Special Link" recipients, disbursements to the low income group having not quite doubled and to the over $1,000 countries having more than doubled in this period.

At the other end of the scale of per capita incomes, from which one would hope to see funds transferred to the poorer countries as donor policies become better adjusted to needs, 1972 receipts of "Special Link" recipients with per capita incomes in excess of $600 increased by $261 million over the 1969 figure of $354 million, while for the 91 Selected Countries there was a decline of $70 million from a 1969 total of $408 million. It is clear where pressure must be applied to secure better treatment for the poorer countries.

Of increasing concern is the growing burden of debt that the developing countries must service. Publicly guaranteed debt of LDCs from all sources—DAC members, other countries and multilateral institutions—amounted to over $80 billion at the beginning of 1972, with annual debt service of approximately $7 billion. The composition of this debt now causes much consternation because the debt, and debt payments, are growing faster than the foreign exchange receipts required to service them. The less the net inflow of ODA, and the more restricted the export opportunities, the more will heavy debt-service obligations cause serious payments difficulties for some LDCs in the 1970's.

DEBT PROBLEMS OF DEVELOPING COUNTRIES *

One difficulty with looking at the *nominal* amount of debt is that it includes credits with greatly differing interest rates and repayment periods, ranging from hard commercial credits to soft IDA loans. One way for allowing for these differences is to calculate the *present value* of future debt service payments due. Using a 10 per cent discount rate, this gives the amount through the present payment of which the debtor country could eliminate its debt in one stroke. The assumption is that the creditor would accept the smaller payment now, instead of the larger sum due over time, because he could invest it at 10 per cent and obtain the same benefit as on the original debt service due. The present value of total debt outstanding at the end of 1971—$80 billion (disbursed)—amounts to around $50 billion.

The difference in softness of the various debt components also shows up when comparing their share in debt outstanding and debt service. Bilateral

* OECD, *Development Co-operation, 1973 Review,* Report by Edwin M. Martin (November 1973), pp. 67–68.

Table III. Debt of Developing Countries Disbursed and Outstanding at
End-1971 and Their Debt Service in 1971

	Debt Outstanding		Debt Service			
			Total		Interest	
	$ bill.	%	$ bill.	%	$ bill.	%
To DAC Countries	63.3	79	10.3	84	2.7	82
a) ODA	25.0	31	1.1	9	0.5	15
b) Export Credits	26.6	33	7.0	57	1.5	46
officially extended	6.2					
officially guaranteed						
private	19.2					
other private	1.2					
c) Other commercially oriented flows	11.7	15	2.2	18	0.7	21
To Multilateral Institutions	9.5	12	0.8	7	0.4	12
Concessional development assistance	2.3	3	0.0	0	0.0	0
Other development-oriented flows	7.2	9	0.8	7	0.4	12
To Communist Countries	5.8	7	0.7	6	0.1	3
To Other Countries	1.9	2	0.4	3	0.1	3
Total Medium and Long Term Debt	80.5	100	12.2	100	3.3	100

ODA of $25 billion owed to DAC Members constitutes 31 per cent of the total disbursed debt but accounts for only 9 per cent of the total debt service. In contrast, debt arising from official and private export credits accounts for one-third of the debt outstanding but for 57 per cent of the debt service.

These global figures are of course not very meaningful when it comes to assessing the impact on individual countries. One-half of the total debt outstanding (including undisbursed) is concentrated on only 10 countries: India, Brazil, Pakistan, Mexico, Indonesia, Iran, Argentina, South Korea, Yugoslavia and Turkey; another 12 countries account for one-half of the remaining debt: Chile, Spain, Israel, Colombia, Cuba, Greece, Liberia, Egypt, Algeria, Philippines, Peru and Venezuela. Each of these countries had total debt outstanding of over $1 billion. Taking the present value of debt outstanding would not alter the fact that debt is heavily concentrated geographically. However, the ranking of the countries listed above would change significantly: countries whose debt is composed mainly of hard lending would move up, e.g. Iran and Argentina.

How to reduce debt service difficulties in the future is another essential part of this Policy Problem's concern with improving the aid relationship. An improvement will depend on measures to increase the quantum of aid, improve the terms of aid, utilize more effective allocational criteria, and harmonize intergovernmental aid arrangements. After considering the following issues, what practical measures can be proposed for a reorientation of aid strategy?

B. THE ISSUES

5. RECIPIENT VIEWPOINT

The aid relationship will, of course, be viewed differently by aid-receiving and aid-giving countries, and by diverse interests within each country. Although a program that would be considered ideal from the viewpoint of the aid-receiving country is clearly not "practical politics," nonetheless it is important to ask whether current aid policy cannot at least be reoriented in the direction of the ideal rather than away from it.

AN IDEAL *

How should the poor countries be assisted in their struggle against poverty? One simple and perhaps most satisfying answer to the recipients would be to say that the poorer nations should be helped by the rich in the same way as the poor within the nation states were helped and are being helped in the industrially advanced countries. On the face of it, at any rate, such a proposition is likely to be accepted by many in the richer countries themselves. It may not be out of place, therefore, to begin by enquiring into the meaning and significance of the answer just given.

In the early years of the Industrial Revolution in the West, it was not uncommon to believe that poverty was, to a large extent, self-imposed so that charity was at best a mixed blessing. The Western

* I. G. Patel, "How To Give Aid—A Recipient's Point of View," in *International Co-operation in Aid*, edited by Ronald Robinson (1967), pp. 88–90.

world has moved away from such a rigid puritanic attitude for many decades now. It is now generally recognised among all modern states that the elimination of poverty is a national objective, that every citizen of a nation state has a right to a certain minimum of social and economic well-being which must be provided by the state and that the resources required for this purpose should be raised essentially by progressive taxation of the comparatively well-off sections of the community. "From each according to his ability, to each according to his needs" is not merely a distant goal but a goal perpetually striven for by democratic societies.

Translated in international terms, such an approach to foreign aid would imply, among other things, the following;

i. the starting point for determining the requirements of aid and its distribution will be the needs of the poorer countries as measured in relation to certain minimum standards of nutrition, health, education, employment opportunities and the like;

ii. the minimum needs as defined above may not be met immediately by transfer of real resources or purchasing power but would be sought to be satisfied in the shortest possible time. While internationally organised relief measures in the event of famines, epidemics and the like might be the first charge on international assistance, foreign aid proper will be deployed for increasing productivity and employment opportunities, priority being given in the distribution of aid to countries which are farthest removed from internationally accepted standards of minimum social and economic well-being;

iii. the funds required for disbursing foreign aid will be collected by taxation of *all* nation states in accordance with their capacity to pay and will not be dependent on the periodic vetoes exercised by national legislatures. At the same time, the richer and the poorer nations together will have their say in deciding the total quantum of foreign aid (that is the current limit of tolerance for international taxation) in the same way as groups within a nation have a say in deciding the extent of national tax levels. But the world will not be divided between "givers" and "takers." Instead, all will give and take according to mutually agreed criteria;

iv. since all human beings are being treated alike, there will be no question of considerations of political ideology or of race or colour or creed coming in the way of distributing aid strictly according to needs;

v. indeed, even criteria of national performance would become largely irrelevant. If the sins of the fathers should not be visited on the sons, there is no reason why the sins of the leaders and the privileged élite in any country should be visited upon the large mass of the poor who may have little effective say in the governance of their country. If performance has any role, it will be related not so much to the quantum of aid to be given but to the nature and degree of the effort that the international community as a whole should put up in order to improve performance;

vi. the richer nations would receive no compensation for their effort and sacrifice except the satisfaction of seeing common human objectives realised. The poor would not feel obliged to make recompense except in terms of contributing their mite to the common endeavour; and

vii. those who are actively engaged in the business of foreign aid will hardly be obsessed with the thought that their duty is to put themselves out of business as soon as possible. A nation does not look forward to the utopia of a withering away of the state at least in regard to its responsibility in the economic sphere. Rather, as it conquers stage after stage of the battle against poverty, it widens its horizons of social responsibility and sympathy.

One has only to set down the implications of the general principle we laid down at the outset to realise how far removed we are at present from a total commitment to international co-operation for eliminating poverty and want in this world. . . .

The ideal approach, therefore, is simply not practical politics. But can we at least take some steps in the right direction and avoid such current practices and fashions which might take us away from rather than nearer to what would be widely agreed as an ideal situation? Ideas have a way of becoming counter-productive in the work-a-day world, even though experience might show that what is considered visionary at one time often comes to be regarded as practical necessity before long. But even if the path of progress has to be charted warily, it is difficult to accept that we have already reached a satisfactory position in regard to foreign aid.

Becoming more specific—but still only at the level of establishing a "blueprint for action"—the General Assembly of the United Nations proclaimed the 1970's as the Second Development Decade, and specified aid requirements for the decade.

FINANCIAL RESOURCES FOR DEVELOPMENT *

Each economically advanced country should endeavour to provide by 1972 annually to developing countries financial resource transfers of a minimum net amount of 1 per cent of its gross national product at market prices

* United Nations, *International Development Strategy, Action Programme of the General Assembly for the Second United Nations Development Decade* (1970), pp. 9–10.

in terms of actual disbursements, having regard to the special position of those countries which are net importers of capital. Those developed countries which have already met this target will endeavour to ensure that their net resource transfers are maintained and envisage, if possible, an increase in them. Those developed countries which are unable to achieve this target by 1972 will endeavour to attain it not later than 1975.

In recognition of the special importance of the role which can be fulfilled only by official development assistance, a major part of financial resource transfers to the developing countries should be provided in the form of official development assistance. Each economically advanced country will progressively increase its official development assistance to the developing countries and will exert its best efforts to reach a minimum net amount of 0.7 per cent of its gross national product at market prices by the middle of the Decade.

Developed countries members of the Development Assistance Committee of the Organisation for Economic Co-operation and Development will exert best efforts to reach as soon as possible, and in any case before 31 December 1971, the norms set out in the Supplement to the 1965 Recommendation on Financial Terms and Conditions adopted by the Development Assistance Committee on 12 February 1969, designed to soften and harmonize the terms and conditions of assistance to developing countries. Developed countries will consider measures aimed at the further softening of the terms and will endeavour to arrive at a more precise assessment of the circumstances of the individual developing countries and at a greater harmonization of terms given by individual developed countries to individual developing countries. Developed countries will consider, in the further evolution of their assistance policy and with a view to attaining concrete and substantive results by the end of the Decade, the specific suggestions contained in decision 29 (II) of 28 March 1968, adopted by the United Nations Conference on Trade and Development at its second session and made in other international forums for further softening of the terms and conditions of aid.

In the light of the relevant decision of the Conference at its second session, financial assistance will, in principle, be untied. While it may not be possible to untie assistance in all cases, developed countries will rapidly and progressively take what measures they can in this respect both to reduce the extent of tying of assistance and to mitigate any harmful effects. Where loans are tied essentially to particular sources, developed countries will make, to the greatest extent possible, such loans available for utilization by the recipient countries for the purchase of goods and services from other developing countries.

Financial and technical assistance should be aimed exclusively at promoting the economic and social progress of developing countries and should not in any way be used by the developed countries to the detriment of the national sovereignty of recipient countries.

Developed countries will provide, to the greatest extent possible, an increased flow of aid on a long-term and continuing basis and by simplifying the procedure of the granting and effective and expeditious disbursement of aid.

Arrangements for forecasting, and if possible, forestalling debt crises will be improved. Developed countries will help in preventing such crises by providing assistance on appropriate terms and conditions, and developing countries by undertaking sound policies of debt management. Where difficulties do arise, the countries concerned will stand ready to deal reasonably with them within the framework of an appropriate forum in co-operation with the international institutions concerned, drawing upon the full range of the available methods including, as may be required, measures such as arrangements for rescheduling and refinancing of existing debts on appropriate terms and conditions.

The volume of resources made available through multilateral institutions for financial and technical assistance will be increased to the fullest extent possible and techniques will be evolved to enable them to fulfil their role in the most effective manner.

6. AMERICAN AID POLICY

In 1970, President Nixon received a report from his Task Force on International Development, chaired by Rudolph Peterson (former Chairman, Bank of America). President Nixon termed the ideas in the Peterson report "fresh and exciting," and he stated that "a new U.S. approach to foreign assistance, based on the proposals of the Task Force, will be one of our major foreign policy initiatives in the coming years."

THE PETERSON REPORT *

March 4, 1970

THE PRESIDENT OF THE UNITED STATES
Dear Mr. President:

You asked us to examine U.S. foreign economic and military assistance programs, our trade and investment relations with the developing countries, and the fundamental problems that the United States faces in this area of foreign policy. You instructed us to look carefully into the underlying rationale for these programs, to take nothing for granted, and to recommend policies that will serve the best interests of our Nation through the decade ahead.

Many with whom we consulted are deeply troubled by particular aspects

* *U.S. Foreign Assistance in the 1970: A New Approach,* Report to the President from the Task Force on International Development, (March 4, 1970), pp. 1–4, 22–28, 32–34.

of U.S. foreign assistance programs and by the apathy and misunder-
standing that seem to surround the issues. Nevertheless, virtually all believe
that the United States has a large stake and serious responsibilities in international development. . . .

A Time for Change

We believe that the U.S. role in international development will be as important in the future as it has ever been in the past; and prospects for success, if looked at in the perspective of experience, are very favorable.

For the first time in history, it appears feasible to approach this world
problem on a worldwide basis. International development can become a
truly cooperative venture—with the countries that receive help eventually
achieving the ability themselves to help others. The Marshall Plan countries
and Japan, which join us today in providing assistance, were yesterday the
recipients of assistance. And some of the developing countries of a decade
ago, no longer needing assistance themselves, are beginning to help
others. . . .

This, therefore, is a time for change, a time for reappraising our programs
and designing them for the decade ahead. It is also a time to stake out in
the most positive terms America's involvement in the way mankind manages
its common problems. In time, U.S. international development policies may
well prove to be the most important—and the most rewarding—determinant
of America's role in the world.

Conclusions

With these considerations in mind we have reached the following conclusions:

1. The United States has a profound national interest in cooperating with
developing countries in their efforts to improve conditions of life in their
societies.

2. All peoples, rich and poor alike, have common interests in peace, in
the eradication of poverty and disease, in a healthful environment, and in
higher living standards. It should be a cardinal aim of U.S. foreign policy to
help build an equitable political and economic order in which the world's
people, their governments, and other institutions can effectively share resources and knowledge.

This country should not look for gratitude or votes, or any specific short-
term foreign policy gains from our participation in international development. Nor should it expect to influence others to adopt U.S. cultural values
or institutions. Neither can it assume that development will necessarily
bring political stability. Development implies change—political and social,
as well as economic—and such change, for a time, may be disruptive.

What the United States should expect from participation in international
development is steady progress toward its long-term goals: the building of
self-reliant and healthy societies in developing countries, an expanding

world economy from which all will benefit, and improved prospects for world peace.

3. The United States should keep to a steady course in foreign assistance, providing its fair share of resources to encourage those countries that show a determination to advance. Foreign assistance is a difficult but not an endless undertaking. Some countries already have become self-reliant and are beginning to help others; U.S. policies should aim at hastening this process.

4. U.S. international development programs should be independent of U.S. military and economic programs that provide assistance for security purposes. Both types of programs are essential, but each serves a different purpose. Confusing them in concept and connecting them in administration detract from the effectiveness of both.

5. All types of security assistance—military assistance grants, use of surplus military stocks, military credits, economic assistance in support of military and public safety programs, budget support for political purposes, and the Contingency Fund—should be covered in one legislative act. The State Department should exercise firm policy guidance over these programs.

6. Military and related economic assistance programs will strengthen military security only to the degree that they help move countries toward greater self-reliance. These U.S. programs should be geared to the resources that the receiving countries ultimately will be able to provide for their own security. In some cases, reduction of U.S. military forces overseas will require temporary offsetting increases in such assistance. The ultimate goal should be to phase out these grant programs.

7. The United States should help make development a truly international effort. A new environment exists: other industrial countries are now doing more, international organizations can take on greater responsibilities, trade and private investment are more active elements in development, and, most important, the developing countries have gained experience and competence. Recognizing these conditions, the United States should redesign its policies so that:

—the developing countries stand at the center of the international development effort, establishing their own priorities and receiving assistance in relation to the efforts they are making on their own behalf;

—the international lending institutions become the major channel for development assistance; and

—U.S. bilateral assistance is provided largely within a framework set by the international organizations.

8. U.S. international development policies should seek to widen the use of private initiative, private skills, and private resources in the developing countries. The experience of industrial countries and of the currently developing nations demonstrates that rapid growth is usually associated with a dynamic private sector.

Development is more than economic growth. Popular participation and the dispersion of the benefits of development among all groups in society are essential to the building of dynamic and healthy nations. U.S. development policies should contribute to this end.

9. While the Task Force shares the aspirations of many who have endorsed high targets for development assistance, we have deliberately decided against recommending any specific annual level of U.S. assistance or any formula for determining how much it should be. We do not believe that it is possible to forecast with any assurance what volume of external resources will be needed 5 to 10 years hence. No single formula can encompass all that must be done—in trade, in investment, and in the quality as well as the amount of assistance. Our recommendation is to establish a framework of principles, procedures, and institutions that will assure the effective use of assistance funds and the achievement of U.S. national interests.

10. The downward trend in U.S. development assistance appropriations should be reversed. Additional resources, primarily in support of international lending institutions, are needed now for a new approach to international development. We believe this, having fully in mind the current financial stringency and urgent domestic priorities in the United States, as well as this country's balance-of-payments position. Over the long term, U.S. assistance for development abroad will be small in relation to expenditures for development at home. Moreover, the two programs can prove to be mutually reinforcing.

11. The United States must be able to respond flexibly and effectively to changing requirements in the developing world, and, in association with other industrial countries, help make possible the progress that individual developing countries show themselves determined to achieve. . . .

Reliance on International Organizations

The Task Force believes that more reliance on international organizations should be built into all U.S. policies relating to international development—whether they concern development assistance, debt rescheduling, tying, trade, investment, or population. This is basic to the new approach to foreign assistance we recommend. A predominantly bilateral U.S. program is no longer politically tenable in our relations with many developing countries, nor is it advisable in view of what other countries are doing in international development. . . .

The Task Force recommends three actions on the part of the United States:

—It should rely heavily on international organizations to work out programs and performance standards with developing countries and should provide most of its assistance within that framework. This will mean a fundamental change in the conduct of U.S. bilateral programs.

—It should provide the necessary increase in resources, on a fair-share basis with other member countries, to permit the international development organizations to increase their current lending within the next few years as fast as their capabilities and the tested needs of the borrowing countries permit.

—It should join with other members to strengthen the capabilities of these international organizations and to build more coherence into their operations.

Operation of an International System

The World Bank Group and the regional lending institutions now account for more than half of total official development lending. This lending is only a part of the total resource flow to developing countries, but it is a key element. It gives international organizations a basis for taking primary responsibility for setting the strategy under which all donors provide assistance to developing countries.

Under an international system of development, international agencies would assume primary responsibility for analyzing conditions and policies in developing countries, for establishing close working relations with appropriate officials in these countries, and for determining total capital and technical assistance requirements and the policies necessary for effective use of investment resources. This would set the framework for the bilateral assistance programs of the United States and other industrialized countries.

To do this, the international organizations will have to take a less parochial view of their mission. They will need to have wider representation abroad and more flexible lending policies, without lowering standards. They will have to give increasing attention to the management, social, technical, scientific cooperation, and popular participation aspects of development. Finally, they will have to be diplomatic, flexible, sympathetic, and persuasive—but prepared to say no and to withstand political pressure from both the creditor and the borrowing countries. . . .

Financing

The international organizations could roughly double their present rate of lending—from $2.5 billion a year to $5 billion a year—over the next several years while continuing to follow sound practices and maintain high standards. This judgment takes into account the capabilities of these organizations, the current international investment climate, the increasing availability of sound development projects, better planning and performance in both public and private sectors of the developing countries, and estimates of the level of foreign investment and bilateral assistance.

The actual rate of expansion would depend on demonstrated need and assurances on the effective use of funds.

This increase in lending would require an increase in U.S. funding from the current rate of $500 million a year to roughly $1 billion a year, assuming, as we should, no increase in the U.S. share in financing these organizations. In addition, there would be a need for the United States and other member countries to subscribe additional callable capital, enabling these organizations to increase their borrowings in the capital market. This callable capital would require U.S. budgetary outlays only in the event that these international organizations defaulted on their bonds.

An increase in International Development Association (IDA) lending is critical to establishing an international framework for development. In view of the debt-servicing problem in a number of the developing countries, concessional lending on IDA terms is badly needed. Furthermore, IDA lending is the foundation for international participation in some of the major development programs.

The current level of country contributions to IDA is $400 million annually. The Pearson Commission recommended that these contributions be increased to about $1 billion a year by 1972 and $1.5 billion by 1975. The Task Force recommends that the United States take the lead in supporting these suggested levels of financing. The U.S. share would be 40 percent of the total. . . .

Bilateral Development Lending: A U.S.
International Development Bank

The Task Force sees a new role and a new organization for U.S. bilateral lending. If the international agencies are to carry expanded responsibilities for development, the U.S. program must assume a supporting role and not become involved in the entire range of country development policies and programs.

U.S. lending under such a system would be concentrated in selected countries, in selected programs—particularly in agriculture and education—and in multinational projects where long-term development is of special interest to the United States. This U.S. lending, however, would be made on the basis of development criteria. A bilateral lending program would put the United States in a better position to encourage countries demonstrating the ability to move rapidly toward self-reliance. It also would enable the United States to continue to take up its share, with other nations, of programs in India, Pakistan, Indonesia, and selected African countries and to support Latin American development, which is of special concern to the United States.

Whenever it is feasible, U.S. lending should support cooperative programs worked out by the developing countries and the international agencies. Current U.S. participation in World Bank consortia and consultative groups for India, Ghana, Indonesia, and Colombia are cases in point. The proposal in the Rockefeller Report to have the OAS Inter-American Committee for the Alliance for Progress assume larger responsibility for formulating programs and coordinating development assistance in Latin America is another example.

Method of Operations

The United States should manage its lending programs as a bank would, although the scope of lending necessarily would include all aspects of development.

Effective assistance for development requires that capital and related technical services be provided together. The U.S. lending agency should be able to finance preinvestment and feasibility studies. It also should finance training and expert advisors to strengthen the managerial and technical competence of the borrowing institutions. For example, a program for efficient water utilization might include funds for the purchase of equipment, for training workers, and for outside experts. A loan to finance fertilizer, seed, and pesticides could well include the provision of advice on agricultural marketing and distribution. In providing technical services related to its lending program, the lending agency would draw on its own staff or arrange for such services from outside sources.

In making loans for development purposes, the United States should recognize that development is more than an economic process. It should take into account not only the extent to which a loan will contribute to economic growth but also the extent to which it will encourage social and civic development and will result in a wide dispersion of benefits.

The U.S. program should emphasize loans in support of the local private sector and promote broad popular participation in development. It could include program loans, loans to development banks and regional private investment companies, and loans for infrastructure and other projects. The United States could also finance training institutes, such as vocational schools and scientific centers.

The United States should be able to provide a range of development lending facilities, with the terms of specific loans adjusted to individual country circumstances. Terms should range from the most concessional interest rates and repayment terms to near-market rates. The latter would be appropriate for countries that no longer need concessional lending but that do not yet have independent access to private capital markets. For these countries, the United States could provide, or join in providing, guaranty facilities that would enable them to borrow on international capital markets.

Financing

Funds for bilateral lending should be available on an assured basis and in ways that permit flexible use, and the characteristics of the sources of funds should correspond to the financing terms appropriate for each borrower. The Task Force recommends the following:

—Appropriations should cover loans requiring the most concessional terms.

—Borrowing from the public should be authorized for loans made on intermediate concessionary terms. The rate at which these funds are loaned would be lower than the rate at which they are borrowed.

—Interest payments and repayments of principal on outstanding loans of AID and predecessor agencies should be available automatically to cover the interest differential on loans made at intermediate terms or for relending on the most concessional terms.

—Guaranty of foreign official borrowing on international capital markets should be authorized as a transitional device to help countries become independent of U.S. concessional lending. . . .

The Quality of Assistance

Over the past decade, most industrial countries have placed limitations on the use of their development assistance and have set terms for such assistance that have greatly reduced its value to developing countries. The most damaging of these practices are: the tying of development loans to procurement in the lending country, the promotion of exports by industrial countries on terms that lead to serious debt-serving problems for developing countries, and the imposition of a wide range of cumbersome and costly administrative restrictions on lending.

If the United States were to act alone in changing many of these practices, it would yield trade and financial advantages to the other industrial countries, thus discouraging domestic political support for development assistance. Other industrial countries are in the same position. However, if all the lending countries acted together, they would minimize the cost to each of restoring more efficient procedures.

Untying Development Lending

Total bilateral development lending that is effectively tied to procurement in the lending countries is estimated at $2 billion—half from the United States and half from all the other industrial countries combined. This amount does not include agricultural commodity development assistance, or official export credits (which are necessarily tied), or technical assistance, supporting assistance, or budget subsidies. The restrictions in development lending are estimated to reduce the value to developing countries of these loans by about 15 percent—or $300 million a year.

The Task Force recommends that the United States propose that all industrial countries agree to untie their bilateral development lending—permitting the developing countries to use these loans for procurement from the cheapest source on a competitive-bid basis.

The balance-of-payments cost to the United States of this proposal is estimated to be relatively small. In any event, the full effect would not be felt until some years from now. It would be even smaller if the United States improved its competitive position in world trade. The creation of new international reserves, which improves worldwide liquidity and was designed to help countries remove restrictions on trade and payments, provides further support for actions to untie developments lending on a multilateral basis.

Untying development lending would help to create a better international climate for development. It could stimulate investment, production, and trade in all developing countries.

The Task Force recommends two actions that the United States could take alone:

—Permit goods and services financed under U.S. development loans to be purchased in all developing countries as well as in the United States.

Latin American countries have recently been authorized to compete in the sale of good and services under all U.S. development loans made in Latin America.

—Remove the procurement restriction in the U.S. investment guarantee program. This restriction unfairly impinges on the flexibility of U.S. investors, discouraging such investment without providing significant balance-of-payments benefits to the United States.

Better Debt Rescheduling Arrangements

The current public and publicly guaranteed debt of developing countries is close to $50 billion—five times the level of a decade ago. The cost of servicing this debt has been increasing at the rate of 17 percent a year, or three times the rate at which the export earnings of these countries have risen. It is clear that these trends cannot continue.

The procedure up to now has been to reschedule the debt of countries about to default, usually as a result of extensive reliance on commercial credits or of financial mismanagement. The relief is short-term in nature and inadequate for dealing with the problem.

The debt situation for a number of developing countries, however, is long-term in nature and partly a consequence of loan terms the countries cannot handle. Keeping these countries on a short leash by emergency debt rescheduling operations does not show the necessary foresight. Countries with serious debt problems, in trying to avoid default, are likely to impose more internal and exchange restrictions and thereby intensify their future difficulties.

The Task Force recommends that the United States propose joint action—by the lending countries, the international lending institutions and the developing countries concerned—to devise a comprehensive strategy for dealing with this problem. This strategy should be put into effect to prevent an emergency—not to deal with one after it has arisen.

Over the decade ahead, joint action probably will be required to deal with the debt problems of perhaps five to ten countries. These countries now account for at least one-third of the outstanding debt. Such action should be initiated soon on a case-by-case basis. It should consist of an interrelated package that includes the following elements.:

—The World Bank and the IMF should convene a meeting of representatives of the countries involved. These institutions should prepare debt-rescheduling proposals on the basis of the debtor country's long-term outlook—both for debt service and for export earnings.

—Each debtor country seeking debt renegotiation should demonstrate by its plans and policies that it is pursuing a coherent development program and appropriate fiscal and financial policies.

—Bilateral government and government-guaranteed credits should be rescheduled over a long term. The international lending institutions, however, should not be required to reschedule their outstanding loans. Rescheduling their loans would endanger the ability of international institutions to continue borrowing in capital markets.

—The IMF should be ready to provide standby credits as a part of this package. This would be useful for setting financial standards and for providing a transitional supplement to the countries' international reserves.

—Governments should agree on a ceiling for guaranteed commercial credits to a participating debtor country in any one year. Minimum maturities for these supplier credits should also be set by multilateral agreement.

—If agreement is reached on the above points, all bilateral lenders should agree to provide the most concessional terms on new lending to the participating debtor country. These countries should also be given priority in receiving IDA loans.

In addition to rescheduling the debts of countries that already have reached or exceeded the limits of serviceable indebtedness, the creditor countries should design their assistance policies to keep other developing countries from facing debt difficulties. The best way to do this is for all developed countries to improve the terms of their development assistance.

The Peterson Report did not exercise any controlling influence over American aid policy. In fact, compared with the objectives outlined in the Report, the actual situation continued to deteriorate. Objectives remained confused; policy instruments were inadequately specified; and political support was not mobilized for an effective program.

Because of the aid controversies in Congress, foreign assistance had been funded throughout fiscal year 1973 by "continuing" resolutions at a level of about $3.7 billion in economic and military assistance. The President sent Congress a request for $2.9 billion for fiscal 1974: $1.6 billion for economic aid and $1.3 billion for military assistance. In October 1973 the Senate approved an aid bill in the amount of $2.03 billion—the lowest amount ever voted by the Senate for economic assistance. In its final form the Foreign Assistance Act for fiscal 1974 authorized a total of $2.39 billion, of which $1.42 billion was for economic assistance and $0.96 billion for military assistance. A notable feature of the Act was an attempt to provide aid for the poorest sectors of developing nations by replacing the old categories of technical and development loans and grants with new functional categories aimed at specific problems such as food and nutrition, population planning, and education and human resources development.

Not only was American bilateral aid severely cut. Even more disturbing, because of its adverse effects on the multilateralization of aid and the softening of terms, was the refusal of the House of Representatives in January 1974 to renew the United States contribution to the World Bank's IDA.[10] Contrary to the Peterson Report, the Administration had already reduced the proposed amount of the United States contribution from 40 per cent of the total IDA contribution to one-third—an American contribution of $1.5 billion to be spread over four years out of a total contribution from the richer countries of $4.5 billion. The bill to authorize such a contribution was defeated in a House of Representatives vote of 248 to 155.

The future of IDA was now in doubt, as funds were scheduled to run out in July 1974, and it was questionable whether other countries would advance their agreed share without the United States.

7. PEARSON REPORT

Recognizing the atmosphere of disenchantment that was surrounding aid in both the developing and developed countries, the President of the World Bank appointed in 1968 the Pearson Commission (named after its chairman Lester B. Pearson, former Prime Minister of Canada) to conduct a "grand assize" that would "study the consequences of twenty years of development assistance, assess the results, clarify the errors and propose the policies which will work better in the future."

On the problems of aid, the Pearson Report made the following recommendations.

PARTNERS IN DEVELOPMENT *

To Establish a Better Partnership, a Clearer Purpose,
and a Greater Coherence in Development Aid

The motives and purposes of aid policies in the past have been many and varied. However, it has increasingly come to be accepted that a primary objective should be the promotion of economic development, which requires a

---

* Lester B. Pearson *et al.*, *Partners in Development: Report of the Commission on International Development* (1969), pp. 17–19, 21–22.

10. On the need for replenishment of IDA, see p. 60 below.

sustained cooperative relationship between rich and poor. Increases in foreign aid should be clearly aimed at helping the developing countries to reach a path of self-sustained growth at reasonable levels. The target for the 1970's should be to raise the annual rate of growth of their national product to at least 6 per cent from the current average rate of 5 per cent. Such an acceleration is clearly feasible for many countries, although some will continue to lag behind and will continue to receive aid for humanitarian and other reasons. Countries growing at a rate of 6 per cent per year will be able gradually to raise their rate of capital formation. If they give adequate attention to the fostering and promotion of exports, they should, before the end of this century, be able to participate in the international economy as self-reliant partners, and to finance the investments and imports they need for continued rapid growth without foreign capital on concessional terms.

This objective cannot be attained simply by foreign aid. It will take hard and protracted effort in the developing countries themselves. Without such effort, development is impossible and development assistance is wasted. This is why increases in development aid should in the future be closely linked to the economic objectives and the development performance of the aid-receivers. But development plans cannot be made without reasonable assurance that resources will be available. Developing countries cannot reach for ambitious goals unless they know that serious programs will find external support. They are entitled to ask what commitments aid-givers are ready to make and how these commitments will be lived up to. Performance is not a one-way street.

The monitoring and assessment of performance is best done in a multi-lateral context in which donors and aid-receivers jointly review the past and plan for the future. We attach great significance to the dialogue on aid performance and recommend that the World Bank and the regional banks take the lead in discussions leading to the extension of joint review procedures in consortia, in consultative groups, or regional organizations, both those which now exist and those which need to be created.

To Increase the Volume of Aid

With the objectives of aid sharpened, a clearer view should emerge of the need for external resources in developing countries. For the 1970's, studies of development requirements indicate that realistic development policies compatible with the 6 per cent target already cited should give rise to a need for external resources, including both official aid and private investment, of the order of magnitude of 1 per cent of the GNP of the wealthier countries. We therefore endorse the 1 per cent target, to which the donor countries have long since committed themselves, and recommend that it be fully met by 1975, at the very latest. For most of the developed countries, this will require no more than a continuation of recent trends in the growth of their flows of aid and private capital to developing countries.

There is, however, a special need for official development assistance on concessional terms, that is, in the form of grants or loans on soft terms. This is what is properly referred to as aid. On the assumption that increases in aid can be more closely linked to efficient use and performance than hitherto, we recommend a substantial increase in official aid flows. Specifically, official development assistance should be raised to 0.70 per cent of donor GNP by 1975, and in no case later than 1980. This compares with average flows of 0.39 per cent in 1968.

We are aware that some donors will not be able to meet such a target without a major effort. Also, aid-givers who in the past have provided substantial amounts of food aid will in addition face the need, as developing countries reduce their need for food imports, of replacing their food aid programs with other forms of aid. We are mindful of pressing domestic needs; nevertheless, we believe this difficult and demanding challenge must be met if the basis for international community is to be secured.

To Meet the Problem of Mounting Debts

Debt service difficulties have already made several debt rearrangements necessary, and similar measures will have to be undertaken in other cases in the near future. When such rearrangements are required, they should seek to restore a framework for orderly development finance and try to avoid the need for repeated reschedulings. Debt relief should be recognized as a legitimate form of aid. If future debt crises are to be forestalled, sound financial policies must be pursued and the terms of aid must be lenient. The cooperation of aid-givers in consortia and consultative groups also calls for greater uniformity of terms.

To Make Aid Administration More Effective

To provide and to make effective use of aid has proved to be a difficult administrative task. Cumbersome procedures on both sides often hamper its constructive use. A meeting of major aid donors and recipients should be held in 1970 to identify major procedural obstacles and means to overcome them. Also, the need for continuity requires that decisions be taken so that aid funds be made available for periods of at least three years.

The tying of aid to purchases in donor countries imposes both direct and indirect costs on aid-receivers and distorts the channels of world trade. Balance-of-payments problems have been the principal reason for tying policies, and the creation of the new Special Drawing Rights (SDRs) in the International Monetary Fund (IMF) may provide an opportunity for a joint attack on the tying problem. We recommend a sequence of steps leading to progressive untying. We also believe aid-givers should permit aid funds to be used for purchases in other developing countries.

Food aid represents a special case of tying. Prospects are that an increasing number of developing countries will become independent of food grain imports or become exporters. Gradually, food aid should be subsumed under general aid programs so as to permit recipients to choose aid-financed imports without distortions in their own or the donor's economy.

Moreover, aid-givers should recognize more widely the need to adapt the forms of aid to the needs of individual recipients which, in many cases, have a special requirement for non-project aid. In particular, IDA should undertake program lending in appropriate instances. . . .

To Strengthen the Multilateral Aid System

The international organizations must be put in a position to provide more leadership and direction and to make development assistance into a genuinely international effort.

A substantial enlargement of the responsibilities of international organizations will require a thorough review of their practices and policies. It also requires that the balance of international aid be shifted toward a greater multilateral component. We recommend that the share of multilateral aid should be raised from its present level of 10 per cent of total official development assistance to a minimum of 20 per cent by 1975. If official aid increases to 0.70 per cent of GNP in that time, this target for aid would involve, on the average, channeling less than one-third of the additional aid through multilateral agencies. Thus it does not amount to a displacement of bilateral aid, though it would result in a fivefold increase in multilateral flows during this period.

The great demand for concessional development finance and the desire for gradual multilateralization combine to place the International Development Association (IDA) in a key position. It now has a proven record of development finance and the present procedure for triennial replenishment should be replaced by a more automatic and regular inflow of contributions. We believe that IDA should continue to handle at least as large a share of multilateral finance as it has so far disbursed. For the time being this means that the next replenishment of IDA should anticipate a growth in annual contributions to a level of $1.5 billion in 1975, compared with a level of $400 million per year at present. Other measures should also be taken to subsidize the interest on some World Bank loans and to provide a steady source of funds for this purpose. We attach similar importance to the further strengthening of the regional development banks, which should be encouraged to become competent in as many fields of development promotion as possible, and should be supported with more funds as they demonstrate the capacity to put them to good use.

The international aid system today, with its profusion of bilateral and multilateral agencies, lacks direction and coherence. A serious effort is necessary to coordinate the efforts of multilateral and bilateral aid-givers and those of aid-receivers. There is a need for consistent reviews of performance and for authoritative assessments of aid requirements. We recommend that the President of the World Bank should, in the course of 1970, invite the heads of the appropriate organs of the United Nations and other multilateral agencies, as well as representatives of bilateral aid-givers and of developing countries, to a conference to consider the creation of machinery essential to the efficiency and coordination of the international aid system.

8. CRITIQUE OF PEARSON REPORT

The Pearson Report received a generally good reception in governmental circles, but several development economists asked some harder questions of the Report. One reviewer, for instance, warned that "we must beware lest the grand assize . . . does not encourage a grand illusion." And he raised a number of doubts about certain presuppositions in the Report: "Is it not naïve and pious to assume that morality and national self-interest coincide? Is not the fundamental presupposition of the strategy of the report—that the need for aid should eventually subside—both unrealistic and lacking in vision? Does not the enthusiastic support of a scheme of generalised, non-reciprocal preferences for manufactured and semi-manufactured products from underdeveloped countries, compared with a lukewarm hypothetical paragraph on the link between Special Drawing Rights and the replenishment of the International Development Association display a curious lack of a sense of priorities? Are not aid, trade and private foreign investment treated in a political vacuum? Are not the targets of 6 per cent growth, 1 per cent capital transfer and 0.7 per cent official aid either meaningless or, if meaningful, unwarranted? Does not the preference for multilateral aid . . . fail to take full account of the present limitations and deficiencies of some of the international agencies?" [11]

Other questions about the Pearson Report are raised in the next extract.

STATEMENT OF HARRY G. JOHNSON *

Mr. JOHNSON. Mr. Chairman, unlike my three distinguished colleagues this morning, I am not a professional in AID business, rather an amateur whose interest arises partly from personal experience in many of these countries and partly from a study I did some years ago for the Brookings Institution on "U.S. Economic Policies Toward Less Developed Countries."

* Joint Economic Committee, *U.S. Policies Toward Developing Countries,* Hearings before the Subcommittee on Foreign Economic Policy, 91st Congress, 2d session, (May 1970), pp. 636–41.

11. Paul Streeten, review of *Partners in Development: Report of the Commission on International Development,* in *New Society* (November 27, 1969), pp. 868–69.

So what I have to offer is not a seasoned, experienced view but rather some general considerations which occur to me in this connection.

I begin with the so-called crisis of aid with which the Pearson report was concerned. And here it seems to me that what the problem is, is one which arises whenever you have transfers from rich people to poor people. There are two different principles in which such transfers can be made, one being the principle of philanthropy, and the other being the principle of the right of human beings to enjoy a decent standard of living.

Now, the philanthropic principle points toward the self-help principle and to the idea that assistance should be limited in time and should seem to have a reasonable payoff in terms of success of those who are receiving assistance.

The human rights concept, on the other hand, stresses the obligation of the rich to give so long as there remains a problem.

Now, within the individual national state we have resolved this conflict of principle by institutionalizing the transfer of income from the rich to the poor. In place of private philanthropy we now have social security which transfers income through a tax system to members of the poor who are in clearly defined circumstances deserving of these transfers.

There are some residual problems which are taken care of by private philanthropy. But in general we have resolved the things by a political process and political institutionalization.

In the international sphere, we do not have an international government and we do not have a way by which political demands for transfers of resources can be reconciled with people's willingness to give philanthropically. And consequently we have a real problem outstanding.

Those concerned with aid have attempted to resolve this problem by developing the notion of a moral obligation of the rich to give to the poor, and a moral right of the poor to receive from the rich. But the fact that it is a moral resolution of the problem and not a political one is disguised by the use of statistics such as the famous 1 per cent of gross national product on the one hand as a definition of obligation and the use of target rates of economic growth on the other as definitions of need.

This way of resolving the problem is fictitious, and its weaknesses are responsible for the crisis of aid. On the other hand the notion that aid is philanthropy clears the way sooner or later for the decision that the amount of aid to be provided should be decided after every other claim has been decided, and that it should be a residual category to be cut down if this is thought necessary.

I do not think myself that the case should rest on pure philanthropy. I think there is an ultramoral claim on the part of the residents of poor countries for assistance from developed countries on the ground that the nation state itself is a very strong instrument of discrimination against those who are not fortunate enough to live in it.

Through immigration policy, through tariff policy, through our own redistributive policies by which we build up the productive capacity of our poor people, we are making life more and more difficult for the people who are not fortunate enough to live in a country such as this one.

From the standpoint of the point of view I am developing, the recommendations of the Pearson report, which are followed by the Peterson report, that aid should be multilateralized is, I think, a step in the right direction toward the recognition that this is a world problem, and that the citizens of the rich countries have obligations, and not simply the possibility of giving when the spirit moves them.

But the multilateralization of aid is only part of the recommendations of the Pearson report. The other part is its obligation on the part of the rich to transfer a certain part of their income to the poor.

And in this respect the Peterson report refuses to follow the Pearson report, and instead it seems to me retrogresses into the charity approach, and furthermore attempts to disguise what is essentially a charitable operation as a business proposition.

Now, it is true, I think, that the present temper of the American public is quite skeptical of aid, and that the Peterson recommendations are an attempt in effect to salvage something from the wreckage. But I feel that it is likely to be very dangerous for the United States to turn inward on itself in this context, and to retrogress into the charitable approach toward the giving of aid.

I do agree with the Peterson report—and this is a matter of personal observation—that in the past of aid policies the American presence has been far too obvious, and very often very obnoxious, and that the multilateralization of aid is a way of giving the aid without having to be there yourself and figuring largely in the politics of the receiving countries.

On the other side of the aid picture, the practice of formulating the moral claim for assistance in terms of private rates of growth seems to me to be far too aggregative, and to be highly misleading. No statistics of this kind can epitomize the moral claim that the poor countries would like to lay on the rich countries for help and development. More important, statistics of growth rates of GNP, and particularly the statistics of the growth rate of GNP in total and not per capita, seem to me to fail to capture the essence of the development process, which is a process of social transformation. It is the kind of social transformation which can only be effected by a myriad of microeconomic changes in the way people use resources, the way they plan their lives, and so forth. And those changes have to be effected mostly by the private citizens of these countries with their governments, if possible, assisting by improving the framework in which private decisions are taken.

If one looks at development in this fashion there is a great deal to be said for the so-called self-help principle, particularly if it is administered on a multilateral basis, so that strictures passed on the policies of particular countries appear as a collective international judgement and not simply as a U.S. view. And I think that the emphasis in aid policy should be placed on efforts to promote private enterprise—and I define the term very broadly to mean the question of incentives for farmers, and all sorts of other things that David Bell has mentioned—that it should be based on providing a framework within which individual initiative can get to work, and that where government policies of intervention are considered desirable these policies should be general policies which establish a code of laws and framework within which private enterprise could not break, rather than efforts to intervene by administrative methods within the functioning of the competitive system.

I also feel that considerable emphasis should be placed on direct private foreign investment, which, I think, has an important demonstration effect and which is frequently complementary with the development of use of local resources, and which, incidentally, provides considerable tax revenue to governments which typically have a problem of raising taxes.

If the self-help principle and reliance on private enterprise are to be the basis of the objectives of development assistance policies in the future, it is incumbent on the developed countries to do the best they can to provide rapidly expanding export markets for these countries, so that they can pay for their imports and for the service of their developmental debts.

The policy proposals here tend to concentrate on the proposal for a preference system for manufactures from these countries in the market of developed countries. I think that scheme should be implemented as fast and as rapidly as possible.

In addition, there are extensive quotas which have been imposed on goods in which these countries have a comparative advantage, which quotas should be removed as soon as possible.

But, I think, to do that one has to recognize that we need to improve the functioning of our own economy. What we need to go for is policies promoting flexibility, capacity to respond to economic change. And these should not be considered purely as trade-related policies but as policies in our own interest in improving our own economy.

The interest is centered on the proposal for trade in manufactures, but it must be remembered that the bulk of these countries' exports are primary products, and that their export potential here is very severely limited by barriers to agricultural imports imposed as a social policy in the developed countries designed to transfer income to farmers.

Now, I think that considerable improvement could be made for the developing countries by eliminating these barriers which, according to all the economic evidence, do very little to achieve the objective they are aiming at, namely, improving the welfare of farm-workers as contrasted with improving the value of farmland.

But I recognize that this is a very difficult problem and it is one which will take some time to resolve.

If we were to establish a more liberal world trade environment and to emphasize the principles of self-help and reliance on private enterprise, I think that this would provide a powerful stimulus to the development of these countries, at least to the economic growth of these countries.

But here we run into what I think is the crux of the development problem, namely, that you can grow by producing more and more people without actually developing in the sense of transforming your society into a modern, competitive-maximizing, efficient technology-using, and productivity-raising society. In fact, growth in the aggregate through growth of population may make the problems which . . . others have called attention to, the problems of unemployment, the problems of lack of employment for youth, the problems of development not communicating itself to the masses, development in the form of accumulation of capital, it may make these problems worse.

In his recent report on the Latin American situation to the Inter-American Development Bank, Dr. Prebisch has argued that the central problem of Latin America is that development is not communicating itself to the mass of the people, and that to solve it we need a great acceleration of industrialization.

My fear is that acclerating industrialization may provide no solution at all, that it may increase the problems of inequality by confining development to a small proportion of the population in industry, and keeping the mass of the population growing as a result of a natural increase in population, in the same sort of situation as they are now.

I also think this is one of the major problems for people in developed countries. If development assistance simply increases the world population, increases the absolute number of poor people in the world, the question arises whether this is a beneficial activity to be engaged in.

It would seem to me far simpler, rather than try to beat population by industrialization, to try to control the population. And if you do that, then the processes of accumulation of capital, increasing education, and so forth, would gradually cure these problems of mass poverty of these countries by increasing the scarcity of labor and providing opportunities for these people to get into the industrial system.

If, on the other hand, population grows unchecked, then you are likely to have a two-sector economy, one sector the advanced modern, educated technology-using sector, and the other the mass of the population.

More effective population control is in my judgment a top priority for development policy. And it needs a great deal of research, not just on the medical and biological technology of birth control, but on the social and psychological factors which may or may not make a family planning program a viable one.

But there are many other areas where research and development expenditures could pay big dividends. Given the magnitude of the development problem, and given the amount of aid even at the highest levels that it has reached in the past, it has really been a drop in the bucket compared with the amount of capital in all sorts of forms needed for development. And given that the general public is not willing to increase aid substantially, it seems to me that research and development is the best way by and large to which to spend development assistance.

The average returns on capital investment in industry are at most about 20 per cent. If we deduct from that the servicing charges, and so forth, on development capital, the actual contribution to the welfare of these countries is going to be fairly small in percentage terms. We know, as David Bell has mentioned, that some research projects have paid off fantastic rates of return, and given the limitation of funds, these may well be the best investments to make. Not only that, but research and development has the great advantage that once you have got the new knowledge it is available to everybody. Sometimes the products in which knowledge is embodied are not available without substantial cost, but the knowledge is there, and it is a permanent contribution, and it contributes something which any country can take up and use without further cost to the donor of aid.

Let me finish by making a few remarks on conventional approaches to development. I have always been in favor of untying aid, and any international agreement that could be reached to that effect would have substantial benefits to the recipient countries without increasing the cost to the donor countries.

There are a lot of detailed questions on concessionary lending which the experts have taken up. And the Pearson report is full of them. The main point I would make here is that we really create the problem for ourselves by insisting on giving aid in what looks like a commercial form, a private enterprise form, namely, loans on concessionary terms. We do not necessarily have the assurance that the use to which these funds are put is capable of paying off that kind of return even though it is concessionary. And so we find ourselves with the problem of having given the aid in the form of loans, and then finding that the debt service charges prove a source of considerable difficulties to the country paying them.

I would much prefer myself to give aid in the form of outright grants. In that case you do not have to worry about debt financing and refinancing, and so forth. And you do not store up problems for the future the way that past aid policy has done.

I would like to put in a final word on the so-called "link" proposal, which is the proposal to distribute some proportion of the new special drawing rights at the International Monetary Fund to the developing countries, and then for the developed countries to earn them back. I know Dr. Prebisch is very much in favor of that proposal, and I am equally strongly against it. The first reason I am against it is that I think that the special drawing rights will have enough trouble getting started without being saddled with a concealed development assistance function.

Secondly, the "link" proposal is essentially a proposal for inflation financing of development assistance, and as one concerned about inflation, I would rather be taxed in some way which legislators can control.

Thank you, sir.

Chairman BOGGS. Thank you very much, Professor Johnson.

Your prepared statement will be placed in the record at this point.

A third critique questions the central theme of the Pearson Report—that aid promotes development through more investment expenditure and that in the absence of aid, the volume of necessary investment expenditure cannot be secured without an intolerable reduction in consumption. Contrary to the Pearson Report, it is claimed that investment expenditure is neither necessary nor sufficient for the economic development of LDCs.[12]

> First and foremost, investment must be unproductive in the absence of the necessary co-operant factors, both in the form of a supply of labour with suitable skills, and also in the wider sense of the presence of appropriate abilities, attitudes, motivations and institutions. Moreover, investment will be unproductive unless there is a market for the ensuing products . . . The presence of these required favorable conditions cannot legitimately be taken for granted . . .
>
> Second, productive investment or an increase in investment need not call for appreciable reduction of consumption. Highly productive capital formation is often not at the expense of consumption but at the expense of leisure, especially in that phase of economic development when subsistence production and customary methods give way to production for the market.

Furthermore, contrary to the assumption of the Pearson Report, it is claimed that aid may in practice retard development rather than promote it: [13]

> Investment expenditures made possible by foreign aid may have a negative productivity. The project or programme may in time absorb a greater volume of domestic resources than the value (to the economy) of its output. This can happen where the domestic resources necessary to maintain or continue the operations of a plant or project have been underestimated, and where for reasons of prestige the venture cannot be jettisoned. That such an outcome is not improbable is suggested both by the total failure of numerous aid-financed projects in South Asia and in East and West Africa and also by the instances in which effective protection of manufacturing industries in developing countries has been found to exceed 100 per cent (which means that the activity absorbs domestic resources in excess of the value of the net output).

---

12. P. T. Bauer and B. S. Yamey, "The Economics of the Pearson Report," *Journal of Development Studies* (January 1972), p. 320.
13. *Ibid.*, p. 322.

But foreign aid can and often does set up much wider and more pervasive adverse repercussions.

Foreign aid means that additional resources are made available to the government of the recipient country. It enlarges the resources of the government relatively to the rest of the economy. It increases the centralisation of power, especially in countries in which comprehensive economic planning is practised. Because the attainment or maintenance of political control is consequentially more important, political tensions are exacerbated, and regional and ethnic conflicts of interest become more pronounced. The greater the volume of resources at the disposal of the government, the higher are the prizes of political power. The increase in the weight or scope of government diverts the energy of able and ambitious men from economic activity to political pursuits. All these tendencies are likely to retard economic progress.

The expectation that aid will be forthcoming to help bail out a country which has got into economic difficulties has also tended to encourage the pursuit of policies likely to endanger or retard economic progress. This encouragement has been the more powerful where the policies in question have a political appeal because of their attractiveness to influential groups.

Policies of extravagant government expenditure or of wasteful protection of particular industries have been more easily instituted and implemented where there has been a reasonable expectation that the adverse economic effects would be counterbalanced, at least in part, by future inflows of aid.

Finally, from quite another political viewpoint, the Report has been criticized as "the quintessence of the liberal economist's approach . . .

The Commission's world is peopled with governments, international organizations and individuals (whose greater freedom to prosper as individuals is in the Commission's view the mainspring of development). There are neither classes nor pressure groups, let alone imperialism or revolutions. It is not at all surprising that the Commission chooses not to use such concepts to analyse the Third World. But its choice must be noted along with the *naïvetés* in analysis which result.

The mechanism of economic improvement upon which the Commission is forced to rely is the disinterested munificence of the governments of advanced capitalist countries who will, it is hoped, step up their annual aid and private investment to 1 per cent of their national income to those Third World countries which encourage individual initiative and if possible provide guarantees against expropriation.

It never seems even to occur to the Commission that, in the past, development and industrialization have always been the outcome of some great social upheaval. Such upheavals then or now have no place in the Commission's world; their view of development has no historical or social dimension. The same goes for their view of aid: noting, and ignoring, the fact that support for aid in the West has collapsed (except for some pressure from exporting capitalists for more tying of aid to national exports), they advocate with a staggering absence of awareness of what is politically possible, that there should be more of it. The trouble is that they believe quaintly that 'we live in a village world; we belong to a world community'.[14]

9. JACKSON REPORT

In contrast with the Pearson Report, the Jackson Report sought major organization reforms of the United Nations Development System. Critical of existing machinery, it offered recommendations for redesigning and centralizing the allocation of aid to the various United Nations agencies, centering the basic programming of international assistance at the country level, and improving the administrative organization of multilateral aid channels. It was directed more to advocating remedial policies than to mobilizing popular support for aid, as the following findings of the report indicate.

CAPACITY OF THE UNITED NATIONS DEVELOPMENT SYSTEM *

The study of capacity means looking back as well as forward. Many impediments are deeply rooted in the UN development system and are unlikely to be removed unless their origins are fully understood. For that reason the

---

* R. G. A. Jackson (ed.), *A Study of the Capacity of the United Nations Development System* (1969), pp. 6–13, 22–23, 25–29, 159–62.

14. R. B. Sutcliffe, review of *Partners in Development: Report of the Commission on International Development, Journal of Development Studies* (October 1971), p. 145.

Study has surveyed the operation from its inception. What constraints and difficulties are revealed? First, there have been the growing pains of new nations and new international organizations. These were inevitable but should be transient. In the case of the UN system, however, they have been sharpened by the addition of a new dynamic—development co-operation— into a structure not designed for that purpose. Second, there is the sectoral autonomy of the Specialized Agencies and the consequent handicaps when they seek to operate collectively. That is understandable and capable of redress if firm measures are taken by governments. Up to now, however, it has been exacerbated by the blurring of the lines of demarcation between existing organizations and the proliferation of new bodies. Third, the scope of the co-operation offered by the UN development system has been curtailed by the reluctance of governments to endow it with capital for the developing countries. That, too, was understandable, but unhappily shortsighted, given the magnitude of the challenge. It is not irrevocable. . . .

The two chief criticisms levelled at the United Nations Development Programme are that it is slow and is not yet making the best use of its resources. On the evidence before the Study, both are justified. On the positive side, it is encouraging that many officials within the system recognize these shortcomings and want to correct them. However, their efforts are often frustrated by the pressures on their time and by the intractability of the organizational structures.

While judgements are difficult, it is possible to identify the general picture in *quantitative* terms—referring primarily to performance in the Special Fund component by UNDP itself and the four principal Executing Agencies (UN, ILO, FAO and UNESCO) which are responsible for about 80 per cent of the operation. Here, it can be shown that the operation has become slower as it increased in size and that, despite many efforts to speed up procedures, the time involved in each of the various stages of a Special Fund project is too long in relation to the urgency of development needs. Thus, the total genesis of a Special Fund project from the time it is first discussed until the moment that it starts operations as an approved project may take up to three or four years, or even more.

From a *qualitative* point of view, there is general agreement on a number of general aspects. As regards the character and content of the programme, for instance, the basic nature of "technical assistance" has changed very little over the years, and probably too much has been expected of it. There is widespread criticism that those concerned with the operation are all too often ignorant of the subtleties of the development process, and insensitive to the needs of the developing countries. This has led to a "donor bias"— i.e., the initiative has come from an Agency and not from the country itself, and a failure to recognize the need for a comprehensive approach to development problems. Another general stricture is that insufficient emphasis has been placed on training. At the same time, the number of institutes is almost certainly excessive, having been started without due regard for local manpower requirements and employment prospects or for the alternative possibilities of multinational institutes. Surveys, too, have been conceived on an excessively long-term basis, without sufficient attention to the resource position of the country.

This leads to a general conclusion about the content of the present programme: there is, in my judgement, about 20 per cent of "deadwood" in the present operation—projects that are not worthwhile if subjected to the acid test: "Is it *essential* for our development?" In a programme costing some US$180 million a year in project costs, they represent an expenditure of roughly US$36 million. Obviously, it will not be easy politically to eliminate these, but it is clearly in the interests both of the developing countries and of the UN development system to do so, in order to get the maximum use from available resources. Even 50 per cent success would permit US$18 million per year to be directed to better use.

The root cause of these deficiencies can be identified by an analysis of the constraints at each of the various phases of the programme:

a. *Programming and project formulation.* The present programming procedures of the UN development system do not adequately reflect the real needs of the developing countries nor is there any form of integrated approach to the problems of each country. All too often, projects are the results of Agencies' "salesmanship" rather than a response to priority needs and this is encouraged by the "project-by-project" approach adopted for the Special Fund component. The consequence is "scatterization" of effort, less than effective impact, and a tendency to the self-perpetuation of projects.

b. *Execution.* Difficulties here stem largely from the heavy operational burdens which have devolved so suddenly on the Specialized Agencies and which surpass the present capacity of several of the larger ones. This leads not only to delays in delivery but also to a decline in quality, especially as regards project personnel who are often not suited or prepared for assignments which exact so much more than technical expertise.

c. *Evaluation.* Quantitatively, so much evaluation is now being attempted that it almost amounts to international hypochondria. It is a definite brake on the capacity of the system. Qualitatively, the position is the more disturbing for very few people have the necessary experience and understanding to undertake this exacting function successfully.

d. *Follow-up.* What should be the most important phase of the programme is often its weakest link, and insufficient attention is paid to it as an integral phase in the whole process of development. . . .

What, then, is the capacity of the present system and what are the prospects for the future? Obviously, no precise judgement can be expressed but I have no doubt about my general conclusion. I am convinced that the capacity of the present operation is over-extended in certain critical areas. I would list the major constraints as follows, noting that not all of them are exclusively the responsibility of the UN development system:

The inability, as yet, to develop fully effective techniques for transferring knowledge and experience.

The slow application of science and technology to major problems.

The difficulty of attracting manpower of the quality and experience which the operation demands.

The absence of an effective system for the control of the resources entrusted to it.

The lack of an organization specifically designed to co-operate with the developing countries.

The diffusion of responsibility throughout the system.

The general reluctance of the Agencies (with one or two significant exceptions) to contract outside the system. . . .

Governments will naturally wish to know what is entailed if they decide to take the new road signposted by the Study. The first essential is to recognize that, above all else, the United Nations Development Programme must be conceived as an *operation.* This entails the adoption of measures designed to ensure an integrated managerial approach toward development co-operation at all levels of the UN development system, and at all phases of the operation, in order to achieve optimum results for the benefit of developing countries and maximum use of resources. Briefly stated, these measures should include:

First, the introduction of a programming method which would enable all inputs from the UN development system to be programmed comprehensively at one time in a programme corresponding to the needs and the duration of each country's national development plan.

Second, effective and prompt execution of approved projects, having recourse, as necessary, to all available methods and resources within and without the system.

Third, controlled evaluation, designed to maintain the accountability of the Administrator of UNDP for the use of all resources contributed to UNDP, to measure results, to judge the effectiveness of the methods used, and to draw conclusions which may be applied with benefit to future operations.

Fourth, effective follow-up conceived as an integral part of each project from the outset.

Fifth, the introduction of an efficient information system.

Sixth, organizational reforms at the country, regional and headquarters level designed to integrate the components of the UN development system more closely. These should combine greater control at the centre with maximum decentralization to the field level, where the authority of the Resident Representative should be greatly strengthened.

Seventh, proper staffing of the operation at all levels, involving far-reaching measures to attract and retain the best qualified people available.

Eighth, a financial framework designed to ensure the smooth running of the operation, through which the maximum possible amount of funds entrusted to the UN development system for development co-operation should be channelled, the head of the central organization being held personally accountable for their use.

Ninth, maximum use of all modern managerial and administrative aids and techniques to ensure an effective, expeditious and economical operation.

Tenth, maximum flexibility on the part of governments and the system alike to permit adaptability to changing circumstances and a speedy and effective response to new challenges and opportunities as they arise.

These might be called the Ten Precepts.

The Ten Precepts define what has to be done. In essence, they cover the remaining two tiers of the Study. Thus, the initial Precepts relate to procedures for planning and operating the programme, while the others deal with its organization, administration, and financing. The Tenth and last Precept adds the indispensable element of imagination and vision which must animate all the rest. . . .

The proposed system rests on two main pillars. First, programming procedures flowing from the country level—the decisive area of action. Second, the integrated programming of all inputs from the various components of the UN development system—UNDP, UNICEF, WFP, Agency programmes financed by Agencies' own resources, and the like—so that they complement one another, fit into the development plans or objectives of the recipient country and bear adequate rapport to the inputs from other sources, particularly those of a capital nature. The role of IBRD, as the arm of the UN system responsible for capital investment, is therefore of the highest importance. . . .

10. THE WORLD BANK

As the major multilateral agency for financing development, the World Bank has assumed an increasingly strategic position in the international aid community. During its first quarter-century of existence since it was established at the Bretton Woods conference, the Bank has grown to 116 member-governments and has acquired two affiliates, the International Finance Corporation (IFC) and the International Development Association (IDA).

The IFC invests—without requiring the Bank's normal government guarantees of repayment of the investment—in productive private enterprises in LDCs, in association with other private investors who can provide management.

The "soft" loans or credits from IDA are designed to place less burden on the balance of payments of the borrowing nation. The level of IDA assistance is determined, however, by the contributions that the Bank's richer members are willing to supply. IDA commitments rose from $100 million in 1961 to about $600 million in 1970–71. Under the third proposed replenishment, the level of commitments was expected to rise to $900 million a year, but there was danger of complete termination in July 1974 of IDA's activities after the House of Representatives failed to approve the United States contribution (see p. 57 above).

By mid-1971, the Bank had made nearly 800 loans and IDA had extended nearly 300 credits, together totaling approximately $20 billion. In the most comprehensive study of the Bank,[15] the question is asked:

> Can it be said that the world as a whole, and the less developed portion of it in particular, is better off as a result?
>
> Despite a scarcity of "hard" evidence, the answer appears to be yes . . . Some of the Bank's influence on methods of promoting development is a result of the fact that it was itself a pilot project—the first institution of its kind. Precedents for its actions were scarce . . . If the Bank was a cautious explorer, it had plausible reasons for caution . . . In fact, one of the most important assets of the Bank has been continuity. The Bank has been 'here to stay.' It therefore remains relatively invulnerable to transitory political and economic trends and to sudden changes in fashion. It can plan ahead and enter into long-term partnerships for the development of vital sectors of the economies of member nations.
>
> Several factors account for this special source of strength. Bond issues give the Bank (though not the IDA) a financial base that is substantially independent of the appropriation processes of member countries. The Bank Group's relations with member governments can become strained by differences of view on how best to promote reconstruction and development. But the strains need not be compounded by the numerous nondevelopmental considerations that enter into bilateral relations. . . .
>
> A member country that engages the Bank in its development efforts can usually count on a continuation and intensification of the relationship. . . .
>
> A related consequence of the Bank's "being here to stay" and having considerable autonomy is that it has been able to obtain a remarkably competent staff. . . .

15. E. S. Mason and R. E. Asher, *The World Bank Since Bretton Woods* (1973).

Endowed with strong leadership, the Bank has put development lending on a businesslike basis and made it respectable. It has pioneered in raising capital in the markets of industrial countries (and more recently in oil-rich underdeveloped countries) for investment in productive projects in poor countries.

To help ensure effective use of its loans and to flag difficulties as they arise, the Bank has emphasized close control of disbursements and close supervision of projects. . . .

[A] frequent criticism of the Bank as a development agency is that it has been too cautious, that it concentrated too long and too exclusively on power and transport expansion, and that it has left the risky projects to others and been anything but bold in exploring new areas for investment. Relevant for the first fifteen years of Bank lending, this criticism has been decreasingly applicable since about 1963. Industry, agriculture, and education have been claiming more Bank Group investment, and new approaches are being tried in the Bank's traditional as well as in its more recent fields of lending.[16]

A closer appraisal of the Bank's operations is presented in the following review of the progress of the Bank during its five-year program for 1969–73.

THE BANK'S FIVE-YEAR PROGRAM *

On April 1, 1973, Mr. Robert S. McNamara began his second five year term as President of the Bank, IDA and IFC. . . . It was noted that Mr. McNamara's first term had been a period of rapid progress in the Bank Group's operations around the world. The progress is reflected in the completion of the program for the five years 1969–73 outlined by the President in his address to the Board of Governors in September 1968. The results show that all the targets of the program have been achieved, and some substantially exceeded.

Specifically, the targets were:

—To double the global total of Bank and IDA lending. The total has increased 128%.

—To triple lending to Africa. It has risen 214%.

—To double lending to Latin America. It has grown 128%.

—To quadruple lending for agriculture. It has increased 317%.

* *World Bank/IDA Annual Report 1973*, pp. 14–22.

16. E. S. Mason and R. E. Asher, *The World Bank at Quarter Century*, Brookings Research Report No. 137 (1973), pp. 3–5.

—To triple lending for education. It has expanded 362%.

—Comparing the two five year periods, lending to developing countries in Asia has increased 123%. The comparable increase for developing countries in Europe and the Middle East is 225%. . . .

The growth in operations in the poorest and "least developed" countries has been made possible in large part by the growth of IDA resources. But there has been a shift also in Bank loans, not to the poorest countries, but to the middle income countries and to the poorer ones among them. Table IV

Table IV. Bank and IDA: Lending by Income Category of Borrower
(*US$ millions and percentages. Fiscal years*)

	Number of Countries	Through 1963 Bank	IDA	1964–68 Bank	IDA	1969–73 Bank	IDA
1970 GNP per capita		Amount of Lending ($ millions)					
Up to $120	28	1,259	335	501	886	842	2,785
$121–$250	22	713	48	471	346	1,582	841
$251–$375	17	745	69	343	104	1,500	286
$376–$500	7	744	18	864	—	2,274	20
$501–$800	9	794	25	722	—	1,466	—
Above $800	14	2,867	—	1,395	—	1,254	—
TOTAL		7,122	495	4,296	1,337	8,918	3,932
1970 GNP per capita		Percent of Total					
Up to $120	28	18	68	12	66	9	71
$121–$250	22	10	10	11	26	18	21
$251–$375	17	11	14	8	8	17	7
$376–$500	7	10	4	20	—	26	1
$501–$800	9	11	5	17	—	16	—
Above $800	14	40	—	32	—	14	—
TOTAL		100	100	100	100	100	100

illustrates the trend by grouping borrowing countries into categories according to their per capita GNP.

No less important than the increases in the volume of assistance have been the qualitative changes in the Bank's activities. The Bank has been taking a much more comprehensive view of the development process. Although economic development is the Bank's main concern, it believes that it is necessary also to promote the social development required to stimulate economic growth. Greater attention has, therefore, been given to the social aspects of economic growth, including population, employment, income distribution, health, malnutrition and the impact on the environment. Increasingly, assistance is being given on the basis of a comprehensive study of a country's economy, or of particular sectors within the economy, in the effort to assure that it has maximum impact at points of greatest need.

The more comprehensive view has led to a marked diversification of the Bank's activities. The diversification is seen in the support given to projects in new sectors such as population planning and urban development. It is seen also in new types of projects in the more traditional sectors, such as agriculture, transportation or industry. In each case, the emphasis has been on innovation and flexibility in responding to the special needs of the country or people in question.

An Integrated Approach

The more comprehensive view, furthermore, has led increasingly to projects that, rather than being confined to a narrow purpose, encompass a variety of activities that often transcend individual sectors. Thus, through an integrated approach, the aim has been to establish a mutually reinforcing framework of action designed to assure that the assistance has the most beneficial impact on the country, the area or the sector as a whole.

Greater attention has been given to types of projects that can help spread the benefits of development more widely, especially among the poorer sections of society. The attention is inspired by the conviction that the object of development is not projects, but people. Development can have no meaning unless it brings a better, fuller and more productive life to the mass of the underprivileged in poor countries.

In no sector has the volume of lending increased more rapidly than in agriculture. The sharp increase has been accompanied by a marked diversification in patterns of lending. In the Bank's early years, the emphasis was on basic irrigation infrastructure, such as dams and canals. But, over the years, there has been a shift toward financing on-farm activities, such as provision of credit and technical services. During the last five years, the shift has accelerated. The Bank has also become more heavily involved in storage, marketing, seed multiplication, forestry and fisheries projects. The importance of agricultural research has been recognized both in individual projects and through support for international research institutions.

Many of the agriculture projects supported by the Bank in recent years offer an outstanding example of the more comprehensive approach. Although the move toward integrated projects which include some non-agricultural components is not wholly new, the number and scope of such projects has been growing. Recent projects for rural development or integrated smallholder development are increasingly directed at the overall development of a specific geographical area which has high potential and is of manageable size. The aim in these projects is not simply to increase agricultural production, by providing such inputs as credit, seeds and fertilizer, or supporting infrastructure in the form of roads, marketing facilities and soil conservation measures. The aim is to help improve the quality of life for the people of the area, by including also facilities for education, domestic water supply, health, or other social services. . . .

Development of Education

In education, as in agriculture, the Bank's activities have been characterized by growth and diversification over the last five years. When the Bank
started providing assistance for the development of education a little over
11 years ago, it concentrated, as a matter of deliberate policy, on two fields.
The first was vocational and technical education and training at various
levels. The other was general secondary education. Other kinds of projects
were considered only in exceptional cases.

Over the years, as the Bank gained more experience, it diversified its activities. A few years ago, it decided that it should broaden its approach further by determining priorities and selecting projects on the basis of a thorough examination of the education system as a whole. In particular, apart
from projects which produce trained manpower directly, it should consider
other types of projects which could have important long-term significance
for economic development. Such projects would be "designed to encourage changes which improve the relevance, efficiency and economy of education systems."

In the earlier years, the overwhelming proportion of the assistance was for
educational "hardware"—for the construction and equipment of school
buildings. But, more recently, greater attention has been given to the "soft-
ware"—to such aspects as improving the curriculum, producing better
teaching materials, and planning systematically the education that is offered. . . .

Population Planning

On the longer view, an important diversification of activity within the last
five years is represented by the Bank's decision to enter the field of population planning. The decision is based on the conviction that rapid population
growth is a major barrier to the economic and social progress of most of its
poorer member countries.

The Bank and IDA have so far approved assistance totalling $65.7 million
for seven projects—in India, Indonesia, Iran, Jamaica, Malaysia, Trinidad
and Tobago, and Tunisia. Help is being given for preparing projects in another five countries. Within five years, the number of projects supported by
the Bank and IDA is expected to rise to about 30. In a majority of cases, the
support will probably be combined with assistance from other external
donors under cooperative funding arrangements. Population planning is a
field in which the Bank cooperates closely with the U.N. Fund for Population Activities.

The volume of lending, however, is an inadequate index to the Bank's activities in this sector. Much of the Bank's contribution is in the form of technical assistance. Advice may be offered on such aspects as the organization
and planning of a program, its administration and evaluation, the training of
personnel, and communications. The assistance is not always linked to a financial commitment from the Bank itself.

A large proportion of Bank funds for population projects has been used to construct clinics, maternity centers, maternity hospitals and training schools, and for the purchase of equipment and vehicles. More recent projects have devoted greater attention to communications, education, and evaluation and research activities. This comprehensive approach reflects the Bank's objectives in the sector. The objectives are to help develop viable family planning organizations and programs, strengthen information and communication activities, and promote a deeper understanding of the many socio-economic factors that influence fertility.

The Bank is well aware of the complex and delicate problems in population planning. Some are rooted in political, social and ethical attitudes. Others are technical in nature. The Bank is, therefore, cooperating closely with several agencies—international, bilateral and private—in order to improve its understanding of the problems. It recognizes that it can provide assistance only to countries which are aware of the serious implications of excessive population growth, and are prepared to do something about it. The number of such countries has shown an encouraging increase. The Bank's activities in the sector are, therefore, expected to expand substantially in the years ahead. Work is also going forward to develop specific projects to combat malnutrition, a field in which the Bank's interest is growing.

Support for Industry

The Bank's lending for industry in recent years has been marked by a number of new features. Firstly, the level of direct lending to industry has increased substantially, and within it support for government-owned industrial enterprises, which began in 1967. In fact, only four of the 21 specific projects financed in 1969–73 have been privately-owned. This is in accordance with a change in policy approved by the Executive Directors a few years ago, under which it was decided that the Bank would be willing to consider providing finance to government-owned industrial enterprises if satisfied that their managements were experienced and efficient.

Secondly, new dimensions have been introduced in the Bank's work on traditional "heavy" industries. Projects in such fields as mining, steel, fertilizers, and pulp and paper, are judged in the context of the optimal pattern of national and international development. The Bank is tending to become involved at earlier stages in the shaping and preparation of projects; and the effects of such industries on the environment are regularly assessed so as to incorporate appropriate safeguards.

Thirdly, to reinforce the support for agricultural development, the Bank has given more attention to fertilizer projects—in India, Indonesia, Pakistan and Turkey. An increasing number of projects in this and related fields are being considered. The Bank has also given new emphasis to the financing of labor-intensive small-scale industries and other industries that are primarily export-oriented. Increasing attention is being given to the impact which industrial enterprises have on employment and social goals.

The most notable feature, however, is that the Bank's support for development finance companies (DFCs) has greatly expanded. In many countries, DFCs are playing a role which goes beyond merely providing finance; they may assist in developing local capital markets, as well as in encouraging local entrepreneurship and the acquisition of appropriate technology. The benefits of their activities—which are concentrated on enterprises far smaller than those that could qualify for direct Bank loans—tend to be widespread. In recent years, the Bank has helped DFCs to develop policies and approaches to meet the increased demand in developing countries for industrial and tourism finance. Several new types of DFCs have been encouraged; and greater attention has been paid to achieving an appropriate balance between the developmental and the financial objectives of these institutions. . . .

Electric Power Projects

The Bank has traditionally helped finance electric power projects with a view not only to providing a portion of the capital requirements, but also to promoting institutional and operational efficiency. Although its assistance has in the past been principally for generation and transmission facilities, it has sought to assure that the development of the sector is taking place on a balanced, coordinated basis. In many countries, significant improvements have been achieved in electric power institutions and in their efficiency.

The Bank now is increasingly directing its attention to the distribution aspects of the electric systems it helps to finance, with a view to stimulating concern for the welfare of the lower income groups among the population. It is planned to seek opportunities to lend for distribution extensions at the margins of urban centers, in the countryside, and in smaller villages. Recognizing that there are benefits to society not adequately measured by the price which customers may be able to pay for electricity, the Bank has taken greater interest in such programs, and particularly in those for electrification of villages. . . .

Improving Water Supply

In the water supply and sewerage sector, as the number of projects has increased, a special effort has been made to extend the benefits to more people, particularly the poor. In most developing countries, among the top three causes of morbidity and mortality are the enteric diseases which are associated with unsafe and polluted waters and with poor sanitation—in both urban and rural areas. The provision of a safe and convenient water supply, and an improvement in sanitation, has usually done much to reduce the incidence of these diseases, particularly among the poor. The latter are frequently forced to use unsafe sources and are the most common victims of diseases transmitted by such water. They are, therefore, the ones who benefit most when properly designed systems are brought within their reach. In helping to build such systems, the Bank has been giving greater attention to the need to dispose of liquid wastes properly and to control pollution. . . .

Urban Growth

Since 1970, the Bank has sought to develop an integrated approach to problems arising from the explosive growth of urban centers in developing countries. Although much of the work is still in an experimental stage, several new types of urbanization projects are being developed. Among the most promising is that of "sites and services" to cope with the acute shortage of housing and other facilities for the urban poor—a shortage exemplified by the very rapid growth in the proportion of city populations existing in squatter settlements. An analysis of urban resources and needs has made it clear that, at least in the poorer majority of developing countries, the shortage cannot be overcome by providing conventional "low-cost" housing. It is necessary to help the urban poor to help themselves in building and improving their homes. To do so, the provision of sites with minimum services for houses, schools, markets and other social needs has to be closely related to employment and transport opportunities. . . .

Responding to the evolving development situation, the President of the World Bank suggested new goals and shifts in emphasis for the Bank's second five-year program during 1974–78.

THE BANK'S PROGRAM FOR 1974–1978 *

Most of our developing member countries are faced with three interrelated difficulties:
—An insufficiency of foreign exchange earnings from trade.
—An inadequate flow of Official Development Assistance.
—And an increasingly severe burden of external debt.
Each of these problems is serious in itself. But together they threaten the outcome of the entire development effort. . . .
Given the nature of this interrelated set of problems in our developing member countries—an insufficiency in foreign exchange due to trade difficulties, the inadequate flow of ODA, and the growing debt burden—the Bank, far from relaxing the momentum of our operations over the next five years, must increase it. And that is what we intend to do.
We plan to expand both our IBRD and IDA lending at a cumulative annual rate, in real terms, of 8%.
For the five-year period FY1974–78, our lending—in 1973 dollars—should total $22 billion for almost 1000 projects.

* Address to the Board of Governors by Robert S. McNamara, President, World Bank Group (September 24, 1973), pp. 5, 9–10, 12–14, 25–28.

The total cost of these projects will approach $55 billion.

Our $22 billion in new commitments will constitute, in real terms, a 40% increase over the 1969–1973 period, and a 175% increase over the 1964–1968 period.

This, then, in financial terms is our plan for the Second Five-Year Program. It will represent the largest program of technical and financial assistance to developing countries ever undertaken by a single agency.

But the qualitative changes in the program will be of even greater significance than the increase in its size. We plan to place far greater emphasis on policies and projects which will begin to attack the problems of absolute poverty to which I referred earler—far greater emphasis on assistance designed to increase the productivity of that approximately 40% of the population of our developing member countries who have neither been able to contribute significantly to national economic growth, nor to share equitably in economic progress.

Identifying the Concentrations of Poverty

This proposed reorientation of development strategy would require far greater precision in identifying the main concentrations of the poorest people in a given society and examining much more intensively the policies and investments through which they can be reached.

Clearly, the bulk of the poor today are in the rural areas. All of our analysis indicates that this is likely to continue to be the case during the next two or three decades:

—At present, 70% of the population of our developing member countries and an equivalent percentage of the poor live in the countryside.

—Although demographic projections indicate that 60% of the population increase in these countries (an increase of two billion people by the end of the century) is expected to take place in the urban areas—largely through internal migration—in the year 2000 more than half of the people in the developing world will still reside in the countryside.

—Rapid urbanization is already creating very serious problems. Under present policies, per capita public expenditures in urban areas are typically three to four times as great as they are in rural areas. Thus, efforts to relieve rural poverty by still greater migration to the cities will result in an even more inequitable division of public expenditures and only exacerbate the existing inequalities of income.

—Within the rural areas the poverty problem revolves primarily around the low productivity of the millions of small subsistence farms. The truth is that despite all the growth of the GNP, the increase in the productivity of these small family farms in the past decade has been so small as to be virtually imperceptible.

But despite the magnitude of the problem in the countryside, focusing on rural poverty raises a very fundamental question: is it a really sound strategy to devote a significant part of the world's resources to increasing the productivity of small-scale subsistence agriculture? Would it not be wiser to concentrate on the modern sector in the hope that its high rate of growth would filter down to the rural poor?

The answer, I believe, is no.

Experience demonstrates that in the short run there is only a limited transfer of benefits from the modern to the traditional sector. Disparities in income will simply widen unless action is taken which will directly benefit the poorest. In my view, therefore, there is no viable alternative to increasing the productivity of small-scale agriculture if any significant advance is to be made in solving the problems of absolute poverty in the rural areas.

But that does not mean there need be an irreconcilable conflict between that objective and the growth of the rest of the economy. On the contrary, it is obvious that no attempt to increase the productivity of subsistence agriculture can succeed in an environment of overall economic stagnation. The small farmers cannot prosper unless there is significant growth in other sectors, both to provide the development resources they will require, and to create the demand for their additional output.

The point is that the reverse is also true—and it is time we recognized it. Without rapid progress in smallholder agriculture throughout the developing world, there is little hope either of achieving long-term stable economic growth or of significantly reducing the levels of absolute poverty.

The fact is that very little has been done over the past two decades specifically designed to increase the productivity of subsistence agriculture. Neither political programs, nor economic plans, nor international assistance— bilateral or multilateral—have given the problem serious and sustained attention. The World Bank is no exception. In our more than a quarter century of operations, less than $1 billion out of our $25 billion of lending has been devoted directly to this problem.

It is time for all of us to confront this issue head-on.

An Action Program in the Bank

What can the Bank do to assist in this effort?

First of all, we expect to lend $4.4 billion in agriculture during our next five-year program (1974–78), as compared to $3.1 billion in the first five-year program (1969–73), and $872 million in the 1964–68 period.

This in itself is a formidable target, but more importantly we intend to direct an increasing share of our lending to programs which directly assist the small farmer to become more productive. In the next five years we expect that about 70% of our agricultural loans will contain a component for the smallholder. We are now preparing these programs in consultation with member governments.

But we recognize that at best our lending can finance only a small portion of the total credit and investment needs of small-holder agriculture. That is why we intend to give particular attention in our economic advice to governments to those sectoral and financial policies which most affect the rural poor so that the resources to be invested by governments will have a maximum impact.

And though experimentation and innovation will remain essential, the broad policies governing the Bank's program are clear:

—We are prepared to do much more to assist governments in the reform of their agricultural financial structure, and to support institutions designed to bring credit to the small farmer.

—We intend to continue to invest in large irrigation projects and in the recovery of saline lands, but we will emphasize on-farm development incorporating a maximum of self-financing so that the benefits of irrigation can reach small farmers more quickly.

—We will support non-irrigated agriculture, including the financing of livestock production, and in particular small-scale dairy farming in milk-deficient areas.

—We are prepared to finance the expansion of training facilities for extension agents who can help raise the productivity of the rural poor.

—We are prepared to finance rural works programs as well as multi-purpose rural development projects.

—We are ready to assist land and tenancy reform programs by providing the follow-up logistical support required by the small farmer, and to help in the technical and financial aspects of land purchase and consolidation.

—We have financed agricultural research institutions in the past and are fully prepared to do more in the future, particularly in the development of an appropriate technology for semi-arid agriculture. We propose to support investigation into the most effective use of water at the farm level, especially in water-deficient areas. We are already assisting one such investigation in Mexico.

—We will, in our lending for infrastructure, strongly urge that account be taken of the pressing needs of the rural areas.

Summary and Conclusions

Let me now summarize and conclude the central points I have made this morning.

If we look objectively at the world today, we must agree that it is characterized by a massive degree of inequality.

The difference in living standards between the rich nations and the poor nations is a gap of gigantic proportions.

The industrial base of the wealthy nations is so great, their technological capacity so advanced, and their consequent advantages so immense that it is unrealistic to expect that the gap will narrow by the end of the century. Every indication is that it will continue to grow.

Nothing we can do is likely to prevent this. But what we can do is begin to move now to insure that absolute poverty—utter degradation—is ended.

We can contribute to this by expanding the wholly inadequate flow of Official Development Assistance.

The flow of ODA can be increased, by 1980, to the target of .7% of GNP—a target originally accepted within the United Nations for completion by 1975.

This is feasible, but it will require renewed efforts by many nations, particularly the very richest.

Further, we must recognize that a high degree of inequality exists not only between developed and developing nations but within the developing nations themselves. Studies in the Bank during this past year reinforce the preliminary conclusions I indicated to you last year: income distribution patterns are severely skewed within developing countries—more so than within developed countries—and the problem requires accelerated action by the governments of virtually all developing nations.

A minimum objective should be that the distortion in income distribution within these nations should at least stop increasing by 1975, and begin to narrow within the last half of the decade.

A major part of the program to accomplish this objective must be designed to attack the absolute poverty which exists to a totally unacceptable degree in almost all of our developing member countries: a poverty so extreme that it degrades the lives of individuals below the minimal norms of human decency. The absolute poor are not merely a tiny minority of unfortunates—a miscellaneous collection of the losers in life—a regrettable but insignificant exception to the rule. On the contrary, they constitute roughly 40% of the nearly two billion individuals living in the developing nations.

Some of the absolute poor are in urban slums, but the vast bulk of them are in the rural areas. And it is there—in the countryside—that we must confront their poverty.

We should strive to eradicate absolute poverty by the end of this century. That means in practice the elimination of malnutrition and illiteracy, the reduction of infant mortality, and the raising of life-expectancy standards to those of the developed nations.

Essential to the accomplishment of this objective is an increase in the productivity of small-scale agriculture.

Is it a realistic goal?

The answer is yes, *if* governments in the developing countries are prepared to exercise the requisite political will to make it realistic.

It is they who must decide.

As for the Bank, increased productivity of the small, subsistence farmer will be a major goal of our program of expanded activity in the FY1974–78 period.

But no amount of outside assistance can substitute for the developing member governments' resolve to take on the task.

It will call for immense courage, for political risk is involved. The politically privileged among the landed elite are rarely enthusiastic over the steps necessary to advance rural development. This is shortsighted, of course, for in the long term they, as well as the poor, can benefit.

But if the governments of the developing world—who must measure the risks of reform against the risks of revolution—are prepared to exercise the requisite political will to assault the problem of poverty in the countryside, then the governments of the wealthy nation must display equal courage.

They must be prepared to help them by removing discriminatory trade barriers and by substantially expanding Official Development Assistance.

What is at stake in these decisions is the fundamental decency of the lives of 40% of the people in the 100 developing nations which are members of this institution.

We must hope that the decisions will be the courageous ones.

C. QUESTIONS

1. a. What is the case, if any, for aid? Is it essentially a matter of moral obligation? Or national self-interest? Or to attain other objectives?

b. What is the case against aid—from the "right" of the political spectrum? From the "left"?

2. It has been observed that while the Pearson Report recognizes that the gap between the developed and developing countries will continue to increase to three or four times its present absolute size by the end of this century, the analysis of the Report nonetheless remains based upon the almost unquestioned assumption that the primary purpose of aid is to enable countries to achieve self-sustaining growth, at which time aid can disappear, even though the gap may still persist or widen.

In contrast, it may be argued that "the continuing gap, not simply the date of attaining self-sufficiency, must set the perspective within which the problem of international development must be viewed. The problem of international development must be seen as a persistent problem of world inequality—the tendency of the rich to grow richer, in part with benefits to the poorer, in part to the disadvantage of the poorer, but on balance very must faster than the poorer. Far from being a short-lived phenomenon, the evidence suggests that this will be a growing characterisitc of the coming decades and will exacerbate present tensions to an unprecedented degree. Far from implying that aid will taper off by the end of the century, the widening gap implies that transfers of income and development assistance—whatever form they may take—will be required in much greater amounts." [Richard Jolly, "The

Aid Relationship: Reflections on the Pearson Report," *Journal of International Affairs* (1970), p. 168.]

Do you belive that an aid program should look forward to its termination? Or should we learn to live with continual aid, in lieu of an international progressive income tax?

3. What is the evidence that aid actually helps development?

4. a. In what ways, if any, do you think it is feasible to increase the quantum of aid? Is there a rationale for United States developmental aid that will mobilize public support?

 b. How would you improve the allocation of aid? Would you emphasize performance criteria? What if a country evidences poor performance but great need? What if a country requires aid as a precondition for more effective performance?

5. a. What exactly is the "burden" of aid?
 b. How should the problem of "burden-sharing" be met?
 c. Does a percentage target for aid have any meaning—given that aid involves various terms and conditions? Would you support the targets of the Pearson Report?

6. What determines debt-servicing capacities? What are the possible measures of debt-relief? What are the arguments against debt-rescheduling?

7. Many economists have concluded that the most obstinate constraint to development is the rate of change of agricultural output. How can foreign aid influence agricultural change? In this connection, consider the Pearson Report, Jackson Report, and activities of the World Bank.

8. What are your views on the following issues:
 a. project versus program aid,
 b. bilateral versus multilateral organization of aid programs,
 c. loans versus grants to developing countries,
 d. country aid versus regional aid.

9. Do you think the foregoing issues should be posed in terms of conflict? Can they be complementary?

10.   Would it be desirable to provide more continuity or au-
tomaticity in aid? How might this be done?

11.   Consider the various schemes for resource transfer from
rich to poor countries. What are the different effects of (a) explicit aid on a government-to-government basis; (b) aid
through a policy of preferential tariffs (see Problem III,
below); and (c) aid through a link with SDRs (see *Problems of
a World Monetary Order*, Problem III).

12.   According to a news report (January 24, 1974) the United
States chargé d'affaires in Jamaica stated that the United States
would cut off aid to Jamaica if it goes ahead with plans for
trade links and an air connection with Cuba. Would you agree
with such action by the United States?

13.   Jamaica's import bill for oil in 1973 was $77 million. It is
estimated that in 1974 the same amount of imported oil will
cost $165 million. The increase of $88 million is more than
Jamaica's total amount of foreign reserves (January 1974).
Should concessional finance be offered to Jamaica? If so,
under what international arrangements?

D. READINGS

Asher, R. E., *Development Assistance in the Seventies* (1970).
Byres, T. (ed.), *Foreign Resources and Economic Development: A Sym-
posium on the Pearson Commission* (1972).
Chenery, Hollis B., "Growth and Structural Change," *Finance and Develop-
ment* (September 1971).
Clark, Paul G., *American Aid for Development* (1972).
Frank, C. R., et al., *Assisting Developing Countries* (1972).
Gardner, R. N., and Max Millikan (eds.), *The Global Partnership: Interna-
tional Agencies and Economic Development* (1968).
Hawkins, E., *The Principles of Development Aid* (1972).
Jackson, Sir Robert, *A Study of the Capacity of the United Nations Develop-
ment System* (1969).
Jolly, Richard, "The Aid Relationship: Reflections on the Pearson Report,"
Journal of International Affairs (1970).
Little, I. M. D., and J. Clifford, *International Aid* (1965).

Mason, E. S., and R. E. Asher, *The World Bank since Bretton Woods* (1973).

Mikesell, R. F., *The Economics of Foreign Aid* (1968).

National Planning Association, *A New Conception of U.S. Foreign Aid* (March 1969).

Ohlin, G., *Foreign Aid Policies Reconsidered* (1966).

Pearson, Lester B., *Partners in Development* (1969).

Peterson, Rudolph A., *U.S. Foreign Assistance in the 1970's: A New Approach* (March 1970).

Pincus, J., *Trade, Aid and Development* (1967).

Streeten, P. P., *Aid to Africa: A Policy Outline for the 1970's* (1972).

Thorp, Willard L., "Foreign Aid: A Report on the Reports," *Foreign Affairs* (April 1970).

Tinbergen, Jan, *Report of the U.N. Committee for Development Planning* (1970).

Wall, David, *The Charity of Nations* (1973).

Ward, Barbara, *et al.*, *The Widening Gap: Development in the 1970's* (1971).

Problem II
Private Overseas Investment and Development: Bauxite Investment in Jamaica

A. THE CONTEXT

Doubts about foreign aid are giving rise to more interest in the contribution that private foreign capital might make to development. The flow of private capital was the earliest form of resource transfer to developing countries, with a long history before the postwar episode of international economic assistance or the more recent effort to transfer resources through tariff preferences. The history of direct foreign investment can be divided into three major periods: the earliest phase of investment in raw material and extractive industries; the postwar period of investment in import-substitution industries; and most recently, investment in manufactures and semi-manufactures for export.

Private overseas investment (POI) has, however, always been controversial; it is now in need of considerable rethinking. It has been said that

> many believe that POI may provide the key to this potential crisis in underdevelopment: in the absence of rising aid, POI may bridge the set of gaps that constrain development

in the Third World: the balance of payments gap, the resource gap, the savings gap, the technological gap, and
hence, in the long run the per capita income gap. Others
have argued that POI has been one of the major factors contributing to development of this crisis: that POI is merely
the twentieth-century refinement or economic outcome of
the gun-boat diplomacy of the imperialist powers of the last
century. On this view POI gives ever-greater foreign ownership of the capital stock, dominating the development of the
market structures, determining the allocation of resources
and the distribution of income, more especially the share
going to foreigners. By producing an ever-greater dependence of the underdeveloped economies upon those of the
developed countries, POI is thought to stand in the way of
national policy efforts at planned growth, and to frustrate
local entrepreneurial talent and the raising of employment.[1]

Many of these controversial elements run through this Policy Problem. But they should be given a more systematic assessment in terms of the particular benefits and costs of bauxite investment in Jamaica, and the alternative negotiating
strategies of the aluminum companies and the Jamaican government.

This Policy Problem relates to one of the most remarkable
episodes of private foreign investment and development since
the second World War: the investment in bauxite mining and
alumina refining in Jamaica by six major North American aluminum companies: Alcoa, Alcan, Reynolds, Kaiser, Anaconda,
and Revere. The discovery of bauxite deposits (the mineral
from which alumina is refined) has been highly significant for
Jamaica's development. Reynolds Metals made the first ship-
ment of bauxite exports from Jamaica in 1952. By 1957, the
island had become the world's largest producer of bauxite, and
now accounts for approximately one-quarter of the world's
bauxite production. By 1965, more than one-half of the United
States' imports of bauxite came from Jamaica, and it has remained the largest single source of bauxite used by the United
States aluminum industry, accounting for over 57 per cent of
United States imports in 1973. During 1972, the bauxite in-

1. Peter Ady (ed.), *Private Foreign Investment and the Developing World* (1971),
p. 3.

dustry contributed almost 15 per cent of Jamaica's GDP; royalties and corporate taxes paid by bauxite companies to the government in 1972–73 were almost $25 million; and bauxite and alumina exports of almost $190 million accounted for almost two-thirds of the value of Jamaica's exports.[2] The island's reserves of commercial grade bauxite are believed to be well in excess of 1 billion tons.[3]

1. BENEFITS AND COSTS OF POI

The substantial exports of bauxite and alumina raise the question whether this mining sector can act as a "leading sector," propelling the development of the Jamaican economy. Economists have expressed different views on the potential for international trade as an "engine of growth." [4] The problem of export-led development acquires an additional dimension when the rise in exports is linked to direct private foreign investment.

The double-edged character of this investment is emphasized by the former Secretary-General of the Commonwealth Caribbean Regional Secretariat in the following extract.

DIRECT FOREIGN INVESTMENT *

[T]he most prominent feature of the international transfer of funds in recent years has been the emergence of the international or multinational corporations engaging in direct investment abroad. . . .

With direct investment, unlike portfolio investment, the multinational corporation owns the physical productive assets directly, and not merely a paper claim entitling it to a flow of interest or dividends and capital repayment. But much more than the direct ownership of

* *From CARIFTA to Caribbean Community*, Report of the Secretary-General (William Demas) of the Commonwealth Caribbean Regional Secretariat (1973), pp. 66–69.

2. Government of Jamaica, *Economic Survey 1972* (1973), pp. 46, 118. The "bauxite industry" refers to both the mining of bauxite and the manufacturing of alumina from bauxite; "bauxite companies" refer to both bauxite and alumina companies.

Dollar amounts are expressed in Jamaican dollars (J$), unless otherwise specified; in 1972, J$1 = U.S.$1.20. In 1973, the Jamaican dollar was devalued and J$1 = U.S.$1.10.

3. Jamaican Geological Survey Department, *The Mineral Resources of Jamaica*, (Bulletin No. 8, 1973), p. 14.

4. See G. M. Meier, *Leading Issues in Economic Development* (1970), chapter 8, and bibliography, pp. 584–85.

the physical plant overseas is involved. Foreign direct investment through the multinational corporation involves the transfer of a whole productive and organisational complex, embracing a bundle of factors of production—not merely capital, but also knowledge, technology, management, know-how and marketing skills. Consequently, the return on foreign direct investment includes, at least conceptually, much more than the return on capital. It also includes payments for management, marketing services and particularly for technology—in the form of patent fees, licence fees, royalties and technical and management charges.

Because of this "package," direct foreign investment is more complex in its effects on the recipient country than either, say, portfolio investment or foreign aid. These last two forms of foreign borrowing raise problems of debt service for the borrowing country. Many developing countries now face serious problems of the burden of debt service in respect of both fixed-interest portfolio investment and foreign aid in relation to their annual earnings of foreign exchange. But the analysis of the effects of this kind of foreign borrowing is much simpler and less controversial than is the case with direct foreign investment. There is no consensus among the "best" economists in the developed countries with regard to the effects of direct foreign investment on both the country of origin and the recipient country. Moreover, because of this and because the subject is one of political economy rather than one of pure economics, such a consensus is unlikely ever to emerge.

From the point of view of progressive, nationally-oriented economists in Third World countries, direct foreign investment is viewed not so much in terms of its effects on real national income and the balance of payments of the recipient country (which are much more difficult to analyse than is usually thought) as in terms of its effects on the long-run capacity of the recipient economy to transform itself mainly by its own efforts—that is to say, to achieve internally propelled growth.

In this kind of analysis the main considerations include structural and institutional factors—such as the effects of continuing large-scale foreign ownership on the pattern of wage and salary rates and on the distortion of the labour market in recipient countries and the effects of these in creating agricultural backwardness and unemployment; the effect on the capacity and scope for indigenous enterprise and entrepreneurship; the effect on indigenous capacity for making technological innovations and for adapting imported technology; the effect on the ability of the recipient country to generate a large enough volume of national savings; the effect on the possibilities for creating linkages between the different economic sectors and activities in the recipient countries (since the multinational corporations tend to import components and inputs from the home country); and, more generally, the effects on national decision-making and on the use and allocation of national resources by economic policy-makers in the recipient countries.

Viewed in this perspective, foreign direct investment on a very large scale taking place over a long period of time (or foreign domination of the economy) is very much a double-edged sword. Such investments can certainly assist by increasing real national income in the aggregate sense, providing some well paid jobs for both manual and white collar workers, introducing some local personnel to managerial and marketing skills (since in many cases the local subsidiary of the multinational corporation is more anxious than the traditional local firm to give opportunity to local talent on the basis of merit); they can pay (particularly in the mineral sector and also, after the end of tax holidays, in the case of the manufacturing sector) good revenues to the Government. In some cases, too, such investments are in a position to gain export markets for manufactures while in all cases, in the case of minerals, a vertically integrated international corporation provides its own markets abroad.

On the other hand, excessive domination of the economy by foreign direct investment can create severe distortions in the labour market of the recipient country by creating enclaves paying high wages and salaries not related to productivity in the rest of the economy. In this way it can destroy as many jobs as it creates; retard agricultural development; and, through trade union action, lead to rapidly rising wages and salaries in the public sector. It can restrict exports of manufactures to both intra and extra-regional markets by restrictive licencing agreements imposed on its subsidiaries or on independent local firms purchasing its technology or its brand names. It can inhibit the local development of a capital market, since the savings of each subsidiary of a multinational corporation are specific to the corporation: such savings are never re-invested in other activities locally but are either re-invested in the same activity or remitted to the head-office. It can create very strong linkages between the subsidiary and the economy of the country of origin and so fail to integrate the national economy by creating internally forward and backward linkages. It can add to problems of unemployment by introducing highly capital-intensive technologies inappropriate to the labour-surplus situation in developing countries.

Consequently, foreign economic domination ought to be sharply reduced in the interest of creating a more soundly and broadly based pattern of economic growth.

On the other hand, the kind of analysis sketched out above also leads to the conclusion that there is still room for foreign direct investment to supplement but not supplant national efforts. After reducing foreign domination in the key sectors of the economies, "normal" foreign private investment, operating within the framework of a clearly laid out Government policy, could still make an important contribution to economic development in the Region, as well as in other Third World Countries.

A strategy for localisation of the economy would, of course, throw a great burden on local savings, local enterprise, local initiative and local managerial capacity. But this is precisely the point of development. Development, properly conceived, means the capacity of the population to face up to challenges and to make efforts and sacrifices. Development is never without tears. Development means learning by doing. In the illuminating formulation of the distinguished Caribbean economist, Felipe Pazos: "The main weakness of direct investment as a development agent is a consequence of the complete character of its contribution. . . ."

Over the last four years the Governments of the Region, particularly those of the More Developed countries, have been instituting programmes of localisation of foreign-owned enterprises.

In Jamaica, it has been for some time now the practice of the Government, in giving concessions to foreign investors in manufacturing and tourism, to make it a condition that part of the equity should be issued to local private investors. The majority of hotels are now in local hands, but since foreign investors have concentrated on the larger hotels, foreign interests hold a majority of the total value of assets of the industry. A programme of localisation is also being implemented with respect to the commercial banks and insurance companies operating in Jamaica: these institutions are now incorporating locally, establishing a capital structure in respect of the locally incorporated companies, and issuing up to 51% of the equity within a five-year period to local private investors. Even prior to this, the Jamaica Citizens Bank was established as a joint venture in partnership with a small American Bank. In addition, in 1971, the Government acquired a 51% equity in the local operations of Cable and Wireless and a new joint venture, known as JAMINTEL, was incorporated locally to this end. The 51% equity is to be paid off by the Government out of its share of future profits of the new company over a fairly long period of time. The same procedure of payment over a number of years had also been applied to the purchases by the Government in 1971 of some 30,000 acres of sugar lands formerly owned by Tate and Lyle. According to newspaper reports, the Government also seems to have acquired interest in the formerly fully foreign-owned electricity company operating in the country. There is no foreign-owned newspaper in the country. But the telephone and Bus Transport systems remain under foreign control. The Government owns the only television station and one of the two radio stations; and the only daily newspaper in the country is owned by private Jamaican investors.

Increasingly, the Government is encouraging the use of local consultants and contractors for development projects executed in the country, except for very large projects and those financed by tied foreign aid. The Government has also taken steps to tighten up on the sale of land to foreigners for real estate and hotel development. The Government of Jamaica established in 1968 an international airline, Air Jamaica, flying between Jamaica and North America. The bauxite and alumina installations, the biggest investments in the country, are all exclusively owned by North American interests. The new Government has set up a National Bauxite Commission to make recommendations on ways and means of maximising the benefits to the Nation from the industry.

The social benefits and costs of foreign investment are now of prime interest to developing countries in order to determine whether, in the first place, the entry of POI should be allowed; and if so, under what conditions, and for what period of time. In broadest terms, the calculation of the benefits and costs depends on both the allocation of the investment within the host country and the form of the investment (e.g., whether it is composed of 100 per cent foreign equity or is a joint venture; whether it has a terminal date for divestment or unlimited life; and other conditions of entry and operation).

In more specific terms, the benefits of direct foreign investment are as follows:

1. Foreign savings are made available to the host country, and these savings supplement domestic resources.

2. Foreign exchange is also made available, and this increases the country's capacity to import.

3. Over time as the investment operates, the increase in real national income is greater than the resultant increase in the income of the investor: the value added to output must then be greater than the amount appropriated by the foreign investor. This increase in national product must therefore have been shared with domestic labor in the form of higher wages, domestic suppliers, or the government through royalty payments and higher tax revenue.

4. The provision of managerial knowledge and skills, including organizational know-how and access to foreign markets. The training, hiring, and promotion of national managers may also be significant.

5. The training of labor, and an opportunity for labor to "learn by doing."

6. The transfer of technology from more advanced countries.

7. The spill-over effects of advanced management, technology and a trained labor force. These constitute significant transfers of nonmonetary resources that may be considered as equivalent to "private technical assistance," with important educative effects extending elsewhere in the host economy beyond the immediate foreign enterprise.

On the other side, the costs of direct foreign investment are:

1. Special concessions by the government that may be necessary to attract the foreign investment but which involve a fiscal cost in the form of tax concessions or greater government expenditure for additional public services, financial assistance, or subsidization of inputs.

2. A negative effect on domestic saving if the foreign investment competes with home investment and reduces profits in domestic industries, or if the foreign investment limits the supply of domestic entrepreneurship.

3. The cost of balance of payments adjustment. Unless the inflow of foreign investment continues at an increasing rate, a time will come when the inflow of new capital is insufficient to cover the return outflow of interest, dividends, and profits. The recipient country then has to generate a surplus on current account in its balance of payments. To do this, the country may have to incur the costs of deflation, direct controls over trade, or devaluation. These indirect costs of balance of payments adjustment are what are most significant for the problem of servicing a foreign investment—not the direct costs. For the direct costs of servicing are not a matter of concern as long as the foreign investment is productive.

4. Political and social costs through the possible loss of national autonomy in domestic policy-making if the foreign enterprise or the foreign investor's government exerts undue influence on the host government's policies. The loss of national identity and control may be psychologically and sociologically undesirable. The recipient country may also believe it is excessively dependent on foreign technology, management and capital.

When negotiating over conditions of entry, operation, and repatriation of foreign capital, the foreign investor and the relevant agencies of the host government should establish a case for or against the investment in terms of a time profile of these benefits and costs.

After considering the benefit/cost ratio of POI, a developing country has then to compare this assessment with the next best alternative. It is essential to be clear on whether what is being assessed is the *investment* project *per se*, or the *"foreignness"* of the investment, or the *"multinational"* character of the foreign investment, or some *alternative* institutional arrangement for acquiring the ingredients of the investment.

It is now notable that opportunities are increasing for the transfer of nonmonetary foreign resources—that is, for managerial and technical knowledge from the more advanced countries. International trade in ideas can be as significant as trade in commodities. One of the greatest benefits to the recipient country is the access to foreign knowledge that private foreign investment provides—knowledge that helps overcome the managerial gap and technological gap. For many countries, however, the cost of foreign equity capital is high, even post-tax. The host country may therefore consider this cost excessive for the foreign managerial and technical knowledge which it desires but which cannot be acquired through a direct foreign investment without the high payment for equity capital with which the foreign knowledge is in joint supply. Accordingly, many developing countries are beginning to focus on alternative sources for capital, management, and technology in order to determine if the cost of the "package" can be reduced. A variety of alternative contractual arrangements might be considered. For some types of investment projects, the use of license agreements, technical service agreements, engineering and construction contracts, management contracts, and co-production agreements can prove of considerable benefit for developing countries—supplying the needed foreign knowledge in many cases at a lower cost than must be paid when the knowledge comes with equity capital.

Management consulting firms, engineering firms, and construction enterprises are important agents for this type of managerial and technological transfer. The cost may be borne on an enterprise-to-enterprise basis. Or it may prove more desirable for payment for the foreign knowledge to be made by the government of the host country and then have the government disseminate the knowledge freely to domestic firms. It is also conceivable that international agencies might assume a more extensive role in scientific research designed to meet the particular problems of developing countries and to develop a technology more suited to the local conditions in these countries. In view of the unemployment problem, there is increasing concern over "appropriate technology" for the less-developed countries.

In general, new contractual arrangements can be made to be extremely flexible devices for securing the transfer of the non-monetary resources of management and technology. Their adaptability to widely diverse circumstances and their utility in meeting a variety of objectives are becoming increasingly appreciated. This is especially true when certain industries are reserved under a development program for public ownership or for majority ownership by local nationals but there is a need for seeking technical information or managerial services from abroad.

In terms of cost/benefit analysis as applied to project evaluation, we can summarize the steps involved in the evaluation of a foreign investment project: [5]

1. Indentification of the expected stream of inputs and outputs resulting from the project along with any nonmarket influences (e.g., externalities, effects on income distribution);

2. Conversion of the input-output streams into streams of net benefits (i.e., difference between benefits and costs) of different types corresponding to the different objectives of development planning;

3. Derivation of one stream of total net benefits by applying appropriate relative weights to different types of benefits;

4. Estimation of the present value of the total net benefit stream by summing up the discounted series of total net benefits, using the relevant social rates of discount;

5. See UNCTAD, *Methods of Evaluating the Economic Effects of Private Foreign Investment* (Report by A. K. Sen), TD/B/C.3/94/Add.1 (20 August 1971), p. 18.

5. Selection or rejection of the proposed project based on the present value estimated.

If negotiations over the entry and operation of foreign investment were to proceed in terms of rational economic calculations, the host country would adopt as its criterion for entry the condition that the present value of net benefits expected from the foreign investment be positive. The life of the foreign investment would be terminated, however, through a divestment or "fade out" requirement at a date when the calculation of the present value of net benefits became negative, or when the present value of net benefits from the domestic ownership of the investment became greater than from foreign investment.

At the outset of the investment, there may be available alternative arrangements for the same project (i.e., different combinations of foreign and domestic ownership and contractual arrangements for management and technology). The best alternative—in the sense of highest present value of net benefits —should then be selected from the set of alternatives. Again, the life of this arrangement should be terminated when the present value calculation turns negative, or when another alternative arrangement yields a higher present value.

All these calculations confront the practical difficulties of determining what shadow prices should be used to reflect social weighting (especially the weight to be given to externalities and merit wants), what social rate of discount should be used to reflect the community's time preference, (that is, the rate at which society is prepared to postpone consumption from the present to the future), and what weight should be given to the effects of the investment on employment and income distribution.

Such calculations clearly become difficult exercises in applied welfare economics. Further, the problem is complicated even more by the various noneconomic, political, and ideological elements that are likely to enter into the host country's evaluation of the effects of the foreign investment.

If divestment is to be required, the transfer of ownership can be done in several ways, as suggested in an UNCTAD report: [6]

6. UNCTAD, *Private Foreign Investment in Its Relationship to Development,* TD/134 (17 November 1971), p. 15.

[T]ransfer from foreign to local ownership is far from cost-less. The most immediate problem is how the transfer is to be financed. The foreign company will expect to be paid a sum corresponding to the present value of its future earn-ings. One possibility is for the country to finance this sum out of its foreign exchange reserves—but the sum will usually be too large for that. Another is to finance it in local currency, in the hope that the firm will reinvest in new de-velopments locally—but often the firm will be unwilling to do this. A third possibility is to finance the sum by the issue of government bonds which can be converted into foreign exchange over a period of time—but this combines elements of both the previous disadvantages. Two other solutions have been suggested. One is that transfer should be effected by the government accepting shares in the company, in lieu of taxes, over a period of years. The disadvantage of this is that the government would have to forego its revenue dur-ing that period. The other is that some international inter-mediary (sometimes described as a "divestment corpora-tion") should be established, to supply a form of bridging finance; the intermediary would make immediate payment to the foreign investor, and be reimbursed over a period of time by the government acquiring the investment. This suggestion is by no means free of drawbacks—notably the very large sums that might need to be available to the inter-mediary—but it may supply some of the answers.

2. MULTINATIONAL CORPORATIONS

The analysis of foreign investment becomes even more com-plex when the agency of the investment is a multinational cor-poration (MNC), as is true for bauxite investment in Jamaica. The distinguishing feature of an MNC is that its operations constitute an international system that combines equity capi-tal, technology, and marketing facilities spread through many countries and responsive to a common management strategy. The growth of MNCs has recently attracted considerable atten-tion, and a number of studies have been undertaken on the organization and functions of the MNC.[7]

7. Raymond Vernon, *Sovereignty at Bay: The Multinational Spread of U.S. En-terprises* (1971); J. N. Behrman, *National Interests and the Multinational Enterprise* (1970); J. N. Behrman, *Some Patterns in the Rise of the Multinational Enterprise* (1971); J. Dunning (ed.), *The Multinational Enterprise* (1971); D. F. Vagts, "The Mul-tinational Enterprise: A New Challenge for Transnational Law," *Harvard Law Review*, Vol. 83 (1970), pp. 739–92; R. O. Keohane and J. S. Nye, Jr. (eds.), *Transnational Relations and World Politics* (1972), pp. 97–114, 325–55.

Certain characteristics of the MNC may be especially relevant for this Policy Problem:

i. The decision-making process of the MNC is global in scope. The entire range of major decisions (finance, investment, production, research and development, and reaction to governmental measures) consider the opportunities and problems that the MNC confronts in all the countries in which it operates.

ii. Decision-making may also be centralized, with the top management of the parent-concern reserving to itself whatever powers over its subsidiaries that it believes important—usually, financial control, inter-affiliate transfer prices, allocation of export markets, and investment decisions.

iii. For the MNC, the relevant profit is that of the total net-worth of the investor's interests, not that of the individual subsidiary alone. The MNC utilizes a "global scanning capacity" in determining its investment plan, sourcing strategies, and marketing based upon expectations of returns and risk factors.

iv. The MNC tends to be less of a risk-averter to the extent that it operates in a number of countries, produces a number of products, and has greater maneuverability with respect to marketing opportunities and conditions of production than does a firm of lesser scope.

In the development of natural resources, the MNC is directed either to selling the product on the world market directly or to using the raw material as an input for its own internationally integrated processing operations, as is the case of bauxite. A major conflict may then arise with the host country over the degree of local processing.

The feature of vertical integration is especially significant. Its occurrence depends on circumstances which let the firm capture rents by supplying the input to itself, reducing risks about the continuity of supply, controlling the quality of the input, or some combination of these benefits.

Professor Caves concludes that

> [W]e can . . . use . . . evidence on the determinants of vertical integration, extracted from studies of industries and national economies, to generate a few predictions which seem

to agree with actual patterns of international investment of the vertical type. We expect it to occur to a greater degree where one or more of the following circumstances are present:

1. The world processing industry consists of relatively few companies of relatively large absolute size.

2. The raw material is found in relatively few deposits which require a large initial investment either to find or to bring to production.

3. The raw material is found in countries that are relatively short of entrepreneurship and social overhead capital. That is to say, if other things are equal, the less developed countries would be the principal recipients of vertical direct investment. Mature countries might receive direct investment for the development of large scale resources, such as iron ore or hydroelectric power for aluminum production, but less developed countries would also receive investments for activities with lesser scale economies such as raw rubber production.[8]

When there is vertical integration the matter of transfer prices becomes an important variable in the MNC's analysis and planning of operations. The traditional foreign trade importers and exporters dealt at "arm's length," establishing a market price. In the earlier stages of development of MNCs, internal purposes independent of government restraints—in particular, cost accounting motivations—dictated the setting of transfer prices. There may be no market sales for comparison but the internal operation of the MNC requires a transfer price or pricing mechanism acceptable to the different divisions of the MNC. It is commonly said that if the MNC is concerned with overall profit, not profit at any particular stage, then the dominant motivation behind the pricing structure is to gain maximum advantage vis-à-vis the different governmental schemes of taxation and regulation of international flows. Transfer prices or cost allocation techniques then acquire an artificial quality.

In this Problem, it will be repeatedly seen that whether justified or not (indeed, this question is a major issue), the MNC

8. Richard E. Caves, "Foreign Investment, Trade and Industrial Growth," in Joe S. Bain (ed.), *Essays on Economic Development* (1970), pp. 14–15.

is suspect—not only because of its "foreignness" but because it is believed that a marked inequality exists in the negotiation relationship between the MNCs and the Jamaican government. This is often expressed vaguely in terms of the "power" of the MNC, its "large size," its "mysterious operations." These concerns can be translated in more specific terms to mean that the MNC has a greater range of options than does the host government through the MNC's practices of transfer pricing on interaffiliate sales, technology ascendancy in a vertically integrated firm, royalty payments for technology, and interaffiliate debt-equity strategy. The individual nation senses futility in making the MNC accountable for its international operations. And while the host government can control only a fraction of the MNC's global operations, the MNC shapes its world-wide operations in light of national policy to maximize global after-tax profits.

A description of the MNC's global organization or the control relationships between subsidiary and parent does not, however, in itself constitute an indictment of the MNC. A foreign investment may yield some unique benefits to an individual nation precisely because of its multinational quality. Instead of prejudging the effects of an investment simply because it is undertaken by an MNC, the very problem is to determine if the MNC's investment yields a net social benefit to the host country.

As an UNCTAD report observes:

> Certain of the characteristics of multinational companies could be of service to developing countries—their command over capital, their ability to supply managerial and technical skills, their expertise in identifying and expanding markets, particularly export markets, their relatively long time-horizons, and their potential for assisting in the process of regional integration. A problem for developing countries is how far they can secure these benefits from multinational companies without becoming dominated by them, or permitting their economic development to be distorted. . . .
>
> The question whether a particular private foreign investment project is socially profitable for the host country, and if so to what extent, cannot be determined *a priori* but requires careful analytical investigation in the circumstances of each case. Projects have to be reviewed in the light of their consistency with the development objectives of the

host country, including such factors as the growth and distribution of income, the expansion of employment opportunities, and the absorption of new skills and technology. . . .

If agreement is to be reached between host countries and foreign companies and is to remain satisfactory to both sides, it must be characterized by stability and flexibility. Host countries are entitled to establish the ground rules for foreign investment, and should do so in a manner which makes it quite clear to foreign investors where they stand on such questions as whether there are any sectors of the economy in which foreign investment is not welcome; what restrictions will be applied to transfers of profit and repatriation of capital; what rates of taxation will be levied; what degree of local participation in ownership and control is envisaged, either immediately or in future; and what may be required by way of employment of local personnel and use of locally produced inputs . . . While governments are free to change the ground rules affecting private foreign investment, they have to weigh the gains achieved thereby in relation to the prospects for any future collaboration with private foreign capital that they may have in mind. In these as in other respects, what is necessary is that governments and foreign investors should have regard to each other's legitimate interests.[9]

Highly pertinent to this Problem is how the powers of the MNC may introduce areas of policy conflict—or policy complementarity—between the MNC and the host government in terms of their goals, time horizons, and their respective domains of decision-making. Some might characterize the situation as if a new international industrial state were transcending the national political state. In transcending the nation-state, the global strategy and centralized decision-making powers of the MNC may diminish the policy autonomy of the nation-state. If so, is this a handicap to the host country's development?

Instead of being in opposition, however, might not the MNC and nation-state serve complementary functions? If they have different goals and utilize different instruments of power, might not the MNC and nation-state be complementary in some functions rather than in competitive conflict?

9. UNCTAD, *Private Foreign Investment in Its Relationship to Development* (November 1971), pp. 2–3, 8–9.

Finally, instead of considering the development of the nation-state in monolithic terms, is it not more meaningful to examine how the MNC affects the interests of different groups in the host country?

As this Problem indicates, the bargaining situation between the host government and MNCs involves more subtle relationships than can be captured by the simple cliché of the MNC versus the nation-state.

3. THE BAUXITE-ALUMINUM INDUSTRY

For understanding this Problem, it is desirable to have some background knowledge of the structure of the world's aluminum industry.

The production of aluminum involves three major stages: mining of bauxite ore, refining of alumina, and smelting of aluminum. Between four and six tons of bauxite are required to produce approximately two tons of alumina which are in turn required for producing one ton of aluminum. The aluminum ingot is fabricated into mill products (sheet and plate, foil, rod, bar, etc.) and then used in final products (building and construction, transportation, consumer durables, containers, and packaging, etc.). Because the largest producers of primary aluminum are vertically integrated from the stage of mining bauxite through the production of aluminum ingot or final products, only very limited quantities of bauxite and alumina are sold on the world market. Without the existence of an "arm's length price" for bauxite, the vertically integrated aluminum producers utilize accounting transfer prices for intracompany use of the intermediate product.

The three stages in production tend to occur in different geographical locations. Although it is technologically possible to separate aluminum from many types of ore, the most economical source to date is bauxite ore. Formed by the weathering of rocks in areas of heavy rainfall—mainly in tropical areas—the bauxite consists of hydrates of aluminum. Bauxite deposits of commercial value are concentrated in a relatively few countries. The bauxite is mined mainly by open-pit methods, with stripping operations undertaken by tractor-driven scrapers, bulldozers, bucket excavators, power shovels, and walking draglines. Aside from the earth-moving equipment, the facilities for crushing and drying to reduce shipping costs are the principal installations along with transportation and ore-handling facilities. The cost of mining bauxite represents a relatively small percentage of total costs of aluminum production.

While the mining of bauxite ore involves a mechanical process, the second stage of producing alumina involves a chemical process, and the third stage of aluminum production is based on an electrolytic process. With existing technology almost all bauxite used for production of aluminum is first subjected to the Bayer process which separates impurities from the aluminum hydrates, and these hydrates are reduced to alumina. The physical facilities for production of alumina consist of grinders, heat and steam plants, mixers, tanks and kilns, and materials-handling equipment. The principal materials required are bauxite, fuel, caustic soda, and water. The product that emerges is a white powder—alumina.

The costs of shipping bauxite and alumina are nearly equal per ton mile, but the aluminum content of alumina is approximately twice that of bauxite, so that transport costs may be reduced by locating alumina plants near bauxite mines instead of near aluminum smelters. Alumina production is relatively capital-intensive, but it does not require plentiful electrical power as does the smelting process.

As with bauxite mining, the total initial capital investment required for an alumina plant will vary considerably according to the special characteristics of its specific location. According to one report, "The investment in an alumina plant alone, excluding related facilities can be of the order of $150 per short ton for a 330,000 ton plant, or about $50 million. But when it is also necessary to provide the bauxite mines, mining equipment, a port, ship channel, town site, railroad transportation, public housing, hospitals, and schools in remote areas, then the investment is much greater, and a much larger plant capacity is required to make a feasible project . . . The 950,000 ton Alpart project in Jamaica is reported to have required nearly $200 million, including bauxite mines and port, but no town site or housing." [10]

10. *Metal Bulletin, Integration in Aluminum,* Winter 1969, p. 83.

At the third stage of production, aluminum is produced from alumina by separating the metal from its oxide by an electrolytic reduction process. The process is highly capital-intensive and an abundant supply of low-priced energy is required for the smelting operation. The capital costs are high, and an integrated aluminum firm of optimal size requires an initial investment of several hundred million to $1 billion. There are, however, significant economies of scale in aluminum reduction. For these reasons, the primary aluminum industry has to date remained characterized by a limited number of large companies mostly located in developed countries where there has been inexpensive electric power sources and the added advantage of proximity to final markets.

Just as bauxite is the major cost element in the production of alumina, reducing alumina is the major cost item in the production of aluminum. In the production of alumina, the costs will vary, of course, in different alumina plants. For illustrative purposes, however, a United Nations study estimated in 1966 that for an alumina plant with access to high-quality bauxite and with an annual capacity of 330,000 tons (close to the optimal size) the average costs of production would be about $59 per short ton of alumina, broken down as follows: [11]

Input	Quantity	Cost ($)
Bauxite	2.1 tons	16.80
Caustic soda	80 kg NaOH	5.10
Steam	2 tons	3.30
Electric power	200 kwh	0.80
Fuel for calcination	130 liters fuel oil	2.60
Labor, operating, maintenance, and indirect	3 man hours	7.50
Maintenance, materials and equipment	—	3.00
Capital Cost:	$43 million	
Depreciation on fixed capital		9.00
Interest on fixed capital		7.20
Miscellaneous supplies and general expenses		3.70
TOTAL		59.00

In this cost breakdown, about 30 per cent of the total average cost is accounted for by bauxite, another 30 per cent by capital costs, less than 15 per cent by labor costs, and the remainder by miscellaneous other items.

The costs of aluminum production have also been estimated for an integrated aluminum complex. Considering a hypothetical plant that would conform to engineering approximations of input requirements in plants with "optimal" capacities of alumina and aluminum production, it has been estimated that the average cost of production in 1966 of one ton of aluminum was as follows.[12]

Input	Quantity (per ton of aluminum output)	Cost (Dollars, per ton of output)
Bauxite	4.2 tons	33.60
Caustic soda	160 kg	10.20
Steam	4 tons	6.60
Electric power	17,900 kwh	62.60
Fuel oil for calcination	260 liters	5.20
Fluoride	35 kg	25.00
Carbon	560 kg	25.00
Labor	20 man hours	57.00
Operating and maintenance supplies	—	24.00
Annual capital cost	—	123.40
Miscellaneous	—	45.40
TOTAL		418.00

In these estimates, the cost function of aluminum production is dominated by the cost of the last stage of reducing alumina to aluminum, which accounts for approximately two-thirds of the average per ton costs of production. Bauxite production accounts for less than 10 per cent, and alumina production for about 25 per cent of total production costs.

11. Cost estimates are presented in United Nations, *Studies in Economics of Industry 2: Pre-Investment Data for the Aluminium Industry*, ST/CID/9 (1966) pp. 9–10, 17–18; Charles River Associates, *An Economic Analysis of the Aluminum Industry* (1971) chapter 2, Appendix A.

12. See references in footnote 11.

Table I. Input-Output Table for Ton of Aluminium:
Mining to Semi-Fabricating [early 1960's]

	Quantity	Value £J	Value Cumulated £J
PROCESS		Mining and drying	
Inputs		2.85	
Value added: (i) Labour		1.58	1.58
(ii) Other		6.27	6.27
Total value added		7.85	7.85
Gross value: Bauxite	4.074 long tons	10.70	
PROCESS		Beneficiation	
Inputs: Bauxite	4.074 long tons	10.70	
Other		11.63	
Total inputs		22.33	
Value added: (i) Labour		4.28	5.86
(ii) Other		17.38	23.66
Total value added		21.67	29.52
Gross value: Alumina	1.9 short tons	44.00	
PROCESS		Smelting	
Inputs: Alumina	1.9 short tons	44.00	
Electricity		20.00	
Other		26.25	
Total inputs		90.25	
Value added: (i) Labour		21.16	27.02
(ii) Other		48.37	72.03
Total value added		69.53	99.05
Gross value: Aluminium	1 short ton	159.78	
PROCESS		Semi-fabricating	
Inputs: Aluminium and Alloys	1 short ton	163.78	
Fuel		9.07	
Other		73.28	
Total inputs		246.14	
Value added: (i) Labour		80.85	107.87
(ii) Other		55.71	127.74
Total value added		136.66	235.60
Gross value		382.71	

NOTE: Values used are in Jamaican pounds; at time of calculation, one English pound sterling equaled £J.1 equaled U.S. $2.80.

SOURCE: Calculated from data in U.S. Bureau of the Census: *Census of Manufactures 1963; and Census of Mineral Industries, 1963;* and from data on the Caribbean producers. Adapted from Norman Girvan, *The Caribbean Bauxite Industry,* Studies in Regional Integration, Vol. 2, No. 4 (1967), p. 3.

It also follows that value added increases markedly at each stage of production. Table I offers some indication of the value added at each production stage; although the values are out of date, the magnitudes serve to illustrate the relative amounts of income created at each stage. It is clear that the greatest value added occurs in the reduction of alumina to primary ingot, and that the production processes of beneficiation and smelting are more labor-intensive than bauxite mining.

It should be noted that Jamaica has some special advantages in bauxite mining: large quantities of reserves; a thin "overburden" on the bauxite deposits so that extraction costs are low; internal accessibility; locational proximity to the large United States market and the hydropower facilities in Canada.

The Jamaican alumina plants have been especially designed, however, for the use of Jamaican bauxite. This bauxite is not readily substitutable for other bauxites in existing alumina plants outside of Jamaica that have been designed to use other bauxites.

Tables II, III, and IV compare Jamaican and world outputs of bauxite and alumina.

Tables V and VI indicate the recent trends in bauxite production in Jamaica and bauxite and alumina exports.

At present, all Jamaican bauxite is exported to the United States by three companies, Kaiser, Reynolds, and Alcoa. Of the alumina which is exported by Alcan, Alpart, and Revere, nearly a third is transferred to the United States, about one-fifth goes to Canada, a third to Norway and Sweden, while the rest is shipped to the United Kingdom, Venezuela, Poland, and the U.S.S.R.

At present six North American companies hold concessions for bauxite ore in Jamaica. Tables VII and VIII give the basic details on the bauxite and alumina operations in Jamaica.

Growth of the world aluminum industry has been rapid, with world aluminum consumption rising at an average rate of almost 10 per cent per annum during the last two decades. The elasticity of demand for aluminum has been high with respect to industrial production. By the mid-1950's, aluminum reached a position of leadership second only to iron among the five most widely used metals of the world. In all countries, other

Table II. Bauxite: World Contribution by Countries (thousand long tons)

Country	1968	1969	1970	1971	1972
NORTH AMERICA					
United States	1,665	1,843	2,082	1,988	1,927
LATIN AMERICA					
Brazil	309	343	492	492	324
Dominican Republic	979	1,076	1,050	1,291	1,200
Guyana	3,663	4,238	4,079	3,757	3,668
Haiti	439	654	621	663	782
Jamaica	8,390	10,333	11,820	12,244	12,345
Surinam	5,571	6,138	5,916	6,611	7,777
EUROPE					
France	2,670	2,753	3,003	3,066	3,258
Greece	1,807	1,807	2,242	3,039	2,700
Hungary	1,928	1,904	1,990	2,057	2,356
Romania	20	49	299	300	893
U.S.S.R	4,900	4,100	4,200	4,400	5,800
Yugoslavia	2,039	2,094	2,066	1,928	2,197
AFRICA					
Ghana	280	242	344	324	334
Guinea	2,084	2,420	2,600	2,600	2,600
Sierra Leone	463	447	433	581	693
ASIA					
China Mainland	374	440	490	540	550
India	922	1,064	1,338	1,414	1,659
Indonesia	865	753	1,210	1,218	1,276
Malaysia	786	1,056	1,121	962	1,076
Turkey	—	2	50	125	400
OCEANIA					
Australia	4,877	7,796	9,239	12,343	14,433
TOTAL	45,257	51,782	56,919	62,109	68,802
Jamaica as a % of world	18.4%	20.7%	21.5%	19.7%	18.6%

SOURCE: Jamaican Ministry of Mining and Natural Resources, *Annual Review of Bauxite/Alumina Industry, Jamaica 1972* (December 1973), p. 17. Data for 1972 from *Metal Statistics* 1962–1972, 60th edition, Frankfurt am Main (1973), p. 12.

Table III. Jamaica's Contribution to World Bauxite Production

Year	World	Jamaica as a Percentage
1952	12,600	2.7 %
1953	13,600	6.7
1954	15,500	13.2
1955	17,500	15.0
1956	18,540	16.9
1957	20,150	22.8
1958	21,075	27.0
1959	22,690	22.6
1960	27,020	21.3
1961	28,945	23.0
1962	30,835	24.3
1963	30,206	22.8
1964	32,826	23.8
1965	36,849	23.2
1966	40,041	22.3
1967	43,889	20.8
1968	45,256	18.5
1969	51,782	20.7
1970	56,919	21.5
1971	62,109	19.7
1972	68,802	18.6

SOURCE: Same as Table II, above.

than the Eastern bloc, total consumption of aluminum nearly doubled from 4.4 pounds per capita in 1960 to 8.6 pounds in 1970. In the more industrialized countries, per capita consumption is naturally several times higher: the United States leads with 46.5 pounds per person in 1970, also double that of 1960. Almost 50 per cent of the world's aluminum consumption occurs in the United States, and about 30 per cent in Western Europe. Based on an estimated production of almost 9 million tons of primary aluminum in the non-Communist world in 1971, the usage of bauxite is estimated at between 40 and 45 million tons. In 1973, American production of aluminum reached a new high of over 4.5 million tons.

In the past, the economic feasibility of an aluminum production unit depended upon easy access to the essential raw materials, the availability of large amounts of low-cost electricity to produce primary aluminum, and opportunities for selling alu-

Table IV. Alumina: World Production by Countries (thousand short tons)

Country	1968	1969	1970	1971	1972
NORTH AMERICA					
Canada	1,100	1,107	1,218	1,220	1,149
United States	6,442	7,334	7,148	7,213	5,700
LATIN AMERICA					
Brazil	89	96	131	200	200
Guyana	297	334	336	336	578
Jamaica (exports)	1,017	1,274	1,892	1,997	2,354
Surinam	896	1,046	1,117	1,406	1,378
EUROPE					
France	1,135	1,219	1,246	1,310	1,117
Germany, West	718	749	835	911	916
Greece	246	331	344	514	476
Hungary	420	450	486	500	570
Italy	324	315	346	289	206
Romania	160	187	231	231	245
United Kingdom	100	112	118	120	116
U.S.S.R.	2,300	1,800	2,000	2,200	2,650
Yugoslavia	130	134	138	138	135
AFRICA					
Guinea	585	631	672	680	663
ASIA					
China Mainland	209	250	280	300	320
India	270	294	360	400	360
Japan	911	1,173	1,416	1,767	1,644
OCEANIA					
Australia	1,443	2,129	2,357	2,944	2,852
TOTAL WORLD	18,911	21,164	22,783	24,863	23,515
Jamaica as					
% of world	5.4%	6%	8.3%	8%	10%

SOURCE: Same as Table II, above.

minum on the major consumer markets in industrialized countries.

Within the Caribbean region, Jamaica, Surinam, and Guyana together produce more than 35 per cent of the world's bauxite. As of 1972, however, Australia surpassed Jamaica's bauxite production, and it is estimated that Australia possesses more than one-third of the world's reserves. In the Boké region of

Table V. Bauxite Production, 1967–1972 (thousand long tons)

Year	Bauxite Exported		Bauxite Processed		Total Bauxite Production	
	Quantity	Per cent	Quantity	Per cent	Quantity	Per cent
1967	7,142	78.3	1,979	21.7	9,121	100
1968	6,212	74.0	2,179	26.0	8,391	100
1969	7,909	76.5	2,424	23.5	10,333	100
1970	7,575	64.1	4,245	35.9	11,820	100
1971	7,590	62.0	4,654	38.0	12,244	100
1972	7,049	57.1	5,296	42.9	12,345	100

SOURCE: Jamaican Ministry of Mining and Natural Resources, *Annual Review of Bauxite/Alumina Industry, 1972* (December 1973).

Table VI. Bauxite and Alumina Exports, 1967–1972

Year	Volume of Exports ('000 long tons)		Value of Exports ($'000)		
	Bauxite	Alumina	Bauxite	Alumina	Total
1967	7,142	825	71,444	41,772	113,216
1968	6,212	867	62,120	50,832	112,952
1969	7,909	1,177	76,013	71,102	147,115
1970	7,575	1,768	75,752	111,141	186,895
1971	7,590	1,751	75,898	104,316	180,214
1972	7,049	2,102	68,375	119,867	188,242

SOURCE: See Table V, above.

Guinea in West Africa, one of the largest bauxite developments in the world is being undertaken. The Boké project is of
interest not only because of its large size but also for the joint
arrangements among the Guinea government, the World Bank,
and a consortium of six North American and European aluminum producers. The loan by the World Bank for the development of Guinea's enormous bauxite reserves is the Bank's
third largest in Africa. The aluminum companies expect to
produce eight million tons a year of bauxite by 1976.[13] Not
only are the mines so large, but the bauxite is also among the
highest quality in the world. Brazilian Amazon bauxite re-

13. *New York Times,* February 14, 1971.

Table VII. Bauxite Ore Production and Export Facilities

Company	Parent Company	Rated Annual Capacity
Alcoa Minerals of Jamaica	Aluminium Co. of America	1.2m LDT
Kaiser Bauxite Co.	Kaiser Aluminium & Chemical Corp.	6.0m LDT
Reynolds Ja. Mines	Reynolds Metal Co.	2.7m LDT

m LDT = million long dry tons.

SOURCE: See Table V, above.

Table VIII. Alumina Operations in Jamaica

Company	Parent Company	Rated Annual Capacity
Alcan Ja. Ltd.	Aluminium Co. of Canada	1,100,000 LT
Alumina Partners of Ja. Ltd.	Partnership between Anaconda Co., Reynolds Metals Co., Kaiser Aluminium & Chemical Corp.	1,161,000 LT
Revere Ja. Alumina Ltd.		196,400 LT
Alcoa Minerals of Ja. Inc.	Aluminium Co. of America	492,000 LT

LT = long tons.

SOURCE: See Table V, above.

serves also appear to have a potential near that of Guinea, possibly the third largest in the world.

Although research is being undertaken on the production of alumina from materials other than bauxite, such as clays, anorthosite and alunite, no alternative refining technique is yet economically competitive with bauxite. For example, in 1972, Alcoa purchased 8000 acres of anorthosite-rich land in Wyoming, but the company said that "bauxite continues to be the aluminum industry's most economical source of alumina." [14] The French metals and chemicals group, Pechiney, also reported in 1974 on a new process it had developed to extract alumina from clays other than bauxite, but this too was not yet a profitable alternative to bauxite.

The world aluminum industry is oligopolistic, with nine major international producers responsible for 90 per cent of total world capacity. The four North American producers—Alcoa, Reynolds, Kaiser, Alcan—alone account for 60 per cent. The multinational corporations operating in the bauxite-alumina industry in Jamaica are vertically integrated, usually with bauxite holdings in other countries besides Jamaica, alumina plants in several countries, and fabricating plants in major marketing areas. Table IX gives some indication of the range of Alcan subsidiary and related companies.

Kaiser Aluminum and Chemical Corporation has bauxite mining interests in Jamaica, Australia, United States, India, and Spain; produces alumina in Australia and the United States, as well as Jamaica; and has fabricating facilities in some 45 plants in more than 15 countries. Alcan has bauxite deposits in Jamaica, France, Brazil, Malaysia, Australia, Guinea. A large bauxite development is planned in the Amazon basin of Brazil. In 1972 approximately 40 per cent of Alcan's requirements of alumina came from its Jamaican alumina plants, 44 per cent from its Canadian plants, 12 per cent from its affiliated company in Australia. Alcoa has mines in Jamaica, Surinam, Australia, and the United States and produces alumina in the United States, Jamaica, Australia, Surinam. The company is also enlarging its resources and exploration in Guinea, French

14. *Wall Street Journal*, June 28, 1972.

Table IX. Alcan Aluminium Limited, Principal Operating Subsidiaries and
Related Companies (31 December 1972)

NORTH AMERICA

Canada

Aluminum Company of Canada, Ltd
Alcan Canada Products Limited
Alcan Ingot Limited
Alcan Pipe Limited *
Alcan-Price Extrusions Limited **
Aluma Building Systems, Inc.**
Roberval and Saguenay Railway Company, The
Saguenay Power Company, Ltd
Saguenay Shipping Limited
Saguenay Transmission Company, Limited
Supreme Aluminum Industries Limited ***

United States

Alcan Aluminum Corporation
V. E. Anderson Mfg Co.*
Fabral Corporation **

Bermuda

Alcan (Bermuda) Limited

CARIBBEAN

Guyana

Sprostons (Guyana) Limited

Jamaica

Alcan Jamaica Limited
Alcan Products of Jamaica Limited
Sprostons (Jamaica) Limited

Trinidad

Chaguaramas Terminals Limited
Geddes Grant Sprostons Industries Limited ***
Sprostons (Trinidad) Limited

LATIN AMERICA

Argentina

Camea S.A.I.C.***

Brazil

Alcan Aluminio do Brasil S.A.
Aluminio do Brasil Nordeste S.A.
Mineração Rio do Norte S.A.

Colombia

Aluminio Alcan de Colombia, S.A.*

Mexico

Alcan Aluminio, S.A.*
T.K.F. Engineering and Trading de Mexico, S.A.*

Uruguay

Alcan Aluminio del Uruguay S.A.*

Venezuela

Alcan de Venezuela, S.A.
T.K.F. Engineering & Trading de Venezuela S.A.

EUROPE

Belgium

Alcan Aluminium Raeren S.A.

Denmark

Aluminord A/S *

France

Aluminium Alcan de France
Alcan-Schwartz, Filage et Oxydation *
S.A. des Bauxites et Alumines de Provence
Société Industrielle de Transformation et de Construction(SITRACO) ***

Germany

Alcan Aluminiumwerke GmbH
Alcan Aluminiumwerk Nürnberg GmbH
Alcan Folien GmbH
Aluminium Norf GmbH **

Ireland

Unidare Limited ***

SOURCE: Alcan Aluminium Limited Annual Report 1972, p. 25.

Italy
Alcan Alluminio Italiano S.p.A.
Alcan Angeletti & Ciucani Alluminio
  S.p.A.

Netherlands
Alcan Europe N.V.

Norway
A/S Ardal og Sunndal Verk (ASV) **
A/S Nordisk Aluminiumindustri ** †
DNN Aluminium A/S **

Spain
Empresa Nacional del Aluminio, S.A.
  (ENDASA) ***

Sweden
Gränges Essem AB ***

Switzerland
Aluminiumwerke A.-G. Rorschach

United Kingdom
Alcan Booth Extrusions Limited *
Alcan Booth Sheet Limited *
Alcan Castings & Forgings Limited *
Alcan Design Products Limited *
Alcan Ekco Limited ***
Alcan Enfield Alloys Limited **
Alcan Foils Limited *
Alcan Polyfoil Limited *
Alcan (U.K.) Limited
Alcan Wire Limited *
P. J. Bailey (Patent Glazing) Limited *
Thomas Bennett Limited ***
Freight Bonallack Limited *
Johnson & Bloy Aluminium Pigments
  Limited ***
E. C. Payter & Co. Limited *
Saguenay Shipping (U.K.) Limited
Tenon Contracts Limited *
Ulamin Light Metal Company (1954)
  Limited ***

AFRICA

Ghana
Ghana Aluminium Products Limited *

Guinea
Halco (Mining) Inc.***

Nigeria
Alcan Aluminium of Nigeria Limited *
Flag Aluminium Products Limited *

South Africa
Alcan Aluminium of South Africa Lim-
  ited *
Republic Aluminium Company (Pty)
  Limited *

ASIA

India
Indian Aluminium Company, Limited *

Japan
Nippon Light Metal Company, Ltd **
Toyo Aluminium K.K.**

Malaysia
Alcan Malaysia Berhad *
Southeast Asia Bauxites Limited *
Johore Mining and Stevedoring Co.
  Ltd *

Thailand
Alcan Thai Company Limited **

SOUTH PACIFIC

Australia
Alcan Australia Limited *
Alcan Queensland Pty Limited
Kawneer Company Pty Limited *
Queensland Alumina Limited ***
Wm Breit & Company Pty Ltd *

Table IX. Alcon Aluminium Limited, Principal Operating Subsidiaries and Related Companies (31 December 1972) (*Continued*)

SOUTH PACIFIC (CONTINUED)

New Zealand

Alcan New Zealand Limited *
Alcan Alloys Limited *
Aluminium Anodizers Limited ***
Aluminium Conductors Limited ***

INTERNATIONAL SALES

Alcan Aluminio (America Latina) Limited—Latin America
Alcan Asia Limited—Japan, Afghanistan, Pakistan and certain areas of Asia

Alcan Southeast Asia Limited—Hong Kong, India, Philippines and certain areas of Asia
Alcan S.A.—Continental Europe (excluding Germany and Scandinavia), Middle East, North Africa
Alcan Metall GmbH—Germany
Alcan (U.K.) Limited—U.K., Scandinavia
Alcan Sales (Division of Alcan Aluminum Corporation)—U.S.A. and Caribbean
Alcan Trading Limited

Unless otherwise indicated, companies are 100% owned
* Less than 100% owned but more than 50%

** 50% owned
*** Less than 50% owned
† 100% owned by A/S Ardal og Sunndal Verk (ASV)

Guiana, Brazil, Costa Rica, and Indonesia. Reynolds has ores in Jamaica, Guyana, Australia, and the United States, and smelting facilities in the United Kingdom, Norway, Canada, and the United States.

The basic pattern for the U.S. corporations is for mining and drying in the Caribbean of bauxite which becomes an intra-company transfer to their other alumina plants in the United States, the production of alumina for their own smelters, and the disposition of the metal in part to their own fabricators and factories and in part to independent operators. Alcan differs slightly in that it beneficiates almost all its Caribbean bauxite into alumina within the area, but it disposes of its output entirely to its own smelters in Canada and to affiliated smelters in Scandinavia. Until 1969 Alcan was the only company processing bauxite into alumina, but since then Alumina Partners of Jamaica (Alpart), Alcoa and Revere have also become important producers of alumina.

Until 1971 there were tariffs on imports into the United

States of bauxite, alumina, and various forms of aluminum, with the tariff rates escalating according to the degree of processing. In 1971, however, imports of bauxite and alumina became free of duty, while various forms of aluminum remained subject to duties. United States imports of alumina from Jamaica have increased from only 43,000 short tons in 1965 to 904,000 short tons in 1973, amounting to approximately 22 per cent of total alumina imports.

4. THE JAMAICAN ECONOMY

Jamaica achieved independence from Britain in 1962, only five years after Ghana emerged as the first black state to obtain sovereignty since Liberia in 1847. In 1963 Jamaica launched a "Five-Year Independence Plan" as its first long-term development program, stating that "the Jamaican situation is a classic demonstration of the race between development and discontent." Indeed, it was: an island economy, previously dominated by plantation agriculture, Jamaica was a classic case of underdevelopment—suffering from the diseconomies of small size, an unfavorable ratio of population to cultivatable land, unemployment, marked inequality, a colonial legacy—but rapidly rising expectations.

The Plan set as its fundamental goals

> . . . economic viability, and social and cultural development and integration . . . In much of the first 5-year period, emphasis will be . . . particularly directed towards the rural agricultural economy in a determined effort to reduce rural migration to overcrowded towns. . . . The immediate task so far as the economic situation is concerned, is to provide employment opportunities and to boost consumer demand as a stimulus for increased output. . . . The new programme involves the substitution of new and more relevant and acceptable values to replace those inherent in a colonial society in which privilege and status were well-entrenched behind social and economic barriers. It involves the development of the necessary social institutions, the improvement of amenities such as housing, water supplies, and roads, and the provision of youth and adult training programmes. It involves a balanced and integrated development which provides adequate opportunities for mobility and which assists in the evolution of a sense of national

unity and a sense of direction among the people of the island.[15]

Of the mining sector, however, the Plan merely stated that
"It is the policy of the Government to encourage the fullest
possible development of mining activities in the island, and to
ensure that in the exploitation of these resources the maximum
possible benefit accrues to the country."

A ten-year summary of Jamaica's development is presented
in the following Tables. Per capita national income (Net National Product) at current prices, rose from $270 in 1963 to
$515 in 1972. Tables X and XI show the increase in the GNP,
and the components of aggregate expenditure of the GNP,
from 1963 to 1972. Tables XII and XIII show the sectoral composition of GDP from 1962 to 1971. Table XIV indicates the
changes in investment by industrial sectors. The trends in the
balance of payments can be seen in Tables XV and XVI.

The Jamaican economy had been traditionally dominated by
two agricultural products, sugar and bananas. But whereas
total agricultural exports decreased from approximately $35
million in 1963 to $28 million in 1972, bauxite and alumina
rose from $42 million to $129 million over the same period.
The increasing contributions of mining to GDP and to fixed
capital formation are also clear in Tables XIII and XIV. The
bulk of the investment in the bauxite-alumina sector has been
financed by inflows of capital from the United States and Canada. As a result of the large inflows of capital into mining and
also into tourism and some manufacturing, Jamaica was able to
sustain during the 1960's a remarkable high ratio of gross domestic investment to GNP—in the range of 20 to 30 per cent
during the decade. Gross domestic investment was approximately $303 million in 1972, amounting to approximately 25
per cent of GNP (Tables X and XI). The financing of gross
domestic investment in 1972 was almost $166 million in na-
tional savings and $139 million in net foreign borrowing.

The aggregate growth rate, as represented by GNP, was
among the highest of all LDCs. But the content or composition
of development has been unsatisfactory. Despite high rates in

15. *Five Year Independence Plan 1963–1968*, pp. 11, 51–52.

Table X. Expenditure on Gross National Product, 1963–1972 (Current Values—$'000)

Item	1963	1964	1965	1966	1967	1968	1969	1970	1971	1972
Personal Consumption Expenditure	389,350	445,688	468,730	500,379	531,551	570,719	639,324	714,864	805,745	893,289
Government Current Purchases of Goods and Services	58,618	63,608	69,838	76,674	89,460	104,522	121,803	124,343	140,251	158,420
Gross Domestic Investment	99,710	120,860	129,026	151,570	177,354	230,489	259,511	273,433	294,111	302,871
Net Exports of Goods and Services	-6,360	-41,602	-31,714	-37,942	-53,588	-85,712	-105,808	-98,174	-150,617	-158,391
Exports	223,832	238,906	258,138	305,566	315,116	344,456	383,720	398,261	455,915	481,402
Imports	230,192	280,508	289,852	343,508	368,704	430,168	489,528	496,435	606,532	639,773
Statistical Discrepancy	-1,086	+420	+1,484	+1,990	-476	+1,562	+1,218	+1,476	+336	+1,787
GROSS NATIONAL PRODUCT	540,232	588,972	637,364	692,671	745,253	821,580	916,048	1,015,942	1,089,826	1,197,996

SOURCE: Department of Statistics, Jamaica, *National Income and Production 1972* (March 1973).

Table XI. Expenditure Components Expressed as Percentages
of Gross National Product, 1963–1972

Item	1963	1964	1965	1966	1967	1968	1969	1970	1971	1972
Personal Consumption Expenditure	72.1	75.7	73.6	72.2	71.3	69.5	70.0	70.4	73.9	74.6
Government Purchases of Goods and Services	10.8	10.8	11.0	11.1	12.0	12.7	13.3	12.2	12.9	13.2
Gross Domestic Investment	18.5	20.5	20.2	22.0	24.9	28.1	28.3	26.9	27.0	25.3
Net Exports of Goods and Services	− 1.2	− 7.1	− 5.0	− 5.5	−7.2	− 10.5	− 11.5	− 9.7	− 13.8	− 13.2
Statistical Discrepancy	− 0.2	+ 0.1	+ 0.2	+ 0.2	—	+ 0.2	—	+ 0.2	—	+ 0.1
GROSS NATIONAL PRODUCT	100.0	100.0	100.0	100.0	100.0	100.0	100.0	100.0	100.0	100.0

SOURCE: See Table X, above.

Table XII. Gross Domestic Product at Factor Cost by Industrial Origin, Sectors and Sub-sectors; 1962–1971
(Current Values—$'000)

Industry by Sub-sectors	1962	1963	1964	1965	1966	1967	1968	1969	1970	1971
Agriculture, Forestry and Fishing(1)	57,418	68,432	68,462	69,082	75,120	77,870	77,516	77,037	79,942	86,130
Mining, Quarrying and Refining(2)	46,204	45,506	52,170	57,736	98,133	102,451	100,084	124,698	159,723	173,148
Bauxite and Alumina Quarrying and Refining (incl. Gypsum and	43,494	42,492	47,916	52,190	91,357	95,881	92,635	116,397	150,147	161,728
Petroleum)	2,710	3,014	4,254	5,546	6,776	6,570	7,449	8,301	9,576	11,420
Manufacture(3)	65,744	78,738	84,304	89,272	99,170	103,273	115,300	121,337	128,844	135,682
Construction and Installation(4)	52,018	52,122	58,100	63,640	69,240	72,866	94,854	105,254	114,015	117,944
Electricity, Gas and Water(5)	5,824	6,332	7,134	8,022	9,002	9,134	10,064	12,938	13,961	15,299
Transportation, Storage and Communication(6)	38,300	37,682	40,486	43,916	48,468	53,214	57,843	63,229	68,800	75,057
Distributive Trade (wholesale and retail)(7)	76,916	77,042	80,200	85,740	91,188	94,122	102,294	109,422	120,055	130,207
Financial Institutions(8)	21,812	18,864	20,866	26,330	29,522	32,750	35,027	45,412	47,902	53,291
Ownership of Dwellings(9)	15,944	17,210	18,886	20,454	21,910	22,384	22,812	24,846	25,063	25,564
Public Administration(10)	34,398	37,174	41,112	44,622	50,250	60,632	69,678	81,276	94,936	101,670
Miscellaneous Services(11)	66,278	72,464	76,174	85,466	90,070	94,382	99,096	103,495	111,221	118,171
GROSS DOMESTIC PRODUCT AT FACTOR COST	480,856	511,566	547,894	594,280	682,073	723,077	784,568	868,944	964,462	1,032,163

SOURCE: See Table X, above.

Table XIII. Percentage Contribution Made by Industrial Sectors to Gross Domestic Product at Factor Cost—Current Price 1962–1971

Item Industrial Sectors	1962	1963	1964	1965	1966	1967	1968	1969	1970	1971
1. Agriculture, Forestry and Fishing	11.9	13.4	12.5	11.6	11.0	10.8	9.9	8.9	8.3	8.3
2. Mining, Quarrying and Refining	9.6	8.9	9.5	9.7	14.4	14.2	12.7	14.4	16.6	16.8
3. Manufacturing	13.7	15.4	15.4	15.0	14.5	14.3	14.7	14.0	13.4	13.1
4. Construction and Installation	10.8	10.2	10.6	10.7	10.2	10.1	12.1	12.1	11.8	11.4
5. Electricity, Gas and Water	1.2	1.2	1.3	1.4	1.3	1.3	1.3	1.5	1.4	1.5
6. Transportation, Storage and Communication	8.0	7.4	7.4	7.4	7.1	7.3	7.4	7.3	7.1	7.3
7. Distribution Wholesale and Retail	16.0	15.0	14.6	14.4	13.4	13.0	13.0	12.6	12.4	12.6
8. Financial Institutions	4.5	3.7	3.8	4.4	4.3	4.5	4.5	5.2	5.0	5.2
9. Ownership of Dwellings	3.3	3.3	3.5	3.5	3.2	3.1	2.9	2.8	2.6	2.5
10. Public Administration	7.2	7.3	7.5	7.5	7.4	8.4	8.9	9.2	9.8	9.9
11. Miscellaneous Services	13.8	14.2	13.9	14.4	13.2	13.0	12.6	12.0	11.6	11.4
TOTAL	100.0	100.0	100.0	100.0	100.0	100.0	100.0	100.0	100.0	100.0

SOURCE: See Table X, above.

Table XIV. Fixed Capital Formation by Industrial Sectors: 1963–1971
(Current Values—$'000)

Industrial Group	1963	1964	1965	1966	1967	1968	1969	1970	1971
Agriculture, Forestry and Fishing	8,386	14,430	11,724	13,024	10,784	9,786	11,145	11,699	12,595
Mining, Quarrying and Refining	21,098	6,378	11,350	21,020	47,523	79,387	89,577	95,449	102,762
Manufacturing	10,166	17,768	15,396	17,402	20,218	21,802	24,830	26,056	28,052
Sugar, Molasses and Rum	2,158	3,772	4,070	4,942	4,146	3,991	4,545	4,786	5,152
Other Manufacture	8,008	13,996	11,326	12,460	16,072	17,811	20,285	21,270	22,900
Construction and Installation	4,222	6,374	9,236	10,246	7,562	9,834	11,200	11,698	12,595
Electricity, Gas and Water	1,682	1,926	2,146	3,412	10,266	13,712	15,616	16,484	17,747
Transportation, Storage and Communication	10,074	14,188	16,946	17,424	12,860	16,677	18,982	19,941	21,468
Wholesale and Retail Distribution	8,180	12,232	10,040	10,504	10,026	7,852	8,943	9,572	10,305
Banking and Insurance	1,300	1,938	1,958	2,264	3,436	2,936	4,184	4,254	4,580
Ownership of Dwellings	12,300	17,434	19,578	20,230	14,930	16,295	18,559	19,675	21,182
Public Administration	10,232	14,000	19,200	23,232	27,050	36,262	41,299	42,806	46,085
Miscellaneous Services	3,960	5,132	6,626	7,242	5,345	6,851	7,803	8,242	8,873
TOTAL	91,600	111,800	124,200	146,000	170,000	221,384	252,138	265,876	286,244

SOURCE: See Table X, above.

Table XV. Foreign Transactions
(Current Values—$'000)

	1963	1964	1965	1966	1967	1968	1969	1970	1971	1972
Export of Goods and Services	223,832	238,906	258,138	305,566	315,116	344,456	383,720	398,261	455,915	481,402
Goods	148,854	156,114	154,892	193,562	194,192	203,568	235,449	244,009	285,473	292,494
Factor Services	17,648	20,824	22,318	16,624	21,452	18,712	18,730	20,035	21,876	23,972
Non-Factor Services	57,330	61,968	80,928	95,380	99,472	122,176	129,541	134,217	148,566	164,936
Transfer Payments	19,120	17,988	17,958	16,132	16,308	22,830	27,957	38,981	45,135	49,715
To Persons and Private Non-Profit Institutions	16,982	15,860	15,478	13,504	13,796	14,308	16,950	27,540	34,336	38,615
To Government	2,138	2,128	2,480	2,628	2,512	8,522	11,007	11,441	10,799	11,100
Net Borrowing from Abroad (Deficit of Nation on Current Account)	6,658	30,554	21,958	30,698	47,292	73,512	91,739	77,987	131,344	138,961
TOTAL RECEIPTS=TOTAL PAYMENTS	236,294	287,448	298,054	352,396	378,716	440,798	503,416	515,229	632,394	670,078
Import of Goods and Services	230,192	280,508	289,852	343,508	368,704	430,168	489,605	496,435	606,532	639,773
Goods	160,268	205,392	205,424	232,712	252,680	319,368	368,586	374,320	458,747	493,165
Factor Services	34,794	37,016	41,040	72,220	73,310	64,696	71,670	73,200	95,447	90,637
Non-Factor Services	35,130	38,100	43,388	38,576	42,714	46,104	49,349	48,915	52,338	55,971
Transfer Payments	6,102	6,940	8,202	8,888	10,012	10,630	13,811	18,794	25,497	30,305
From Persons and Private Non-Profit Institutions	792	706	1,148	1,144	1,000	1,028	2,178	5,239	12,497	13,749
From Government	5,310	6,234	7,054	7,744	9,012	9,602	11,633	13,555	13,365	16,556

SOURCE: See Table X, above.

Table XVI. Capital Account
($ Million)

Item	1969	1970	1971
Trade Balance	—74.4	—89.2	—106.7
Services	—40.5	—56.2	—51.2
Net Goods and Services	—114.9	—145.4	—157.9
Private Transfers	14.7	21.8	21.8
Official Transfers	—2.8	—3.6	—4.5
Current Account (net)	—103.0	—127.2	—140.6
	10.3	—1.2	6.8
Private Capital (net)	97.4	135.3	150.6
Net Errors and Omissions	—6.8	5.4	..
Total Current and Capital Transactions	—4.7	6.9	16.8
Allocations of SDRs	..	5.3	4.7
TOTAL	—4.7	12.2	21.5
Monteary Movements (increase in assets)	2.1	—17.6	—21.5

SOURCE: See Table X, above.

the aggregate indices of GNP and capital formation, there remain pressing problems of agricultural stagnation, high levels of unemployment, and continuing maldistribution of income.[16] At the same time as food imports have increased, sugar continues to dominate agriculture, perpetuating according to some critics the weaknesses of a "plantation society." [17] Nor has the manufacturing sector grown significantly: the share of GDP originating within the manufacturing and processing sector actually declined between 1968 and 1971. Most distressing is the fact that although real GDP grew at a rate of almost 8 per cent per annum between 1950 and 1965, and the labor force scarcely grew at all because of heavy migration to the United Kingdom and North America, the rate of open unemployment was higher at the end of the 15-year period of so-called development, than it was at the beginning.[18] The government acknowledges an unemployment rate of 25 per cent, and some

16. See O. Jefferson, *The Postwar Economic Development of Jamaica* (1972). Jefferson maintains that these problems will remain acute unless there are radical shifts in official policy.

17. G. L. Beckford, *Persistent Poverty: Underdevelopment in Plantation Economies of the Third World* (1972).

18. Gene M. Tidrick, "Wages, Output, and the Employment Lag in Jamaica," Williams College Center for Development Economics, Research Memorandum No. 40 (December 1970), p. 7.

students would put the rate of urban unemployment in Kingston at 30 to 35 per cent.

To aggravate the situation, there remains a high degree of inequality in the distribution of income. An early study of distribution of family incomes in 1963–64 indicates that the top 20 per cent of families enjoyed 56 per cent of the total household income, while the bottom 60 per cent accounted for only 22 per cent.[19] Some would contend the income distribution has become even more unequal since the earlier period.

Exports and imports have both averaged a very high percentage of GNP, but the economy has had to confront a growing deficit on current account. The major item offsetting the current account deficit has been the private capital inflow. In 1972, however, the trade deficit widened markedly at the same time as the capital inflow diminished with the completion of investment in Alpart's new facilities. Between May and November 1972 the country's foreign exchange reserves fell from $150 million to $80 million. A summary of the balance of payments is presented in Table XVII.

The newly elected Prime Minister Michael Manley announced in November 1972 a severe restriction policy on imports, exchange controls, and a tight monetary policy. Outlining the deterioration of the balance of payments situation, the Prime Minister said that it was clear that the present situation was a symptom of the failure of the basic economic policies which were followed in the past—a failure to put the economy on a basis where it would have been capable of supporting self-sustaining growth. Following are excerpts from the Prime Minister's statement to the House of Representatives.

NEW ECONOMIC POLICY STATEMENT *

"It became clear just before Budget time that certain weaknesses in the country's external accounts had begun to be manifested and remedial measures were proposed in July. These were restricted to monetary measures and therefore could only have had indirect effects on the economy. In addition, the Government proposed a price freeze.

*The Daily Gleaner (Jamaica), November 10, 1972.
19. Central Planning Unit, *Economic Survey Jamaica 1971* (1972), p. 153.

"The monitoring of the economy has continued since July and this has confirmed the earlier findings that our balance of payments situation was deteriorating to the point where further corrective action was needed. For the period 1st January to 31st October 1972, our net foreign reserves fell by $51.1mn. Our net reserves at 31st October amounted to $81.1mn. or a little over two months imports. There have been two principal reasons immediately responsible for this poor performance.

"First, we have continued to import much more than we earn abroad. The trade deficit from January to July 1972 amounted to $122.3 mn. compared with $88.8 mn. in the same period last year and this happened at a time when capital goods imports decreased. Secondly, the large capital inflows which went into the bauxite industry fell off substantially for the simple reason that their latest expansion programme was complete.

"I have indicated that these were the immediate reasons, but further thought shows quite clearly that the present balance of payments situation is merely a symptom of the failure of the basic economic policies which have been pursued in the past: a symptom of the failure to introduce changes in the economic structure which we inherited in 1962 and to put the economy on a basis where it would have been capable of supporting self-sustaining growth.

"I will elaborate on some of these major areas of failure:

(a) Passive domestic policies which did not cope with international economic forces, particularly the deterioration in the terms of trade of our main export crops. These policies did not develop a strategy to deal adequately with both the tariff and non-tariff barriers which had been put up against our exports;

(b) We completely failed to modernise our export agricultural sector so that productivity could be increased and the farmer given an incentive to supply the markets which were available. We are in the unusual situation in which our main problem is not currently the availability of markets for our primary exports but our inability to supply the existing markets;

(c) We have failed to meet the domestic food requirements of our people and here again we are in the unique position amongst most of the countries of the world in which our staple foods are not those produced by us. In 1962 our imports of food amounted to $30.4 mn. Whilst the population increased by 12% during this period our imports of food in 1971 amounted to $76.3 mn. or an increase of 150%—an increase much greater than the population and price increases taken together;

(d) There has been failure to seek out new export opportunities and to diversify in a meaningful way the export package in terms of both new products and markets;

(e) Failure to develop an industrial base which was related to the

processing of the basic raw materials that we had or could produce in
the country and which manufactured products that could satisfy the
demands of the masses of the population;

(f) Failure to stem the orgy of consumption of imported luxury
goods;

(g) There was patent failure to promote continued expansion in
the rate of savings consistent with what would have seemed achieva-
ble given the rates prevailing prior to 1962. The rate of personal saving has not increased.

More Savings

Without increased saving there was no hope of accumulating the
capital which was needed for development of the productive sectors
of the economy. This, in turn, resulted in an excessive reliance on
imported capital inflows which would have been more tolerable if all
these capital inflows in turn expanded productive capacity but a substantial portion of these inflows was used to finance the importation
of consumer goods. This has had the undesirable result that we have
mortgaged our future by having to find interest, dividends and profits
to service most of the foreign capital inflows which have been con-
sumed and which did not increase our productive capacity.

Diagnosis of Economic Failure
Review of the Effects of the Failure

"(a) Unemployment skyrocketed although Jamaica experienced
large-scale out migration and only moderate population increases
since 1962. Net migration from Jamaica between June 1962 and December 1971 amounted to 188,400. At April 1972 a survey undertaken by the Department of Statistics showed the unemployed as
being 203,000 out of a labour force of 822,000 or 25%. This should be
compared with the position in 1960 when unemployment was approximately 13%.

Imagine for a moment what would have been the position if the
188,000 who migrated from 1962 and their children were still with
us!

(b) Worsening income distribution: We have no definite figures on
the growth in the imbalance of incomes, but all the indirect indications are there: the high unemployment just cited and the starvation
of the rural/agricultural sectors by the failure of agricultural policies.
Indeed, much of the slums, unemployment and violence in the
urban areas can be directly related to the failure to deal with the
rural problems.

(c) Deterioration of attitudes: In many ways it is in this area that
we find the greatest failure. For there was total failure in winning the
commitment and dedication of all sectors of the people to working

wholeheartedly for the welfare of our country. We find many among the wealthier classes seeking only to maximise profits as quickly as possible but siphoning this off to build nest eggs abroad. Many of our middle income groups, seeking only to ape the rich in their consumption habits but having to borrow to do so and therefore being completely thriftless, and many in the low income groups imbued with a freeness mentality.

If courageous rather than weak policies had been pursued since 1962, Jamaica today would have been able to move ahead.

Programme of Action

"The Government is not going to postpone taking measures which should have been taken years ago. Some of these measures will be painful but necessary to permit sustainable, soundly based economic development.

"It is clear from the diagnosis that I have given that our main problem has been the inability of the productive sectors of the economy to produce the goods and services which are required both for local consumption and for export. The policy to be pursued by the Government will have as its ultimate goal the building up of this economic capacity and the maximum utilisation of all our resources, both natural and human so that we can satisfy the reasonable needs of our people.

"The strategy to be adopted must of necessity be a phased one. In the short run the Government will reinforce monetary policy by limiting the size of the import bill. This limitation must have regard to the potential foreign exchange earnings from our export and other foreign exchange receipts, and we must never again find ourselves in the position where we finance our consumer imports from capital inflows.

"More important, however, will be the restructuring of the composition of the import bill so that priority is given to raw materials and capital goods imports which are needed to support our economic expansion. In addition, the Government will, for the first time, be integrating its foreign trade programme with its agricultural, industrial and hotel development programmes. We recognise that merely taking negative action will not contribute to Jamaica's progress. Rather, we now see this as a tremendous opportunity to correct the imbalances in the economic structure.

5. THE PROBLEM

This Policy Problem centers on the negotiating relationships between the Jamaican government and the multinational corporations investing in the bauxite-alumina industry. What are

Table XVII. Balance of Payments (J$mn.)

	1969	1970	1971	1972*
A. *Merchandise*	− 74.4	− 89.2	−108.2	−121.0
Exports (f.o.b.) (adjusted)	232.2	285.1	286.1	302.4
Imports (f.o.b.) (adjusted)	317.6	374.3	394.3	424.3
B. *Services (net)*	− 40.5	− 56.2	− 51.4	− 59.2
Travel	65.4	66.7	77.2	91.4
Investment Income	− 72.5	− 81.8	− 85.7	−100.6
Other	− 33.5	− 41.1	− 42.9	− 50.0
C. *Goods and Services (net)*	−114.9	−145.4	−159.6	−180.2
D. *Unrequited Transfers (net)*	11.9	18.2	17.3	19.5
Official	− 2.8	− 3.6	− 4.5	− 5.3
Private	14.7	21.8	21.8	24.8
CURRENT ACCOUNT BALANCE	−103.0	−127.2	−142.3	−160.7
E. *Net Capital Movements*	98.5	134.1	160.2	112.4
Official	10.3	− 1.2	4.0	17.6
Private	88.2	135.3	156.2	** 94.8
F. *Total A through E*	− 4.5	6.9	17.9	− 48.3
G. *Allocation of SDRs*	—	5.3	4.7	4.7
H. *Total F plus G*	− 4.5	12.2	22.6	− 43.6
I. *Change in Reserves* (minus sign means increase)	11.3	− 17.6	− 36.4	43.6
Holdings of SDRs	—	− 5.3	− 5.3	4.8
IMF Gold Tranche Position	− 1.7	− 0.1	− 3.1	11.0
Government	0.3	− 3.1	0.4	2.0
Bank of Jamaica	3.5	− 9.1	− 13.5	1.3
Other Banks	9.2	—	− 14.9	24.5
Net Errors and Omissions	− 6.8	5.4	13.8	—

* Provisional.
** Includes net errors and omissions.
SOURCE: *Bank of Jamaica, Report 1973* (1973), p. 9.

the most signicant issue-areas from the standpoint of increasing the contribution of private overseas investment to a country's development? What policy decisons have been made by the actors in this problem? How should the courses of action taken be evaluated? What should be the future resolution of the problem?

The relationships between a host government and a foreign investor involve a bargaining process in a "nonzero-sum game" of possible outcomes (that is, there can be mutual gains, instead of one party's gain being the other party's loss). But on what factors does Jamaica's bargaining power depend? And specifically, how should Jamaica utilize whatever bargaining leverage it has? Just how, in the words of Jamaica's first five-year plan, was the country to ensure that in the exploitation of the bauxite resources "the maximum possible benefit" accrues to the country?

Answers to such questions call for an assessment of the past performance of this type of foreign investment and a consideration of future policies toward it. It is necessary to consider just what are the contributions of foreign investors in an export-oriented resource industry such as bauxite. Although this particular case involves foreign investment in an extractive industry, much of the problem can readily be generalized to other types of foreign investment—for instance, in import-substitute industries (as in many LDCs during the past twenty years), or in manufacturing industries (as contemplated in Problem III, below). Indeed, the general problem can be stated as follows:

> What matters for a correct assessment by a host government of the potential contribution to development of the multinational producing enterprise is not what historically preceded the direct foreign investment, but what the next best alternative would be. Any operational assessment of its potential contribution must start from an assumption about this alternative. . . . A clear formulation of the alternatives is an essential prerequisite to the proper appraisal of the value of foreign enterprise. The important point for analysis and policy is to envisage the various alternatives, against which any operational assessment has to be made and to assess the benefits and the costs of each, measuring what is measurable and judging what is not.[20]

An evaluation of the contributions of alternative arrangements must underlie any rational approach to an analysis of policy options and negotiating strategy.

20. Paul Streeten, "Costs and Benefits of Multinational Enterprises in Less-Developed Countries," in J. Dunning (ed.), *The Multinational Enterprise* (1971), pp. 248–50.

Expressed in broad categories, the issues over which the Jamaican government and the multinationals might negotiate are (1) the extent to which, and the conditions under which, the multinationals are granted accessibility to Jamaica's bauxite resources; (2) the regulation of the multinationals' operations in terms of such requirements as local employment, local content in production, support of agricultural and other auxiliary activities; (3) payment to the government of taxes and royalties; (4) the degree of joint ownership or a future divestment process.

From an examination of several case studies of foreign investment in petroleum and mineral industries, one student of the problem has summarized a number of issues in foreign investor–host government relations.[21] These issues may have some bearing for the immediate problem as well. They are as follows:

1. Tax increases, tax uncertainty, and retroactive taxation have been important issues. Taxation affects the level of production in the short run and the volume of investment in the longer run.

2. Price policies are closely related to the division of the rent from resource operations. Because a large portion of the sales of the producing companies are to processing or refining or marketing affiliates in other countries, there is a conflict over the price to be employed for the calculation of earnings for tax purposes.

3. The level of production is an important issue in cases where integrated firms have several sources of supply for meeting their marketing requirements.

4. The desire of host countries to conserve their material resources, either for domestic use or as a source of future export earnings, has created conflict with foreign investors or deterred resource development.

5. Host countries have generally been frustrated by their inability to control the operations and policies of integrated firms beyond those of the domestic producing affiliates.

21. Cf. Raymond Mikesell, *Foreign Investment in Petroleum and Mineral Industries* (1971), p. 26.

6. The widespread feeling of developing countries that foreign investors cannot be trusted to develop their resources in the national interest has led to demands either for government ownership of the producing facilities or for the limitation of foreign participation to a minority role.

7. Labor relations have been a source of conflict and a deterrent to production in many of the cases studied.

8. Conflicts may also arise as a consequence of the policies of the government of the foreign investor, or from political relations between the governments of the host countries and the foreign investor.

These policy options and the actual agreements between the Jamaican government and the bauxite industries may be examined more fully in the next sections.

B. THE ISSUES

6. FIRST INTEREST IN JAMAICAN BAUXITE

The red earth areas which cover almost two-thirds of Jamaica's surface were identified as bauxite in late 1942. According to the historical account of its operations in Jamaica, Reynolds Metals Company first heard of Jamaica bauxite deposits in January 1943 and showed immediate interest.

REYNOLDS METALS COMES TO JAMAICA *

Reynolds Metals Vice-President in charge of bauxite operations and its Chief Geologist reached Jamaica for the first time on 10th February, 1943. During the next few days they made a preliminary investigation of bauxite deposits.

On 17th February, they conferred with H.E. Governor Sir Arthur Richards and on the following day, 18th February, submitted a letter to the Colonial Secretary entitled, "Reynolds Metals Company's Bauxite Proposal." In this letter, only a month after Reynolds first became aware of the possible existence of bauxite in Jamaica and after only a week of actual geological investigation, these statements were made to the Jamaican Government:

---

* *Reynolds Jamaica Mines Ltd., Its Origin and Development, 1943–1953,* Reynolds Metals Company Economics Research Department (August 1956), p. 13.

1. "Our preliminary investigation indicates that the bauxite deposits are much more extensive than the rough estimate of 5,000,000 to 10,000,000 tons reported to us by Washington officials . . . Although our investigation has been limited as to time and area and we have not yet had an opportunity to drill test holes, our Chief Geologist, Dr. O. C. Schmedeman, on the basis of his preliminary study and observation of large areas with bauxite outcroppings, assures us that in all probability the reserves will aggregate more than 100,000,000 tons.

2. "Presently available information indicates that the grade of bauxite ranges from 45% to 50% alumina and 1% to 5% silica. We have taken a large number of samples to verify these percentages.

3. "Mining Conditions: Since most of the deposits are covered by only one foot of overburden and the bauxite is unusually soft, mining would be essentially earth moving, requiring little or no blasting and only the simplest type of excavating equipment. The deposits are so widespread that alternate methods of transportation can be utilized. The ore can be hauled over separate branches of the Jamaica Government Railway or it can be trucked directly to nearby harbours and ports."

Reynolds Metals then requested:

". . . permission to explore in Jamaica, with the understanding that we will be granted permanent concessions on a basis of equality with the Aluminum Company of Canada. We recognize the position of the Billiton Company in the Parish of St. Ann and the Aluminum Company of Canada in the Parish of Manchester. We have discovered promising outcrops of bauxite in the Parishes of St. Catherine and St. Elizabeth and would like to obtain an exclusive concession on one of them after having the privilege of more fully exploring both. We also desire the opportunity of selecting other parishes on a basis of equality with the other aluminum producer concerned.

"We would expect to pay appropriate royalties or compensation to property owners and the Colonial Government."

The proposal concluded with a strong plea for prompt action to help meet the wartime need for more aluminum and an offer of fullest co-operation by Reynolds Metals Company:

"Since it is urgent to produce high grade bauxite in order to obtain maximum output of aluminum required for military aircraft, we would like to have permission to proceed at the earliest possible date.

"We are returning to the United States on Monday, but we shall be prepared to return promptly at your request. In the meantime we shall be glad to submit whatever additional information you may require if you will communicate with us at the address given below. We shall be most happy to have you or your representative visit our plants in the United States. We are prepared to send a representative to London to facilitate a decision there if we receive advice from you or your Government that such procedure is considered desirable."

As a result of a single week of geological investigation by Reynolds Metals the working estimates of Jamaica bauxite reserves jumped from about five to ten million tons to over 100 million tons. As soon as Reynolds had arrived at these estimates, it transmitted them to the Jamaican Government.

After further exploration, Reynolds reported to the Jamaican government in 1944: "It has been our consistent policy to deal frankly with your Government, and we are now prepared to advise you that the deposits appear to exceed 200,000,000 tons." The report to the government also outlined Reynolds's efforts to develop a process which would make it possible to use Jamaica bauxite commercially:

> Reynolds Metals Company is conducting an extensive research programme to devise a method of treating this new type of ore. We have employed the best technicians in the United States and are conducting experimental work in conjunction with the Massachusetts Institute of Technology where outstanding experts and research facilities have been made available to us. We have expended substantial sums of money in this work, with very promising results to date. Although the orthodox types of bauxite, such as occur in British Guiana, Dutch Guiana and Brazil, are preferable, we are now confident that Jamaica bauxite will have value if it can be mined and shipped at reduced costs.[22]

The report concluded that "we hope the necessary legislation and regulations can be framed and put into force within the next six months so as to enable us to determine our method of production and operation and commence the purchase and installation of equipment as soon as it is available after the War."

Another six years were to elapse, however, before negotiations could be concluded between the government and the company. A summary account of the course of the subsequent negotiations, from Reynolds's viewpoint follows.

22. *Reynolds Jamaica Mines Ltd., Its Origin and Development, 1943–1953*, p. 17.

SUMMARY OF NEGOTIATIONS *

In September 1945, although no Government policies or procedures on bauxite mining had been established as yet, Reynolds retained the services of a leading engineering firm to make preliminary surveys and designs of facilities. In February 1946, these plans were completed and Reynolds was ready to proceed as soon as the necessary mining legislation was enacted. The initial mining legislation (The Minerals [Vesting] Law and the Mining Law—Chapters 38 and 41 of 1947) was passed in September and October 1947.

Jamaica's royalty, when established in 1947, was the highest of any on Caribbean bauxite. The following tabulation shows how they compared in 1947:

	Royalty Terms	
	Per Ton Mined (U.S. Currency)	Period
CARIBBEAN BAUXITES		
Jamaica	20.2¢	5 yrs.
Haiti	17.1¢	60 yrs.
Dominican Republic	15.2¢	60 yrs.

Jamaica's royalty also exceeded those being paid on most of the bauxites which aluminum producers in the United States and Canada were using at the time. These bauxites, from South America and Arkansas (United States), had already proven themselves economical through decades of actual usage while Caribbean bauxites were still in search of an economical process. Nevertheless the royalty rates on these bauxites in actual use were:

	Per Ton	Period
Arkansas (U.S.)	10¢	No termination date fixed
British Guiana:		
Most of the production (old leases)	3.9¢	21 years
On privately owned lands	None	
Under new leases issued after 1947	9.9¢	21 years
Surinam	18.3¢	50 years
(Depending on mining conditions)	or 36.6¢	

Other terms and conditions prescribed by Jamaica's Mining Law were also more severe than those prevailing in Haiti, Dominican Republic, British Guiana or Surinam:

(a) Jamaica is the only country requiring purchase of private lands to obtain mining rights, which also means paying local land taxes.

* *Reynolds Jamaica Mines Ltd., Its Origin and Development, 1943–1953,* Reynolds Metals Company Economics Research Department (August 1956), pp. 4–6.

The other countries permit mining on leased lands at these annual rentals per acre:

Haiti	16.2¢
Dominican Republic	4.1¢
British Guiana	11.8¢
Surinam	21.9¢

(b) Jamaica is the only country requiring that agricultural productivity be maintained on unmined lands and restored on mined out areas. No land use requirements are imposed by the mining laws of the other countries named above.

During the years since 1946, the processing problems of Jamaica bauxite were being studied at a special research laboratory established by Reynolds Metals at Listerhill, Alabama. Higher temperatures and pressures had to be tested through the pilot plant stage to find a way of extracting alumina from Jamaica bauxite commercially. Procedures and equipment also had to be developed for improving the settling and filtering characteristics of Jamaica bauxite. A November 1948 report by United States Bureau of Mines engineers, while noting that progress was being made at the Reynolds laboratory, stated that these results "are merely preliminary" and that only "actual tests in a commercial plant" would be conclusive.

In 1948 Reynolds Metals offered to assume the financial risk of using the as yet unproven Jamaica bauxite, by seeking loans for building its Jamaica facilities first from Colonial Development Corporation, West Indies, Ltd. and then from the Economic Corporation Administration ("ECA" — the United States Government agency administering the Marshall Plan programme). In January 1949, Reynolds Metals notified the Jamaica Government that it was confident of being able to get an ECA loan if it could work out an agreement with the Jamaica Government covering the construction of a pier at Ocho Rios, the granting of a Mining Licence under the Mining Law, exemptions from customs duties on machinery and certain supplies needed for the project and a "fair formula for determining our income tax liability for 25 years after operations commence."

A proposal "to develop immediately" its bauxite mining enterprise in Jamaica was submitted by Reynolds Metals to the Government on 6th April, 1949. Reynolds reported that ECA was ready to loan Reynolds £ 2,775,000 towards the project and that consent to the financing had been obtained from "all seven interested agencies of the United States Government." It was explained that before so large a capital investment could be made by Reynolds Metals, it would need assurance from the Jamaica Government "that the use of Jamaica Bauxite will remain competitive throughout the primary term of the Mining Leases, particularly during the 20-year period in which Reynolds must repay the ECA advance."

The basic conditions requested by Reynolds Metals were essentially the same as stated in January 1949 with additional details as to the income tax formula. Reynolds Metals offered to accept the formula suggested by the Colonial Secretary's memorandum of 3rd February, 1949, 3/-per ton "provided it covers the 25-year primary period of Mining Leases." In exchange for this long-term tax rate commitment from Government, which would correspond with Reynolds Metals' long-term financial commitment to ECA, the Company offered ". . . at the end of the first five years to increase or decrease the assumed profit of 3/-d. in exact percentage of the increases or decreases in the published market prices of aluminum in the U.S. market. . ."

Reynolds Metals also stated that "every effort will be made to man supervisory posts with Jamaicans" and that "the Company proposes to pursue an intensive agricultural policy on the lands which are not actively mined." It estimated an initial production of 400,000 tons per year, bringing Jamaica a yearly dollar income equal to £160,000 which would reach £320,000 when the then estimated capacity, of 800,000 tons, was reached.

The Government indicated its general agreement by letter of 29th September, 1949 from the Colonial Secretary, with these major modifications. The royalty was not to be stabilized for the 25-year period of the Mining Lease "as the provision in the Mining Regulations for revision at 5-year periods is based on legislation now generally in force throughout the Colonies." The income tax formula was changed to a United States Currency basis, the proposed 3 shillings assumed profit per ton being converted to 60 cents. This shift to a United States currency basis was significant in view of the then imminent devaluation of the Pound Sterling. After some further modifications, preliminary agreement was reached as to the proposed terms and conditions.

While Reynolds Metals was interested in expediting the final agreement, it wanted to be sure that there was complete understanding and that the commitments by all parties would be as firm as its financial obligations would have to be to ECA. Consequently, the solicitor for Reynolds Metals suggested, by letter of 7th November, 1949 to the Colonial Secretary, that "it will be essential to pass a law to give adequate protection to our clients that the concessions will not be disturbed." With the dissolution of the Legislature scheduled for later in November, in view of forthcoming General Elections, it developed that the necessary legislation would not be introduced until the new Legislature was in session. Reynolds Metals preferred the further delay in order to get the assurance of legislative sanction for the basic arrangements it was prepared to make with the Government.

On 24th January, 1950 Reynolds Metals signed an agreement committing itself to deliver about £ 5,600,00 worth of commercially pure aluminum ingot to the United States Government stockpile in exchange for a 20-year loan of £ 4,000,000 of ECA funds (plus 4% interest) to be used to construct its Jamaica facilities. Reynolds Metals thereby assumed the full risk of delivering standard quality aluminum, regardless of whether Jamaica bauxite proved commercially usable. At that time, no government and no other aluminum company was willing to make any commitment on that basis. The financial commitment to ECA also involved a long-term contract by Reynolds Metals to buy Jamaica bauxite from Reynolds Jamaica Mines so as to assure the repayment of the 20-year ECA loan.

The legislation required before Reynolds Jamaica Mines could commence actual construction was presented to the House of Representatives on 8th May, 1950 with a supporting message from the Governor, Sir John Huggins. It was passed by the House of Representatives on 23rd May, by the Legislative Council on 2nd June and, when the Governor signed it on 11th June, became the "Bauxite and Alumina Industries (Encouragement) Law."

7. THE INITIAL LAW (1950)

The first law governing the bauxite companies covered the customs duty and tonnage tax concessions, and the special income tax formula which had been the subject of considerable prior negotiation. Excerpts from the law follow.

THE BAUXITE AND ALUMINA INDUSTRIES (ENCOURAGEMENT) LAW.*

12th June, 1950

1. This Law may be cited as the Bauxite and Alumina Industries (Encouragement) Law.
2.—(1) Where the Governor in Council is satisfied that any person is engaged in or is desirous of engaging in the winning in Jamaica of bauxite or the producing in Jamaica of alumina from bauxite so won, and that it is expedient so to do, he may by order declare such person to be a recognised bauxite producer or a recognised alumina producer, or both, as the case may be, with effect from such day (which may be anterior to the enactment of this Law) as may be specified in such order, so, however, that no order shall be made under this section unless the person to whom such order relates has signified in writing his approval of such order and of the conditions, if any, contained therein.

* Government of Jamaica, Message No. 35, House of Representatives (1950).

(2) Every order under subsection (1) of this section shall be subject to such conditions (including but not restricted to conditions requiring the payment by the producer to whom the order relates to the Government of Jamaica of any sum of money) specified therein as the Governor in Council may think expedient for securing that the total area and the fertility and the productivity of land available in Jamaica for agricultural and pastoral purposes shall not be diminished to any greater extent or for any longer period than can in the opinion of the Commissioner of Mines economically be avoided, by the occupancy by such producer of any lands in Jamaica or by the winning of bauxite in Jamaica by or on behalf of or for the purpose of being supplied to such producer, and for securing the speedy and full development of the bauxite resources of Jamaica and the speedy and most effectual development of an alumina industry in Jamaica. . . .

3.—(1) No tonnage tax, customs duty or other similar impost shall be payable in respect of the importation into Jamaica by any recognised bauxite producer—

a. at any time withín five years next after the day with effect from which he is declared to be a recognised bauxite producer, of any of the articles specified in Part I of the Schedule to this Law;

b. at any time within five years next after the specified day, of lubricating oils, grease, blasting materials and chemicals and such other materials (except petrol) necessary for the winning, treating and transportation in Jamaica and shipping of bauxite as may be declared by Order of the Governor in Council. . . .

4.—(1) No tonnage tax, customs duty or other similar impost shall be payable in respect of the importation into Jamaica by any recognised alumina producer—

a. at any time within five years next after the day with effect from which he is declared to be a recognised alumina producer, of any of the articles specified in Part II of the Schedule to this Law; . . .

7—(1) Notwithstanding anything to the contrary, where the Governor in Council is satisfied that by reason of the manner in which or terms upon which or persons to whom any recognised bauxite producer disposes or proposes to dispose of any bauxite won by him in Jamaica it is not practicable accurately to assess for the purposes of any law relating to income tax his rate of profit upon bauxite so won, the Governor in Council may direct that during such period as may be specified in such direction the rate of profit assessable for income tax purposes upon all units of bauxite (specified in such direction) disposed of by such producer shall for such purposes be deemed to be such sum as may be so specified:

Provided that no order under this section shall apply to any bauxite won in Jamaica and utilised in the manufacture in Jamaica of alumina.

(2) No directions under subsection (1) of this section shall be revoked or varied during the period specified in such direction pursuant to the provisions of subsection (1) of this section except with the prior approval of the producer to whom such direction relates. . . .

Schedule

Part I

All plant, machinery, building materials not intended for the construction of dwelling houses, tools, mechanical diggers, overhead conveyors, rails, rail cars, pipes, pumps, wharf materials, drilling and blasting equipment, explosives and accessories, trucks and cars not intended to be and in no circumstances used upon a public road and not required to be licensed under the Road Traffic Law, and any other items of, or for the construction of, plant and equipment necessary for the winning, treating, transportation in Jamaica and shipping of bauxite.

Part II

All plant, machinery, building materials not intended for the construction of dwelling houses, tools, mechanical diggers, overhead conveyors, rails, railcars, pipes, pumps, wharf materials, drilling and blasting equipment, explosives and accessories, trucks and cars not intended to be and in no circumstances used upon a public road and not required to be licensed under the Road Traffic Law, and any other items of, or for the construction of, plant and equipment necessary for the manufacture, transportation in Jamaica and shipping of alumina.

Reynolds was declared "a recognized bauxite producer" under the terms of the 1950 law. Kaiser and Alcan also began operations in 1953. In accordance with the law's provisions, a royalty tax and income tax were levied on bauxite production (see p. 153 below). The arrangements for bauxite exports yielded a total tax-take of two shillings and eightpence per ton. One economist has claimed that "there is little doubt that this was an unnecessarily low payment; in 1950, for example, the Government of Surinam received U.S.$2.04—over fourteen shillings—per metric ton exported. That the companies were able to concede such a low tax payment demonstrates the strength of their bargaining position. . . . Since the dried bauxite ore is transferred from the branches of the vertically-integrated MNCs in Jamaica to other branches in the United States for beneficiation, there is no market transaction involved. To tax the bauxite-exporting operation, the Government and the companies must agree on a system of imputing a notional value on the ore. In this process, the Government is at a distinct disadvantage. The paucity of commercial transactions in bauxite anywhere in the world means that there are few 'reference' prices which can be used as guidelines; the fact that bauxite is not homogeneous means that ores with which Jamaican ore could possibly be compared are of different chemical composition and grade. Most of the technical information which could help the Government to negotiate adequately with the companies is controlled by the companies themselves." [23]

8. NEW AGREEMENT REACHED (1957)

A few years after the 1950 law, the government of Jamaica commissioned two eminent economists—Professor J. R. Hicks and Ursula K. Hicks—to "survey the existing system of Government finance . . . and to make such recommendations as would enable the Government of Jamaica to make the most efficient use of (its) sources of revenue." The Hicks's Report, published in 1955, made some specific recommendations for modifying the 1950 agreement in order to increase revenue from bauxite and alumina producers.

A SPECIAL TAXATION PROBLEM—BAUXITE *

The extraction of bauxite differs from all other productive activities carried on in Jamaica by the fact that the proportion of capital to labour employed is extremely high. In other Jamaican industries it is not especially high, and it is not desirable that it should be—for a given amount of capital will employ more labour in industries with a low capital/labour ratio than in industries which have a high one. But in the case of bauxite, technical necessity causes the proportion of capital to labour employed to be high (not merely in comparison with other Jamaican industries, but as compared with most industries in any country). There is accordingly little prospect that bauxite mining will ever offer employment to any really large number of Jamaican workers; but since it employs so much capital, it can be expected to earn rather large profits in Jamaica, and to be in consequence a rather prolific source of taxable capacity. Whatever may be the case with other industries, a wise economic policy should not look upon bauxite as an important source of employment; the main advantage

* J. R. and U. K. Hicks, *Report on Finance and Taxation in Jamaica,* Government Printer, Kingston, Jamaica (1955), pp. 97–102.

23. Norman Girvan, *Foreign Capital and Economic Underdevelopment in Jamaica* (1971), p. 62.

which it can confer upon Jamaica is not to be a source of employment, but to be a source of revenue. At least in the long run, bauxite revenue could become sufficiently large to be of substantial help in the solution of Jamaica's budgetary problem. Bauxite is a low-grade mineral; it will never be a "gold-mine" or bring in riches like oil in the Middle East; but it should be able to exercise a distinctly comforting effect on the Jamaican budget.

As things are, the bauxite producers pay taxes (or may pay taxes) in three ways: (1) a royalty payment, at so much per ton of bauxite extracted (2) income tax (3) land tax upon their properties. We may begin by saying something about land tax, an issue upon which the bauxite companies have a grievance, which we think to be a justified grievance. Bauxite extraction is an exceptionally extensive form of production; not only do the companies use large amounts of land in their actual workings, but in addition they have had to take over large areas which they are not at present working, in order to secure future supplies. They have thus become some of the largest landowners in the island. Now at the time when prospecting for bauxite was undertaken in Jamaica, and when the plans for development were drawn up (up to the middle forties) land tax was very nearly a flat rate tax, at a low poundage, normally less than 3s. in the £10. Since that time, it has become a highly progressive tax, which is imposed at much higher rates upon large than upon small properties. This change was something which the bauxite companies could hardly have foreseen and it has borne heavily upon them. Though for the time being the scale of land tax has been "frozen," this is not a condition which is likely to be permanent, or which indeed ought to be permanent. The companies have thus become very sensitive to the possibility of an almost indefinite burden being laid upon them under this head.

In a later chapter we shall be recommending what we think to be a workable plan for the reform of this land tax system. We hope that this reform will give the bauxite companies a fairer deal under this head than they seem to get (and certainly think that they get) at present. Though the actual amount of land tax which they would pay under our plan would not be much reduced from what it is now, it should be somewhat reduced but this reduction is less important than the greater security which the reformed system should bring. For it is our general belief that the total tax paid by the companies under all heads is too low, not too high; so that the fact that there should be some alleviation of their position as a result of our proposals with respect to land tax strengthens the case for some increase in taxation under the other heads—to which we now turn.

In order to explain the rather complicated situation which exists with respect to these remaining taxes, it is necessary to begin with a few remarks about the structure of the industry. The whole process of extracting aluminium from bauxite is divisible into three stages: (1) the extraction of the bauxite from the ground (2) the reduction of the bauxite to alumina (aluminium oxide) (3) the smelting of the alumina to make aluminium metal. Of these three processes, the last (smelting) requires an enormous supply of cheap hydro-electric power, such as could not be provided on a small island like Jamaica. But the second (the alumina process) can be carried on in Jamaica, and is actually carried on in Jamaica by one of the three companies— Alumina Jamaica Limited, which is a subsidiary of the Alcan Company (Canada). The position of this company, as a source of revenue for Jamaica, is fundamentally different from that of the two American companies (Reynolds and Kaiser) which do not do their alumina process in Jamaica, but merely dry their bauxite before exporting it.

This important difference between the organisation of the Canadian and American companies can be partly explained by the obvious factor of distance. While the Americans have a short haul from Jamaica to Gulf ports, the Canadians have to take their material through the Canal to British Columbia, so that they naturally prefer to take it in the more refined and less bulky form. But the shortness of the distance (which is of course only relatively short) is hardly enough in itself to explain the policy of the American companies; for the direct export of unrefined bauxite involves the interposition of an extra stage—that of drying the bauxite—which is itself a considerable matter, and which is avoided on the Canadian plan. We are accordingly inclined to believe that there must be some further explanation; it is probably to be found in the American tariff, which falls much more heavily upon alumina than upon the crude bauxite. The inability of the American companies to follow the Canadian example, and to do their alumina process in Jamaica, is probably to be explained by the protective policy of the American government.

For Jamaica this is a serious matter, and as time goes on, its seriousness will become more obvious. If all three companies did the alumina process in Jamaica, instead of only one, there would not only be more employment, there would also be more taxable capacity. The amount of capital invested in Jamaica, per ton of bauxite mined, is much greater when the bauxite is exported as alumina than when it is exported raw. The company which carries on the alumina process in Jamaica must therefore be expected to earn much larger taxable profits in proportion to its output. It is clearly to Jamaica's interest that her bauxite should attract industry, at least to this extent; the advantage which thus ensues is recognised by allowing the company which converts its bauxite to pay royalty on rather more favourable terms. Whether the difference, as it is now (a royalty of 10d. a ton is paid by Alumina Jamaica, and 1s. a ton by the American companies), is a sufficient difference is one of the things we shall be considering later.

We pass on to the question of income tax, which is (at least in principle) of much greater importance. The Canadian company pays income tax, or rather will pay income tax, like any ordinary company operating in Jamaica. Since it has received the ordinary initial allowances (under the general income tax law) on the heavy investment of capital which it has undertaken, this income tax liability is not yet effective; but the day will come, and is not far away, when the revenue which Jamaica derives from this company will begin to be substantial. We see no reason to regard this arrangement as other than satisfactory. It contrasts with the very peculiar arrangement by which the other companies have commuted their liability to Jamaican income tax. Instead of paying income tax on their actual profits, they pay tax on a notional profit of 60 cents per ton of bauxite exported; at the present rate of Jamaican income tax, this works out at a rate of 1/8d. per ton in tax. In effect, this is nothing but additional royalty, in place of income-tax; taken together with the ordinary royalty, it makes a total tax payment of 2/8d. per ton, without any additional liability to income tax. This arrangement has been embodied in an agreement, which is to run for 25 years. There is accordingly nothing which can be done about it directly, whatever we may think of it, since it would be out of the question for the Jamaican government even so much as to hint at a desire to break the contract. But this agreement is so much the crux of the whole question that we must consider what are the reasons which have led to its adoption—to its adoption in the case of the export of raw bauxite, but not in the case of the converted alumina.

In both cases, the profits which the companies can be said to earn in Jamaica depend upon the price at which the bauxite (or alumina) is transferred. Since in both cases the material is transferred to what is in effect another part of the same concern, the "price" is an internal price, which may well have a strong element of convention about it, and which the companies have considerable power to fix in such a way as suits their own convenience. Obviously a high "price" is in Jamaica's interest, but it does not follow that the company's interest will always go the other way. For though a high price means more tax to be paid in Jamaica, it means less tax to be paid in America (or Canada); with tax rates as they are at present, it does not appear that it would be to the interest of the companies to keep down their Jamaican profits in order to increase the profits on which they would pay tax elsewhere. So far, it seems to us, the two cases are exactly on a par.

Where there is a real difference is in the nature of the product. Alumina is a homogeneous product; the alumina produced in Jamaica is substantially identical with that produced elsewhere. Thus even if it is sold upon a narrow market, between buyers and sellers who are not quite "at arm's length," the price at which Jamaican alumina is sold is capable of being checked up, at least to some extent, against the prices at which alumina is passing in other parts of the world. The amount of argument that can go on about it, between the company and the tax authorities, is therefore limited. But the Jamaican bauxite is not just like other bauxite; thus if it were necessary to put a price upon it, every time tax had to be assessed, there would be a danger of interminable negotiations about the quality of the product, negotiations in which the Jamaican government would find great difficulty in finding evidence to support its view, if it did not agree with the price which the companies proposed. This does seem to be the substantial reason why a special method of computing tax is necessary. Even if the United States companies were brought within the ordinary Jamaican income tax, it is likely that some indirect means of evaluating the profits which they could be said to make in Jamaica would have to be employed. It might be possible to start from the alumina content of the bauxite they export, and work back by some indirect estimate of the cost of transport to the United States and conversion there; but it should be noticed that these are things about which the companies would be bound to be better informed than the Jamaican government could be. Alternatively, the tax authorities might proceed from the capital which the companies have invested in Jamaica, applying a conventional rate of profit to that capital—but what rate? In practice, these processes are not alternative ways of fixing the taxable profit; they are at the most bases for arguments, that could be employed in negotiation, for challenging a proposed figure that the tax authorities believed to be too low.

We accordingly conclude that there is in practice no effective means of taxing the companies which export raw bauxite, except by negotiating a figure which is bound to be fixed somewhat in the dark. It is quite proper, in such circumstances, to make an agreement which will remain operative for a number of years; otherwise there is bound to be confusion, with overlapping negotiations going on all the time. Nevertheless we feel that the 25 years period of the present agreement is quite excessive, especially at the beginning of the industry's operations, when the government can be certain of having some more information to bargain with, after quite a few years have elapsed. As far as we can see, the agreement which has been fixed up for this long period was not, from the point of view of the Jamaican government, at all a good bargain.

The Jamaican agreement does not look like a good bargain when it is compared with those that have been made by Surinam or British Guiana; and the poor "quality" of Jamaican bauxite, on which the companies founded their case for a low rate of taxable profit, is a matter on which there seem to be two opinions. Profits depend upon costs as well as upon proceeds. Thus it is not irrelevant when assessing profits, that Jamaica bauxite is easy to get, having little overlay. So far as we have been able to weigh the evidence, it looks to us as if a better bargain could have been made by the Jamaica government in this matter of income tax.

But it is no use crying over spilt milk; and on the side of income tax the milk has been spilt. The 25 years' agreement has to be taken for granted. Nevertheless, this does not close the whole issue, for on the side of the royalty things are more open. As we have seen, the "income tax" paid by the United States companies has become, in effect, an additional royalty; thus it is not a matter of great importance which form a payment takes. If, as we believe, the companies made too good a bargain in the matter of income tax, they should be in a position to pay a larger royalty; we consider that an attempt to raise the royalty should be made at the earliest possible moment.

A rise in royalty will have to be negotiated, as the "income tax" agreement was negotiated; for the purpose of this negotiation the government should arm itself with expert assistance, and the fullest possible information. We do not pretend that we have such information at our disposal. But from what we have learned, we do not see why the revenue from bauxite royalties (apart from income tax) should not be put up from the rate of about £70,000 (at which they are at present running) to something like double that figure (at present output). This would be an important contribution towards stopping the present gap in the Jamaican budget.

Something must, however, be added in conclusion about the differential element in the royalty—at present, it will be remembered, the companies which do not convert their bauxite in Jamaica pay 1s. a ton, while that company which does convert pays only 10d. We are decidedly of the opinion that this differential should in principle be preserved. As we have said, it is decidedly in Jamaica's interest that her bauxite should be converted into alumina within the island; it is reasonable to give some incentive in order to encourage conversion. If, however, we are right in thinking that the main bar to conversion by the American companies is the American tariff, it will not be easy to induce these companies to change their policy; it is not to be supposed that a modest differential, such as that existing at present, will make much difference. But we see no reason why such pressure as Jamaica can exert should not be brought to bear. There is accordingly a strong argument for a larger differential (say one-third instead of one-sixth): in view of the fact that the company which does the alumina process in Jamaica will be contributing more abundantly in other ways to the Jamaican revenue, this wider differential would be perfectly justified. Nevertheless, the main object of those who negotiate on Jamaica's behalf should be to secure the maximum possible revenue, both now and in the future, from all three companies (and from those who may come after them); a widening of the differential should only be approved if it is a means of increasing total revenue; it should not be regarded as an end in itself.

Anxious to shape a more favorable tax agreement, the Jamaican government reopened negotiations with the bauxite companies in 1957. The Minister of Trade and Industry told the House of Representatives that "We in Jamaica are not people who can lightly contemplate the tearing up or renouncing of agreements. On the other hand, we do not expect major international companies that operáte in our country to do so in a manner inimical to our country's interest." He called on the companies to sit down at the negotiating table in a spirit of good will.

"Specifically, the Minister charged the companies with acquiring excessive land having little to do with their annual needs in an effort to keep out other companies. He accused the companies of deliberately underestimating their reserves in the yearly reports that they are required to give the government. He hinted changes in the law might be forthcoming that would provide for heavy penalties for such false information." [24]

The Chief Minister and Minister of Development gave this background to the negotiations:

> Since 1950, the Companies rapidly established themselves in Jamaica and greatly expanded their activities. Whilst this was most gratifying, it became increasingly clear that Jamaica was not receiving under these arrangements a return which was consistent with the value of our bauxite and the magnitude of the Company's operations. The arrangements were nevertheless not disturbed until the first five-year period for purposes of a revision of royalties prescribed under the mining regulations came to an end. This date was the 1st March, 1957.
>
> The Government, however, began a study of the situation from January, 1956. It was essential for Government to equip itself with information about the bauxite industry in general and the companies operating here in particular so as to be able to negotiate rationally and on equal terms with the bauxite companies. Whatever may be said now of the previous agreement, it is obvious that the Government negotiators at that time had neither the information nor the advice to enable them to negotiate on equal terms with the Companies engaged in the business.

24. *New York Times,* November 28, 1967.

The first step taken then, was to engage the services of a consultant to advise the Government. This was not as easy as might appear. Broadly speaking, the bauxite and aluminum industry in America is controlled by four very large companies. There are very few people in the world today unconnected with the companies who have detailed knowledge of this industry. The Government was, however, fortunate in locating one such independent person and he proved of invaluable assistance to us. Information was collected from all sources. This was checked, classified, analysed and studied and by the time negotiations were to commence there was very little of interest to us that was not known about the intricate and vast ramifications of this industry.

It became clear from our survey that it was desirable to deal with both royalty and income tax.[25]

The previous 1950 agreement with the bauxite companies had these arrangements:

a. A royalty of 1/- per ton of bauxite exported and of 10d. per ton on bauxite converted into alumina locally. The royalty was fixed for five years.

b. For purposes of income tax, it was to be assumed that bauxite companies made a profit of 60 cents per ton of bauxite. At an income tax rate of 40 per cent (the rate existing in 1957), this yielded an income tax of 24 cents per ton or 1/8d. The combined yield of royalty and income tax therefore amounted to 2/8d. per ton of bauxite.

The negotiations of 1957 resulted in a new agreement which increased the royalty and income tax on exported bauxite from 2/8d. per ton to approximately 13/- and over; placed the royalty rates on exported bauxite on a regressive scale with higher levels of output; slightly increased the differential royalty rate in favor of locally processed bauxite; and introduced an "escalator" clause tying one-half of the royalty and income tax to the market price of aluminum.

Although the 1957 revision of the tax agreements raised the combined royalty and income tax payments to Jamaica to about five times the previous payments per ton of bauxite, the tax payments to Jamaica by the United States companies still remained below the tax due the United States government be-

25. Government of Jamaica, Ministry Paper No. 2, *Negotiations with the Bauxite Companies* (1957).

fore credit for the tax paid to Jamaica. As a result, tax was still paid in Jamaica and the United States on bauxite profits.

SUMMARY OF AGREEMENT REACHED *

1. *Interpretation:* The term "Bauxite Companies" refers to the Kaiser Bauxite Company, Reynolds Jamaica Mines Limited and/or their parent and associated companies.

2. *Term:* The Agreement is for a period of 25 years from the 1st April, 1957.

3. *Income Tax:* In exercise of the powers conferred upon him by Law, the Governor in Council will direct that during the period of the Agreement the rate of profit assessable on the Bauxite Companies in Jamaica for Income tax purposes (herein called "Profits") on each long dry ton of Jamaica bauxite disposed of by them on or after the 1st of January, 1957 shall be deemed to be the sum of:

(a) a fixed amount of $1,925, and

(b) a variable amount established initially at $1,925 which will be adjusted upwards or downwards in direct proportion to the base price of aluminum pig of 99% average guaranteed minimum purity as quoted in New York by the "American Metal Market" for delivery in the United States by United States producers. The initial price of aluminum pig with respect to which the upward or downward adjustment shall be computed shall be the price published on 1st January, 1957 (namely, 25 cents per 1 lb.). Any change in the price of aluminum pig shall apply from the date of publication of such price change to all bauxite disposed of on or after such date until the next date of variation.

Example: If the price of 25 cents per 1 lb. becomes 30 cents the variable $1,925 would become—$\dfrac{\$1,925 \times 30}{25} = \$2.31$

The Profits, being the total of the amounts specified in (a) and (b) above, shall apply only so long as the aggregate of all taxes imposed by the Income Tax Law of Jamaica and the aggregate of all other taxes payable by the Bauxite Companies on or measured by income or profit from the disposition of bauxite imposed in Jamaica and by the Federation of British Caribbean Territories does not exceed 45% of the Profits calculated in the above manner.

If the aggregate of such taxes at any time exceeds 45% of the Profits, then the Profits shall be reduced to the extent necessary so that the aggregate of such taxes does not at any time exceed 45% of the Profits.

The Profits shall be deemed to include all the income arising from the disposition of bauxite, the ownership or occupation of the land on which

* Government of Jamaica, Ministry Paper No. 2, *Negotiations with the Bauxite Companies* (1957).

the bauxite is situated and any other assets held for the purpose of or in connection with any of the foregoing, and profit or loss (including rents) resulting from any activities carried on in compliance with the order declaring the companies to be Recognised Bauxite Producers.

The Profits are stated in terms of United States currency and income tax shall be payable to the Government of Jamaica in United States Dollars.

4. *Royalty:* The Royalty payable by the Bauxite Companies shall be as follows:—

(a) If the tonnage of bauxite in any calendar year does not exceed one million long dry tons, the royalty shall be 4/- per long dry ton.

(b) If the tonnage in any calendar year exceeds one million long dry tons but does not exceed two million long dry tons the royalty for the entire tonnage exported shall be 3/- per long dry ton.

(c) If the tonnage in any calendar year exceeds two million long dry tons, the royalty for the first two million long dry tons shall be 3/- per long dry ton and for the tonnage in excess of two million shall be 2/- per long dry ton.

9. AMENDMENTS

The next changes in the agreement between the Jamaican government and the bauxite companies were made in 1967 through an Act to amend the Bauxite and Alumina Industries (Encouragement) Law. The special amendments of the earlier legislation were:

(1) The Government could henceforth make special income tax arrangements with the companies that produced alumina, because the normal income tax provision of the 1957 agreement had made no special income tax arrangement for this second-stage product;

(2) The Government should be able to determine for the purposes of any law relating to income tax what is "a fair and reasonable assessment of the value of alumina based on the market conditions prevailing at the time" when "any recognized alumina producer is a company which disposes of alumina manufactured in Jamaica."

(3) The 1950 law had allowed exemptions from tonnage tax, customs duties, and other taxes on imports used by bauxite and alumina producers. To the extent that these importables were now being manufactured in Jamaica, the earlier exemptions were removed, and the companies were forbidden to import goods which are produced in Jamaica at comparative prices.

During 1967, the American companies—Reynolds, Kaiser, and Anaconda—also announced plans to form a consortium for the purposes of producing alumina in Jamaica. Previously only Alcan had produced alumina, but the American consortium of Alumina Partners of Jamaica (Alpart) started construction of an alumina plant that would entail new investment in Jamaica of more than U.S.$175 million.

Jamaica's alumina capacity was also to be increased with the conclusion in 1967 of an agreement between the Jamaican government and Revere Jamaica Alumina Limited, a 100 per cent owned subsidiary of Revere Copper Brass, Inc. One of the terms of the agreement called for the construction of an alumina plant of 600,000 tons per year capacity, with initial investment of around U.S.$125 million. The company was assured the right to mine bauxite to keep the alumina plant operative for at least 40 years. The Jamaican government retained, however, the right to dispose of bauxite reserves within the company's concessions which are adjudged to be additional to its calculated requirements under the terms of the agreement.

Most significant were the revisions of the bauxite tax agreements during 1969–71 for the purpose of having all of the taxes on profits from bauxite in Jamaica paid to Jamaica and none to the United States government. Under the treaty against double taxation between Jamaica and the United States, the United States income tax on profits of United States subsidiaries operating in Jamaica is reduced or eliminated by a foreign tax credit to the extent that the tax paid under Jamaican law does not exceed the tax payable under the United States law. A major issue had arisen during the years between the 1957 and 1969–71 tax agreements over the capture for Jamaica of all of the income tax on bauxite profits as recognized under United States tax law and under the treaty against double taxation between the two countries. The Jamaican government was concerned with capturing as much as possible, short of causing the foreign investment to be diverted to another bauxite-supplying country or causing the aluminum companies to resort to alternative materials for alumina.

Under the agreements between Jamaica and the United States bauxite companies, the Jamaica income tax revenue from bauxite and alumina is limited by the transfer prices used for bauxite and alumina. Under United States income tax law, the income taxes paid to Jamaica by the United States companies operating in Jamaica can also be claimed as tax credits by the parent corporations up to the rate of 34 per cent, presently applicable to companies qualifying as United States Western Hemisphere Trade Corporations. The American companies can entirely avoid domestic taxation of their income from Jamaica if the foreign tax credits equal or exceed their domestic tax liability. If the United States Internal Revenue Service would not question the appropriateness of higher transfer prices, it is conceivable that both government revenues to Jamaica and corporate after-tax profits to the parent firms could be increased by having a higher transfer price and greater profit retention in Jamaica as the base for Jamaican corporate income taxation. (The Jamaican bauxite and alumina prices become elements in cost of production of aluminum in the United States which is subject to the present United States corporate income tax rate of 48 per cent.) However, while both the Jamaican government and the United States companies would gain, the United States Treasury would lose by the amount of 14 per cent of the taxable profit on bauxite and alumina (48 per cent less 34 per cent).

The result of the revised tax agreements of 1969–71 was to increase payments per ton of exported bauxite from the United States companies from an original U.S. 38¢ per ton to about $1.80–$2.00 per ton in 1958–68 and then to $2.50–$2.60 per ton during much of the period 1968–73.[26] The level of payments of combined royalty and income tax per ton of exported bauxite from Jamaica since 1957 has been estimated to be among the highest received by any government, and probably greater than all but two countries, the Dominican Republic and Surinam. In relation to investment of less than $10 per ton of Jamaica bauxite, the tax-royalty payments to the government of between $1.80 and $2.60 per ton exported has been the equiv-

---

26. Government of Jamaica, Series of Ministry Papers on Bauxite Industry; Samuel Moment, *World Bauxite-Alumina Reviews*, annual, privately circulated. This section is indebted to the latter source.

alent of giving the Jamaican government more than an 18 per cent to 26 per cent return on the companies' investment.

The intracompany transfer prices for bauxite used by the United States companies determine the taxable profits as calculated in the United States, and are subject to dispute by the United States Internal Revenue Service. These transfer prices are determined by the individual companies, and it is difficult to relate them to the equivalent of prices of bauxites sold in arm's length transactions from other countries because of different characteristics of the bauxites, different mining and freight costs, and different costs per ton of bauxite for conversion into alumina at different alumina plants. It can be submitted, however, that the tax payments to Jamaica would have been less if the bauxite had been sold only to third parties instead of passing through intracompany transfers to the individual producers. This is because the known commercial transactions in other bauxites throughout the world have been at lower prices than the transfer prices used by the United States companies for United States tax purposes, and because third parties would not have been able to obtain the combined tax advantages that United States companies were able to claim through depletion allowances and Western Hemisphere Trade Corporation tax incentives under provisions of the United States internal revenue code.

10. ASSESSMENT

There are various views on the impact of the bauxite industry on Jamaica's development. And in line with the different assessments, there are also different proposals of policies that the Jamaican government should follow with respect to the bauxite industry.

The occasion of the opening of the Alpart plant in 1970 provided an opportunity for the government to outline its position.

SHEARER SETS OUT GUIDELINES FOR BAUXITE INDUSTRY DEVELOPMENT *

Guidelines for the future development of Jamaica's bauxite reserves and of the alumina industry as a whole were given by the

* *Daily Gleaner* (Jamaica), March 9, 1970.

Prime Minister, the Rt. Hon. Hugh Shearer, when he spoke at the official opening of the Alpart plant at Nain, St. Elizabeth, on Friday.

Mr. Shearer stated four main priorities: First, as much bauxite as possible must be converted into alumina and, when possible, into aluminium; secondly, Jamaica must get the fullest possible benefit; thirdly the companies must train Jamaicans to occupy the highest positions; fourthly, the companies must be good citizens.

A policy statement on the utilization of bauxite lands was also made by the Prime Minister. He noted that as mining proceeded the companies would find themselves with mined-out areas and lands which were no longer necessary for their mining operations.

"Very shortly, Government and the companies will have to discuss the best way we can proceed to ensure that these lands are returned to Jamaican ownership if they are not an essential part of the companies' operations," he said.

"I hope all three companies understand that we operate within a democratic framework; that citizens organize themselves in a variety of ways to improve their individual positions, and you must expect that from time to time pressures build up within these groups for more favourable treatment in the different areas of activity in which they come into contact with the operating companies."

After welcoming "the important contribution" which the partners of Alpart have made to the industry, Mr. Shearer continued:

"Overseas investors in any country wish to know that they are not just tolerated but that they are wanted, and it is this fact that I wish to convey to the partners today.

"Reynolds and Kaiser have been old friends of Jamaica, and I trust the third partner—Anaconda Company—will feel equally at home here.

"These contacts may relate to land acquisition, agricultural leases, transactions with farmers, trade union activity and so on, but following our traditions here we hope and expect that settlement of any disputes in these fields will be done around the negotiating table.

Relations

"The Government itself must constantly be looking at its relationship with the companies to see whether in the light of the developments here and in other countries, both sides have an arrangement which is to their mutual interest. The Government and the companies from time to time will have to discuss ways and means by which the Government can participate more effectively in the bauxite and alumina operations, whether by way of ownership of equity or by some other means.

"We are aware that in the past ten years large new sources of bauxite have been discovered in other countries and that competition from bauxite-producing areas for investment has intensified. We obviously must be keeping our eye on the competition, but as you will have seen from the figures I have given you and from planned increases, we have more than held our own and we have continued to be the world's largest producer of bauxite.

"We are mindful of the fact that what we have is a wasting asset: That these large sums of money which we have been receiving will some day come to an end when the reserves are exhausted. It is the Government's responsibility to spend these sums wisely so that permanent assets are created which will in turn be capable of producing an income to replace revenues now received from this industry.

"The country will be interested in knowing that notwithstanding the fact, as I have mentioned previously, that 104 million tons of bauxite have been mined over the last 18 years, our latest calculations show that proved reserves at present are far in excess of reserves which were proven in 1957.

Identification

"It should be mentioned here that the mere existence of bauxite in the ground does not constitute reserves until they are identified and proven because, obviously, one cannot mine until one knows where the bauxite is. So that by proved reserves, I do not mean physical presence of bauxite in the ground, but rather the identification of additional bauxite available for mining.

"In addition to this fact, it has been agreed with at least one company that bauxite classified as high silica bauxite—i.e. bauxite containing more than 4 per cent silica—will be mined. A lowering of the quality of bauxite which is mined would result in an increase in available reserves, since up to that time high-silica or non-commercial bauxite had not been counted as part of the reserves.

"I would like to take the opportunity of setting out what I regard as some of the important issues which should guide the Government and the companies in the use of our bauxite reserves.

"First and foremost, we must seek to transform as much of the bauxite as possible into alumina, and when the technical problems of cheap power for smelting are solved we should convert as much as possible of the alumina into metal.

"A ton of bauxite converted into alumina produces revenue to the Government twice as great as a ton of bauxite exported as bauxite: the return in terms of foreign exchange is four times as great, and whereas one man is required to mine 4,000 tons of bauxite if exported as bauxite, four men are required to mine and process 4,000 tons of bauxite into alumina.

"If we go to the next stage of smelting, we would be processing a commodity where the final value is seven to seven-and-a-half times greater than the value of alumina.

"The Government has been examining for some time now the feasibility of producing metal from alumina and will be continuing its work in this field of major importance. Already provision has been included in the agreement with one of the companies for the supply of alumina to a smelter should a smelter be shown to be a viable project.

"In view of the fact that we are dealing with a wasting asset, the greater the amount of value which we can add to a ton of bauxite, the better off we will be. The proper use of our bauxite reserves must therefore be number one on our list of priorities in this industry.

"Secondly we must ensure that whether the bauxite is exported as bauxite or is converted into alumina or finally into metal, at each stage the Government and the country must insist on securing a fair share of the value of the product consistent with the fair requirements of the investors of capital for an adequate return on their capital.

"Thirdly, the companies should at all times maintain adequate programmes to ensure that Jamaicans are trained to occupy the highest positions in the companies.

"Fourthly, we would expect the companies to be good citizens of the country in constantly seeking out ways and means by which they can co-operate in other areas of economic development by using to the full in their operations, materials and equipment which are available in Jamaica and, where possible, developing manufactures directly or indirectly related to their mining and processing operations.

Big Landowners

"The companies as a group represent the largest land-owning class in Jamaica. As an island with limited land room it is expected that the companies will give utmost co-operation to the Government in ensuring that all lands with a potential are properly developed either directly by themselves or by lease to farmers.

"The Government is also concerned that the benefits from the location of massive plants like this in a new area should bring immediate benefits to the surrounding countryside and to the people living there. The Government would wish to see the development of settled communities with proper housing, schools, medical services, town centres with shopping and community centres.

"Such development would indicate that those working in the plant regarded employment there as offering a long-term career, and the ancillary developments which would result would provide a fair size town of settled people attached to the area in which they work and live.

"As mining proceeds, the company will find itself mined-out areas and lands which are no longer necessary for their mining operations. Very shortly Government and companies will have to discuss the best way we can proceed to ensure that these lands were returned to Jamaican ownership if they are not an essential part of the companies' operations."

Mr. Shearer at this point announced the expansion of the Alpart plant, already published.

Ending his speech, he said:

"Mr. Chairman, let me conclude by congratulating the engineers on the splendid work they have done in putting up what I understand to be one of the most technically advanced alumina plants in the world—virtually on schedule. In this respect our Jamaican workers displayed a high degree of competence and acquitted themselves well. I congratulate them all.

"I am glad to know that the investors behind this project had confidence in our stability to warrant their making the huge investments which were necessary for this plant and for the extension which I have just announced.

"You have my best wishes for a smooth and efficient operation.

"I have very great pleasure in declaring the plant open."

SIGNING OF ALPART PACT, TURNING-POINT *

Signing of the agreement with Alumina Partners of Jamaica for the operation of the plant at Nain, St. Elizabeth, represented a turning-point in the arrangements made by the Government for the future of the industry.

So said the Hon. Robert Lightbourne, Minister of Trade and Industry, in his speech at the dedication ceremony of the Alpart plant on Friday afternoon.

Mr. Lightbourne said 1966 was "a highly significant year in our history," for in that year Jamaica disproved the long-accepted theory that the aluminium-producing companies of the United States would not engage in the production of alumina in Jamaica.

"By signing our agreement with Alpart, we agreed that an American consortium of companies, two of whom were already operating in Jamaica who merely shipped out ore, would henceforth also produce alumina in Jamaica," he said.

"By that agreement, also, we arranged to double alumina production in Jamaica, and to do that in the very first phase of this plant.

"Arriving at an agreement with Alpart meant considerable changes from the agreement which had been made with Alcan. This was necessitated by the tax laws of the U.S.A. which differ substantially in respect to the Canadian laws, where money is concerned.

"I am pleased to say that we managed to arrive at an agreement mutually acceptable.

"But the Alpart agreement meant more than expanding our bauxite industry by merely producing more alumina instead of shipping out of ore.

* *Daily Gleaner* (Jamaica), March 10, 1970.

"Without meaning to be in the least bit derogatory to our old friends Alcan, who, let us be fair, came here when we were far less developed, the introduction of Alpart meant a Jamaican industrial participation in the building and establishment of the plant itself, and not merely the use of unskilled labour, with everything else pertaining to the plant coming from abroad.

Requirement

"I can recall that, at the outset, this policy was not readily accepted, something over which both sides can now look back and smile at. It was not believed at that time that Jamaica was sufficiently developed to undertake what was required.

"One of my proudest and happiest days came when the head of the major contracting company, Kaiser Engineers, invited me to this site and showed me what had been done, and he told me he was glad that I had insisted on the policy of Jamaica doing as much as it was capable of doing in this project.

"He told me that both the quality of the work and the time in which it had been done, were things which Jamaica could be proud about. . . .

"Today, I am happy to be able to say that what happened through the breaking of new ground at Alpart, has become the accepted norm in the case of both Revere and Alcoa."

Co-operation

Mr. Lightbourne made passing reference to his "quest to develop as many ancillary industries as possible," a quest of which all the aluminium companies were aware. He said he had already received co-operation from several of them towards that end.

"We may not as yet be in full agreement in all instances with all the companies, but I submit that if I did not use every effort to pursue such a course I would not be fulfilling my obligation as the Minister of Trade and Industry for my country," he said.

Speaking on the effect of alumina operations in St. Elizabeth, Mr. Lightbourne said that when the day came when the parish would have a total production of some 3,000,000 tons of alumina, "St. Elizabeth, for so many years the ugly duckling, will indeed be the swan of Jamaica.

"I hope that the great economic expansion which is bound to follow will prove a good thing for St. Elizabeth and her sons, as well as for all Jamaica," he said.

Earlier in his speech, the Minister spoke of the realization that bauxite was a wasting asset and that while it was important to develop the industry to meet the immediate and urgent needs of the country, it was equally important to be concerned as to whether

Jamaica would be sufficiently developed economically by the time that this wasting asset was completely depleted.

Two Courses

For that reason, he had decided, on becoming Minister, to take two courses. One, to ensure that Jamaica got as much as possible in return for its bauxite, and, two, to ensure that the rate of overall development would be pursued at a rapid rate.

That was why, he said, the year 1966, when the Alpart agreement was signed, was "a highly significant and important year to us."

On the question of aluminium production, Mr. Lightbourne said that this was "my ultimate dream—a dream which I know every Jamaican shares with me."

"I am aware of the economic problems associated with the price of electricity in manufacturing aluminium. Even as late as during my visit over the past two weeks to the United Kingdom I had discussions over electricity for the purpose.

"I do not think I am giving away any secrets when I say that several of the aluminium companies with whom I have periodically worried over this matter, have in recent times told me of their readiness to co-operate, once we can put together a reasonable economic package.

"I cannot say anything further on that subject today," he added.

The Leader of the Opposition, Michael Manley (who was to become Prime Minister in 1972), also indicated how Alpart could make a greater contribution.

MANLEY POINTS OUT WAYS FOR ALPART TO CONTRIBUTE MORE TO JAMAICAN LIFE *

Speaking at the official opening of the company's new plant at Nain, St. Elizabeth, Mr. Manley said Alpart had opportunities to serve Jamaica at the fields of labour relations, in community development, and in the encouragement and establishment of industries ancillary to the bauxite and alumina industry.

Not only Alpart but all the bauxite and alumina companies in Jamaica, he said, should make a contribution to the development of the infrastructure of Jamaica, helping to provide basic facilities such as schools and houses.

"I would like to see the bauxite companies undertake major contributions to infrastructure and particularly in the fields of Education, training and Housing", he said.

* *Daily Gleaner* (Jamaica), March 9, 1970.

Sophisticated

"I ask the question: Why can't the bauxite companies collaborate and establish a major institute for technical and vocational training? I ask: Why do they not start major schemes of community development for their workers based on low-cost housing."?

On the subject of labour relations and community relations Mr. Manley said Alpart had an opportunity to co-operate with the unions in making "this plant a model of advanced, sophisticated labour relations.

"Quite apart from wages you should collaborate to explore new techniques in human relations on the plant floor, and should co-operate to engage in community activities," he said.

Mr. Manley said these areas of activity were some of the things that might help to guarantee the success of the operation.

Another area to which he suggested that the bauxite companies might look was that of ancillary industries.

This he said had to do with cases where some of the materials other than bauxite which go into the alumina process could be produced locally and where the bauxite companies, with their access to capital and expertise, could collaborate with local capital to establish local "feeder" industries.

Describing this approach as "a challenge to our ingenuity and your interest," Mr. Manley said:

"I give you one simple example. Starch is used as a floculating agent in the alumina process. We import huge quantities of flour to supply this need, which I believe is 28 tons per day at Alpart alone.

"Cassava which can be grown right here in St. Elizabeth is a natural supplier of starch. We should develop our own locally-based cassava and starch industry, providing employment and development and savings in Foreign Exchange," he said.

"These are some of the ways in which indifference—as the antithesis of love, rather than hate—could give way to the positive pursuit of the country's benefit, as another way of contributing to the development of the country whose assets you necessarily deplete year by year."

Mr. Manley said a lot of attention was being given to the development of an aluminium smelter, and the fabricating side of the industry, as important to the future of Jamaica's economy.

"I have spoken of this before and see it as vital to the long-term future," he said.

But there were many things that could be done in the short run which were either not being done or were inadequately done. It was in this context that he spoke of the contribution which could be made by the bauxite companies in other fields.

Mr. Manley expressed the hope that the future would witness success of the operation, prosperity for the workers, and benefit to the country.

"It is my prayer that Alumina Partners of Jamaica may show the day to new levels of concern for the future of Jamaica, new adventures in partnership with the people of our land." he ended.

Alpart's position was also presented at the opening ceremony.

ALPART PLEDGES TO CONTINUE
SERVING NEEDS OF JAMAICA *

"We thank the Government for their many support services. We thank the more than 50 contractors, of which 38 were Jamaican and Jamaican joint-venture companies, for successfully completing their 139 contracts," he said.

"We thank Kaiser Engineers Americas Incorporated for completing the largest capacity alumina plant ever to come into production at one time.

"Each of us look to Alpart for different reasons: Our employees seek a stimulating and rewarding way to make a living. Our partners want a reliable supply of high-quality alumina. Our investors ask a reasonable return on their investment.

Competitively

"The business community looks to Alpart for the opportunity to sell goods and services competitively, and the government looks to Alpart for its contribution to the balance of payments and to help serve the growing economic and social needs of this nation.

"In the healthy business environment set by Government, with well-trained employees, and with responsible labour unions, Alpart can and will serve each of these purposes well.

"A few months ago, two men on the moon pointed a television camera at the Earth, and millions of people saw for the first time the earth in its global wholeness.

"We saw one world; and if we concentrate our thoughts on the philosophical aspects rather than the technological side of that achievement, that television picture of the earth, can help us to see that we are one people on this earth inter-linked and inter-dependent.

"That television picture can help us to see that the whole world should borrow Jamaica's motto: 'Out of many, one people.'

"You have seen today an example of this new spirit of global inter-

* *Daily Gleaner* (Jamaica), March 10, 1970.

dependence and unity of purpose. Alpart is a perfect product of its time.

"It was in December of 1966 that the work of land clearing began on this site; and in May of 1969, the initial operation of the plant began. Today you have seen the plant in full operation.

Operation

"Even for those of us in this business, Alpart's facilities are impressive. The knowledge of many thousands of many-years of experience of men from many nations was used in the design, erection and operation of this plant.

"When we consider that materials, equipment and technology from all over the world are incorporated in this plant: for example, boiler tubes from Japan, structural steel from Italy, motors from Switzerland, conveyors from Germany, valves from Australia, cement and skilled labour from Jamaica, equipment and technology from the United States—we can understand that the Alpart plant represents a complex exercise in international cooperation.

"Ten years ago, a plant such as this would have been built almost completely from designs, materials and equipment produced in the owner's home country. But the world's accelerating progress towards an interdependent, competitive and unified economic system makes that an outmoded practice.

"The businessman who considers only local sources of equipment or materials, who refuses to look beyond state or national boundaries for his requirements, will soon find himself running a poor second to his more alert competitors who are not so constrained.

No Alternative

"The great economic and social demands upon business today make it necessary that business produce as efficiently, as reliably and economically as possible so that people all over the world can live better.

"Business has no other alternative than to search for the best materials, the best technology, the best prices, the most efficient workforce that it can find.

"In competitive business and the aluminum industry is perhaps one of the most highly competitive on an international scale, it is of increasing importance that new production facilities such as this plant be built at the lowest possible capital cost and that these new plants operate at maximum efficiency in terms of the use of materials, energy, size of workforce, and productive capability.

"For example, we have Australian valves in Alpart's plant, not because we thought it would enhance international cooperation to buy the valves there. We used Australian valves because an Australian business man demonstrated that his firm could produce high-quality valves, meeting our requirements and delivery dates, at lower costs than those bid by his international competitors.

"We haul our bauxite in trucks bought from a Jamaican, because that firm, bidding in international competition, gave us the most attractive bid.

"Thus it is that interdependent worldwide technologies and management concepts have converged to create the productive facilities you have seen today. This plant at Nain is a focal point of the best the world's technology has to offer.

Efficiently

"Going back to the Australian valve manufacturer, he fully realized that he was bidding on Alpart's valves in competition with valve manufacturers from many countries. This heightened international competition, forced the manufacturer to produce more efficiently than when he dealt just in the Australian market.

"We have here at Nain a plant which helps to make Jamaica one of the world's leading producers of alumina. But we must be mindful that we are in competition with the alumina producers of Australia, United States, Greece, Yugoslavia, Surinam, Guinea and other parts of the world.

"We have the most modern facility the world's technology can produce. We have an economic climate established by Jamaica's first two Prime Ministers and supported by present government, which is favourable to the development of private enterprise.

"We have a young, intelligent and enthusiastic Jamaican work force; we have responsible labour unions; and we have available to us the technology and management skills of three great partner companies.

"We are off to a start which promises much to the partners, to Alpart's employees, and to Jamaica. As we continue to work together, each sensitive to the problems and needs of the other, we can continue to build upon the foundation we dedicate here today. And in so doing, Alpart can better serve the needs of Jamaica and the world."

Proceeding beyond ceremonial speeches, an economist would have to appraise the bauxite industry in terms of benefits and costs, along the lines already indicated in section 1, above. An economist would conclude that Jamaica benefits to the extent that the parent firm is not able to capture all of the rents accruing to the resources invested in Jamaica. The marginal social benefits that accrue to Jamaica from the foreign investment would then exceed the private return to the foreign investors.

The parent firm brings to Jamaica not only capital but also managerial, technological, and marketing knowledge. These resources must be paid for, in interest, profits, royalties or licensing fees, and salaries to foreign managers. But the bauxite industry may have failed to capture all the rents for three principal reasons: because it invests in the provision of skills to Jamaican employees without being able to capture the full lifetime productivity of these skills; because it cannot appropriate to itself all the productivity gains that it induces in Jamaica; and because Jamaica does succeed in capturing some of its profits in taxes.[27]

Addressing himself to this issue for the aluminum industry in general, Professor Raymond Vernon evaluates the situation.

THE STRUGGLE OVER THE REWARDS *

The tension between the developing countries and the foreign-owned enterprises in the raw material industries derives from many causes. Not all of those causes are economic. To the extent that economic causes are involved, however, they exhibit a marked similarity from one raw material industry to the next.

On the side of the foreign enterprises, one generally sees a small group of very large firms, eager to achieve both growth and stability under oligopoly conditions. On the side of the developing countries, one sees a ceaseless effort to capture as much of the rewards of the oligopoly as the situation allows. Both sides—both the foreign-owned enterprise and the exporting country—can benefit from the existence of an oligopoly since the object of the oligopoly is to maintain stability and to extract a relatively high price from buyers. But the question of sharing the rewards is at stake in the struggle between the enterprise and the country. And the outcome of the struggle differs from one industry to the next, according to the relative strengths of the two sides.

Oil, copper, and aluminium represent the three industries in which United States-based enterprises have their heaviest overseas stake. At the same time, these three industries illustrate the different outcomes of the struggle over the rewards.

In the case of aluminium, the basis for oligopoly was evident from the very first. The efficient production of aluminium demanded huge

* UNCTAD, *The Operations of Multinational United States Enterprises in Developing Countries*, A Study by Raymond Vernon (1972), pp. 4, 9–10.

27. More generally, see R. E. Caves, "Foreign Investment, Trade and Industrial Growth," in Joe S. Bain (ed.), *Essays on Economic Development* (1970), pp. 30–32.

smelters. The technology of smelter construction was esoteric and complex. The construction of smelters entailed large quantities of capital and absorbed unprecedented quantities of electricity. Obviously this was an undertaking for giants, beyond the reach of most developing countries. Besides, a country that possessed bauxite, the raw material, had nothing like the bargaining position of a country that possessed crude oil or rich copper ore. In petroleum and copper, the cost of the raw material was a very considerable part of the cost of the final product, while fabrication costs were secondary; in aluminium, the opposite was the case. Whereas refining costs in oil amounted to 6 or 7 per cent of production costs, and in copper to 15 per cent of production costs, the comparable figure for aluminium was about 60 per cent.

The giants that appeared in the aluminium industry early in the twentieth century at first seemed almost invulnerable in their negotiations with developing countries. For decades, the North American companies exercised a near monopoly over world production. Later, some Europeans joined the tiny circle of producers. But the increase in numbers did little to loosen the industry structure. As in oil and copper, cartel agreements were in effect for a period before the Second World War. Even after the formal termination of the agreements, the main participants in the industry commonly formed partnerships, sometimes to operate joint bauxite mines, sometimes to run jointly owned smelters. In the late 1960s, there was scarcely a major aluminium producer in the world that did not have some fairly direct link with all the others.

Even this degree of cohesiveness was not enough to guarantee a sense of security among the aluminium producers. Like the producers of copper and oil, those in aluminium also turned to vertical integration in order to buttress their position. In the 1960s, some of the major producers could be seen rapidly acquiring aluminium fabricators, thereby assuring themselves of the existence of a captive group of customers.

Information on the terms of the agreements between the developing countries and the aluminium producers is relatively sparse. There are indications, however, that royalties are commonly paid on the basis of some fixed sum per ton. For the purpose of calculating income taxes due to the producing country, bauxite and alumina are often priced on the basis of formulas that link them to the world price for refined aluminium. To that extent, the developing countries may be the beneficiaries of some portion of the ologopoly rent that the companies capture when selling the refined aluminium, as well as beneficiaries of the price stability that the oligopoly obviously imposes on the market.

On the other hand, it is perfectly clear that the countries in which the bauxite is mined would have great difficulty in capturing much of the final value of the aluminium produced. For one thing, there are the high relative costs of processing the bauxite. Moreover, the oligopoly rent that is incorporated in the price of the aluminium is not a rent that the bauxite-producing country can readily claim.

Unlike the countries that possess copper or oil, there is little that bauxite-producing countries have to offer which greatly affects the strength of the oligopoly. Though a considerable part of the world's bauxite production is concentrated at a few producing points such as Jamaica, bauxite is available in many places on the earth. From the viewpoint of any aluminium producer, some bauxite deposits are to be preferred to others; but the difference between the best and the second best is not fatal from the company's viewpoint. Much more important to successful operation are cheap electric power and an appropriate smelter. The developing countries that control bauxite, therefore, have little with which to bargain unless they have the potential also for generating the power and for acquiring the smelter. Even then—even after they have mustered the capital and the technology—there will still be the question of markets. A single efficient aluminium smelter is so huge in relation to world demand that the developing country would have much more uncertainty about finding the appropriate outlets for the output of an aluminium smelter than of a copper refinery or an oil refinery.

The appearance of invulnerability that flavours the relations between the aluminium companies and the developing countries therefore has some grounding in the technical conditions of the industry. It is bolstered further by the protectionist policies that many countries pursue with regard to aluminium smelting, partly because the industry is thought to be important for defence, and partly because the industry is so easily prone to predatory dumping practices. . . .

For a specific assessment of the Jamaican bauxite industry, an economist would have to analyze—at a minimum—the available data on production, employment, and contribution to national income. The production of bauxite rose from only 381,000 long tons with an export value of £0.4 million in 1952 to more than 9.2 million long tons and an export value of £18.7 million in 1967. Production of alumina increased from 139,000 short tons and an export value of £2.9 million in 1954 to 924,000 short tons and an export value of £20.9 million in 1967. The continued expansion, especially in alumina exports, between 1967 and 1972 is indicated in Table VI above.

Employment in the bauxite and alumina industry, excluding construction activity, was 5493 persons in 1970; 6162 in 1971, and 6756 in 1972. This is clearly only a very small percentage of the total labor force, estimated at more than 808,000 in the 1972 labor force survey. Total employment in the various activities of the bauxite and alumina companies is given in Table XVIII below. It is interesting to note that whereas one man is employed to mine approximately 4000 tons of bauxite, four men are employed to process an equivalent amount of bauxite into alumina.

Table XVIII. Employment in Bauxite and Alumina

	1969	1970	1971
Mining, Processing and Related Activities	5,114	5,493	6,162
Construction	3,438	5,910	3,938
Agriculture and Agricultural Processing	2,027	1,987	1,529
TOTAL	10,579	13,390	11,629

SOURCE: *Economic Survey, Jamaica, 1971*, p. 23.

Some other indications of the bauxite industry's contribution to the Jamaican economy are presented in Tables XIX to XXII which consider the direct income creation by the bauxite industry through payments for materials and supplies, wages and salaries, taxes and royalties, and capital expenditure within Jamaica.[28]

Table XIX. Contribution of Bauxite-Alumina Industry to Gross Domestic Product, 1967–1971

Year	G.D.P. from bauxite and alumina ($'000)	Percentage of total G.D.P.
1967	95,881	13.3
1968	92,635	11.8
1969	116,397	13.4
1970	150,147	15.6
1971	161,728	15.6

SOURCE: *Economic Survey, Jamaica, 1971*, p. 58.

28. For earlier statistics from 1953 to 1967, see Girvan, *Foreign Capital and Economic Underdevelopment in Jamaica*, chapter 3.

Table XX. Capital Investment of Bauxite and Alumina Companies, 1971–1972
($'000)

Item	Total Capital Expenditure		Local Capital Expenditure	
	1971	1972	1971	1972
Land Development	1,307.1	2,489.9	1,307.1	2,489.9
Buildings and other construction	72,401.4	39,353.4	46,873.8	20,043.2
Machinery and Equipment	21,811.3	2,637.3	4,362.2	216.0
Other	470.5	989.6	470.5	237.4
TOTAL	95,990.4	45,470.2	53,013.6	22,986.0

SOURCE: *Economic Survey, Jamaica, 1972*, p. 47.

Table XXI. Non-capital Expenditure of Bauxite and Alumina Companies, 1971–1972 ($'000)

Item	Total Expenditure		Local Expenditure	
	1971	1972	1971	1972
Wages and Salaries	31,652.3	36,083.5	28,716.3	33,711.8
Supplies and Materials	38,100.8	54,502.7	8,192.9	11,465.4
Other Services	14,443.9	9,702.7	6,935.2	7,101.2
TOTAL	84,197.0	100,288.9	43,844.4	52,278.4

SOURCE: *Economic Survey, Jamaica, 1972*, p. 46.

Table XXII. Payments of Bauxite and Alumina Companies to Government
($'000)

Year	Royalties	Corporate Taxes	Total
1969–70	2,457.6	18,863.5	21,321.1
1970–71	3,236.9	28,153.0	31,389.9
1971–72	2,642.0	31,592.3	34,234.3
1972–73	3,186.6	21,317.0	24,513.6

SOURCE: *Economic Survey, Jamaica, 1972*, p. 46.

The most extensive critical evaluation of the bauxite companies' operations has been made by Norman Girvan.[29] In his wider work on the political economy of the relationships between aluminum companies and bauxite-producing countries, Girvan contends that these relationships lead to "a cumulative process of development and enrichment" for the aluminum companies, and for the advanced countries in which they are based, but to "a cumulative process of underdevelopment and dependence" for the bauxite countries.[30]

On the particular issue of the local share realized by Jamaica from the bauxite industry, Girvan first argues that this is unduly low because each subsidiary or branch company in the industry is fully integrated with its overseas parent and "is thereby divorced from the national economy not only in respect of its output but also in respect of its inputs and also in its choice of factor proportions." Inputs tend to be imported from abroad for intracompany reasons, and the foreign enterprise uses capital-intensive techniques because the range of technology available to the firm is North American and European capital-intensive technology, and because capital is far more abundant and cheaper to the firm than it is to the Jamaican economy. "Given the use of capital-intensive techniques, the share of returns to capital in value added is high; given foreign capital ownership, this share accrues abroad." [31]

Further, Girvan argues that while the bauxite industry is "highly qualified" to assume the potential role of being a "leading sector" in Jamaica's development, the realization of this potential has been "virtually nonexistent" because "the bulk of the value added and external economies has been exported to North America . . . [T]he export of Jamaican bauxite and alumina made possible a substantial demand for the products of intermediate goods industries, the substantial creation of employment incomes, the substantial creation of incomes

29. Norman Girvan, *Foreign Capital and Economic Underdevelopment in Jamaica,* and other articles listed in Readings (p. 190, below).

30. Norman Girvan, "Making the Rules of the Game: Company-Country Agreements in the Bauxite Industry," *Social and Economic Studies* (December 1971), p. 378.

31. Norman Girvan, *Foreign Capital and Economic Underdevelopment in Jamaica,* pp. 47–49.

and wealth for corporate shareholders, and the creation of government revenues, mainly within the United States and Canada." [32]

In proposing alternative resource-allocating arrangements, Girvan has argued for both regional integration and nationalization of the industry. The objective would be to control decisions of the industry in order to increase the Caribbean area's share in value added. The region would in essence become a multinational firm, and regional integration would replace company integration in the utilization of the region's bauxite reserves. It is argued that this would correct the corporate fragmentation of the region's bauxite resources. "There is evidence that the Caribbean area has the basic natural resources to become a major producer of alumina, a significant producer of crude aluminium, and to begin the production of fabricated products, over the next twenty-five years . . . [A]fter the first ten years Jamaica might begin to add value to her alumina by smelting with nuclear power." Instead of being restricted only to the set of investment opportunities that have been intra-corporate rather than intra-regional, Girvan contends that "it may be possible that the Caribbean *conceived as a region,* has a comparative advantage in the production of alumina, aluminium and fabricated products whose realisation is inhibited by the organisation of production. For while the theorems of comparative advantage indicate specialization by countries *under conditions of full internal mobility and zero international mobility of factors,* the conditions in the Caribbean are nearer the opposite. Within each Caribbean territory, as a rule, *there is zero internal mobility of bauxite factors controlled by different companies, and full international mobility of factors within each company.*" [33]

32. *Ibid.,* p. 80. A more detailed analysis of local disbursements of bauxite and alumina enterprises in Jamaica during 1957–61 is offered by H. D. Huggins, *Aluminium in Changing Communities* (1965), pp. 122–55.

33. Norman Girvan, "Regional Integration vs. Company Integration in the Nationalization of Caribbean Bauxite," in S. Lewis and T. Mathews (eds.), *Caribbean Integration,* Institute of Caribbean Studies, University of Puerto Rico, 1967, pp. 112–15. Italics in original.

The same text is also available in Girvan, *The Caribbean Bauxite Industry* (1967), pp. 17–19.

It is noteworthy that the present Prime Minister of Jamaica has also supported a united regional policy. Writing before his election, Mr. Manley contended that

> . . . if unemployment is to be significantly reduced and the dangerous gap between the agricultural population and the industrial elite is to be narrowed, radically different policies have to be pursued. These will have to involve new thinking about the use to which internal resources are to be put; a complete reexamination of the sort of foreign capital which should be invited to participate; and the relationship between foreign capital and the national interest as regards ownership and control. . . . The region would benefit enormously if it could learn to handle major foreign capital interests secondary to a common policy. A classic example is the bauxite and alumina industry. The Caribbean region, including the Dominican Republic, Haiti and Surinam (which is next door to Guyana), produces 52 percent of the bauxite consumed in the Western world and 43 percent of world consumption. As the raw material of the aluminum industry, bauxite has a critical part to play in the economic future of Jamaica and certainly of Guyana and Surinam. But it is a wasting asset, which has to make its contribution to general development as rapidly as possible. Interestingly enough, the workers of the region have been much quicker to recognize this than the politicians.
>
> Perhaps because bargaining power is "the name of the game" in trade unionism, the Bauxite Workers Union in Jamaica pursued a more than ordinarily aggressive wage policy against the giants of the industry—Alcoa, Kaiser and Reynolds of the United States and Alcan of Canada—from the very outset of bargaining in 1952. Later, when the companies began quoting the wage rates in Guyana and Surinam against Jamaican union claims in the mid-1950s, the Jamaican Union responded by forming the Caribbean Bauxite Mining and Metal Workers' Federation. In the last ten years, this body has played a significant part in bringing regional strength to the collective bargaining process, and this in turn has led to spectacular gains in wages and fringe benefits for the region's 15,000 bauxite and alumina workers.
>
> Clearly, this is a lead that the politicians and governments of the region would do well to follow. In terms of royalties, taxes and general contributions to infrastructure, the aluminum companies can do far more in the Caribbean region. The ability of the region to bargain, however, to increase the contribution of the industries to general welfare, has been

considerably affected by the fact that no coherent policy within a united political front exists. And here, let me make it clear that I am not talking in the spirit of wreaking some sort of spiteful vengeance on the aluminum industry; rather, I am concerned to find by legitimate bargaining that point at which the conflicting interests of the industry and the region may be reasonably resolved.

So long as this and similar industries remain exclusively owned by foreign, multinational corporations, the search for this point of "mutual justice" will be virtually impossible. The very presence of such economic power in foreign hands represents a threat to the sense of independence of a country and a serious obstacle to its freedom of action in economic planning. On the other hand, the corporations have made large investments and provide access to markets and technology. The key, therefore, must lie in joint owner-ship. It is only when control and ownership are shared rea-sonably between those who supply the initial capital and know-how on the one hand, and those who supply the raw material and the labor on the other, that mutuality of interest can exist. There is perhaps no greater challenge to man's ca-pacity for wisdom than this. Indeed, the future of the world may be profoundly influenced by the ability of the third world to pursue this goal with calmness and with skill and equally by the ability of the metropolitan world to compre-hend the aspirations that lead to the claim for joint owner-ship and to coöperate wholeheartedly with the process. Where the metropolitan world and its overseas corporations have not learned this lesson in the past, expropriation has often sooner or later been the result. If the world refuses to learn from the past, the old device of revolutionary expro-priation may continue to be invoked, not as dogma, but out of practical necessity.[34]

As a supplement to his argument for regional integration, Girvan has also proposed that the potential collective bargain-ing power of the Caribbean producers be used to transfer own-ership and decision-making from the international companies to the public agencies of the region. It is maintained that Ca-ribbean control over the industry is necessary in order to use the profits of the industry for Caribbean development. It is "essential and urgent" for the Caribbean people "to be in a

34. Michael Manley, "Overcoming Insularity in Jamaica," *Foreign Affairs* (October 1970), pp. 107–8.

position to make their own decisions in the industry, and develop their own technologies." As a first step, Girvan urges the formation of an Organization of Bauxite Exporting Countries (OBEC) "with a minimum target of an agreement on the pricing of bauxite and its products, and an ultimate target of a change in the international distribution of ownership and the international division of processing, within the industry." The next step is to decide the degree of national ownership and control—whether nationalization should be "partial" (with minority company ownership and some management or marketing agreements) or "full" in which 100 per cent share ownership is acquired and the government also assumes the functions of management and marketing immediately. Full nationalization, it is said, has the advantages of establishing immediate total control over profits, decision-making, and marketing. But the choice between partial or full nationalization will "depend on the particular government, the particular industry, and the particular circumstances of the take-over. This will determine how far the government can rely on internal popular support, whether the technology necessary for production and expansion is monopolized by the parent firm or can be mobilized from other sources, how far new or different markets can be found, and what are the degree and nature of external opposition." [35]

Nationalization has been rare in the aluminum industry; but in 1971, Guyana appropriated 100 per cent ownership of the shares of Demerara Bauxite Company, a wholly-owned subsidiary of Alcan. For many in the Caribbean there may be considerable appeal in the statement that the Prime Minister of Guyana broadcast just before negotiations began with Demerara:

> By far the most important and vital resources of a nation, apart from its people, are its natural resources. In the case of Guyana, these are in forests and minerals chiefly—a pattern which repeats itself when one looks around the world in most of the developing countries.
>
> For all these countries ownership and control by them of

35. Norman Girvan, "Bauxite: The Need to Nationalize, Part I," *Review of Black Political Economy* (Fall 1971), pp. 76–77, 88–92.

their natural resources are essential to their survival and therefore of relevance to all mankind. Today, the world community frankly acknowledges this. . . . The General Assembly [of the United Nations] recognized "the sovereign right of every State to dispose of its wealth and its natural resources." . . . The Assembly [also] declared that "The right of the peoples and nations to permanent sovereignty over their natural wealth and resources must be exercised in the interest of their national development and of the well-being of the people of the State concerned."

Mineral resources invariably supply the raw materials for industrial development and are therefore an important base for economic growth and progress. But they are wasting assets and non-renewable. . . .

If, therefore, Guyana does not get the maximum benefit from its minerals, it has, to this extent, lost part of its wealth forever. . . .

We must own, and control the exploitation of our resources. We have seen in Guyana and in other underdeveloped countries, foreign owned extractive industries prosper while the native population remained poor and destitute. . . .

Guyana is entitled to a fair price for her bauxite.

Guyana is entitled to have a significant part of her bauxite processed into aluminium in Guyana within the foreseeable future—it should have been done ages ago.

Guyana is entitled to have more alumina processed here.

Guyana is entitled to have other industries, manufacturing from her raw materials goods for the bauxite-aluminium industry. . . .

It is time that Guyana's bauxite made a truly significant contribution to the development of Guyana and to the improvement of the quality of life of the people of Guyana.

But these and other benefits Guyana will never reap if she does not have a substantial share in the ownership, and therefore policy, of these Companies.[36]

Under the terms of settlement for the transfer of ownership, Alcan received notes from the government for 107 million Guyana dollars, payable over 20 years, with 6 per cent interest.[37] The new Guyana Bauxite Company (Guybau) reported 1971 profits of $7 million; and according to the company, production has been maintained, and a new alumina production

36. Broadcast address to the Nation by Prime Minister L.F.S. Burnham, November 28, 1970.
37. *International Financial News Survey* (1971), p. 239.

record was achieved in January 1972.[38] The actual condition of the properties would have to be audited, however, to analyze the standard of maintenance.

It must also be recognized that a considerable portion of Guybau's output is a unique ore—calcined bauxite—which does not enter the aluminum industry but is sold to the refractory and abrasive industries. By avoiding a marketing problem, Guybau may be the exception that proves the rule that it is difficult for an independent producer to be successful without an internationally integrated supply, processing, and marketing organization. Guyana's example has not been followed by other Caribbean countries.

JAMAICA UNIMPRESSED BY GUYANA TAKEOVER *

The enormous foreign investments in the bauxite and alumina industries in Jamaica and Guyana have always been subject to debate. The nationalists (especially those in the University of the West Indies) claim that these industries should be under local control since domestic resources are being exploited. The conservatives feel that local expertise could not do as good a job as the foreign companies, but that continuing efforts should be made to get as much benefit as possible from what has been called a diminishing capital asset.

So far there has been no way of telling which is right. However, with the recent nationalisation by Guyana of the Demerara Bauxite Company, a wholly-owned subsidiary of Alcan, the next few years will provide a means of comparison. There was no official reaction by Jamaican Government officials to the announcement late last year that Prime Minister Burnham would nationalise DEMBA.

Bad Name

Unofficial reaction here was that Guyana was giving the entire West Indies a bad name and that foreign investors would be hesitant to put their money into an area where nationalisation was taking place. At the same time, it was felt that the Guyanese would never be able to keep DEMBA in operation: local expertise would be insufficient, and there would be difficulty in securing foreign markets, even if the transport problem was solved.

Jamaicans point out the fact that over the years there has been increasing investment in bauxite and alumina production, and that the country has benefited. Since 1969, the bauxite and alumina indus-

---

* *The Financial Times*, September 9, 1971.
38. "Guybau Makes a Sound Start," *World Development* (February 1973), p. 14.

tries have been the largest contributors to the gross domestic product. In 1970, the contribution was £80m., or 16.8 per cent of the total. Capital expenditure increased from £11.2m in 1966 to £22.5m. last year. Wages and salaries have more than doubled from £5.3m. to £11.5m., while the number of persons employed increased from 5,013 to 12,039. While the numbers employed are relatively low given the size of the investment, the bauxite and the alumina companies pay salaries which are about twice those paid in other sectors of the economy. Taxes and royalties paid to the Jamaican Government totalled £15.9m. last year, or over 10 per cent of total Government revenue.

One reason for the increasing income to the country is the heavy increase in investments by existing companies operating here, and several new companies. Alumina was first exported from Jamaica in 1952 by Alcan. This company has since expanded its two plants to 30 times their original output.

Recently, a consortium of Reynolds, Kaiser and Anaconda invested some £75m. in an alumina plant which equals the output of both Alcan's plants. The plant is to be further expanded. Meanwhile Alcoa is putting the finishing touches on an alumina plant and Revere expects to go into production shortly. It is estimated that after all the investments have been made, the total will be in the neighbourhood of £500m.

Although Jamaica is the world's largest exporter of bauxite, the Jamaican Government has actively promoted investment in alumina productions since the Government gets more revenue from this. Recently the Government announced that a new tax arrangement had been negotiated with Reynolds whereby tax revenue will be almost doubled. Jamaica will now be getting about £1 per ton. Similar agreements are also being negotiated with the rest of the companies. Last year Jamaica exported 11.8m. tons of bauxite; therefore, any increase of taxes on exports will mean considerably more revenue for the country.

There has been some talk that the Jamaican Government negotiated the increased tax after the nationalisation of DEMBA so as to show that efforts are being made to get more out of the companies. But in fact these negotiations began some years before, although it may be possible that they were speeded up a little.

Under an early Jamaican law, the bauxite mining companies are required to return land to the same state of productivity as when they acquired it. In July, Prime Minister Hugh Shearer announced that agreement had been reached with the bauxite companies whereby the mined out lands would be made available for Jamaican ownership as soon as possible. The bauxite and alumina companies here are the island's largest land owners, and this has given cause for concern. Not because the bauxite and alumina companies do not make good use of the land, but because of the growing need for good farming land.

Goodwill

Perhaps one of the reasons for the good relations which have existed between the bauxite and alumina countries and Jamaicans in general is that the companies realise they have certain obligations, and that by becoming involved in the local economy and society they will create goodwill.

Since the time that Reynolds first came to Jamaica, the impact of governmental policy has been mainly to secure greater royalty and tax payments and to increase alumina processing capacity. Country-company relationships have become more acute, however, as the underlying problem of underdevelopment has persisted in Jamaica; the government has become a much keener bargainer; and more indigenous talent is available to analyze the situation.

Nationalization, or an alteration of the basic pattern of company ownership, has not been considered feasible policy by the government. And yet, there is still the desire to increase the social net benefit of bauxite investment. Once again in January 1974 the Jamaican government reported that it was making an assessment of new prices which it may ask for bauxite and alumina to offset the large increase in the country's fuel bill.

GOVERNMENT TO RE-NEGOTIATE BAUXITE PACTS *

The Prime Minister, the Hon. Michael Manley, announced yesterday that the Government will re-negotiate the present contracts with the bauxite and alumina companies. "The Government of Jamaica cannot regard itself as bound by these contracts any longer," he told the annual conference of the Jamaica Teachers Association.

Mr. Manley made the announcement after a detailed analysis of the economic crisis the country faces as a result of the "astronomical increases in oil prices." He said the country was faced with a crippling fuel bill that could run as high as $160 million to $170 million, compared to $50 million in 1973.

It was against the background "of these stark economic and finan-

* *Daily Gleaner* (Jamaica), January 4, 1974.

cial facts" that Mr. Manley announced that the contracts are to be re-negotiated.

The Prime Minister said he was aware that the contracts were entered into in good faith and that he personally regarded contracts as sacred, particularly in the sense that it was on this basis that the rule of law rested.

However, Mr. Manley said the contracts with the bauxite and alumina companies were made in "a world that no longer exists." He added: "The fundamental economic equations have changed. The contracts have been abrogated by history and factors that make them no longer relevant."

It was at this point that Mr. Manley declared that the Government can no longer regard itself as bound by the present contracts. "If we are to survive, then we must get new contracts with new benefits."

Discussions between the Government and the heads of the bauxite and alumina parent companies were due to begin soon.

Discussions did proceed until May 1974 when negotiations broke down after the companies rejected a formula for "production levies," or taxes, pegging the charge for mined bauxite at 7.5 per cent of the United States price for aluminum ingot, and having the rate rise to 8.5 per cent in two years, from its 1973 rate of approximately 2 per cent of the price for aluminum. Further, a royalty of 50 cents a ton of bauxite would be charged. The companies accepted the concept embodied in the Jamaican proposal that the bauxite tax should be tied to the price of aluminum ingot, but they differed considerably on the formula, offering a 3.5 per cent basis. The government's formula would bring estimated revenues of approximately $230 million during the period January 1, 1974, to March 31, 1975. The companies counter-offer would have raised Jamaica's bauxite revenue from less than $25 million in 1973 to approximately $80 million in 1974.

After rejecting the companies' offer, Prime Minister Manley said the government planned to exercise its sovereign right to tax, and he proposed legislation to Parliament which embodied the same provisions as the government's bargaining position. Most of the contracts still have 10 to 20 years to run. The companies therefore said they would seek binding arbitration of the dispute before the World Bank's International Center for the Settlement of Investment Disputes.

Again, as in the earlier negotiations, the problem remained: what is the next best alternative?

C. QUESTIONS

1. Professor Harry Johnson has suggested that the potential gains to a particular nation from the operations in it of branches of a multinational enterprise have become highly significant because of "the fragmentation of the contemporary world into nation-states. Among these nation-states the movement of labour is severely restricted by immigration laws; the movement of goods and services restricted by tariffs, quotas, and other kinds of regulations; and the movement of portfolio capital increasingly restricted by balance-of-payments considerations. The major remaining avenue open for other nations to share in the affluence of the most developed nations, with the hope of eventually achieving comparable standards of living, once migration, trade, and borrowing of capital by itself are severely impeded by restrictions, is the international diffusion of advanced technology and managerial methods. The activities of the multinational enterprise are now the major way in which the transmission and diffusion of advanced knowledge occurs; for the international corporation has a hard-headed commercial interest, and not merely an ineffectual humanitarian interest, in promoting economic development in this way, its motivation being to tap new and profitable markets and to take advantage of the availability of relatively cheap labor." [Harry Johnson, "Economic Benefits of the Multinational Enterprise," in *Nationalism and the Multinational Enterprise*, edited by H. R. Hahlo *et al.* (1973), p. 169.]

a) What is your general reaction to this statement?

b) More specifically, do you think it justifies the operations of the multinational bauxite enterprises in Jamaica? What other factors might you want to consider?

c) Would you want to distinguish among the effects of the multinational enterprises in LDCs according to whether they operate in the host country's extractive industries, import-substituting industries, or export-substituting industries (as in Problem III, below)?

2. A group of Caribbean social scientists have given considerable attention to the characteristics of the plantation economy. [See Lloyd Best, "A Model of Pure Plantation Economy," *Social and Economic Studies* (September 1968); G. Beckford, *Persistent Poverty* (1972)]. It is contended that the pervasive influence of the plantation resulted in dependence and underdevelopment. But while a "plantation society" in Jamaica was historically centered on sugar, it is now argued that a "branch plant society" is being created by foreign investment. Thus, one study of the MNCs states that "as it crosses international boundaries, [the MNC] pulls and tears at the social and political fabric and erodes the cohesiveness of national states. . . . In conclusion, it seems that a regime of multinational corporations would offer underdeveloped countries neither national independence nor equality. It would tend instead to inhibit the attainment of these goals. It would turn the underdeveloped countries into branch-plant countries, not only with reference to their economic functions but throughout the whole gamut of social, political and cultural roles." [S. Hymer, "The Multinational Corporation and the Law of Uneven Development," in *Economics and World Order from the 1970's to the 1990's*, edited by J. Bhagwati (1972), pp. 129, 133.]

a) What is your general reaction to this statement?

b) More specifically, do you think it justifies the exclusion of MNCs from Jamaica? What other factors might you want to consider?

c) Would you want to distinguish among the effects of the multinational enterprises in LDCs according to whether they operate in the host country's extractive industries, import-substituting industries, or export-substituting industries (as in Problem III, below)?

3. a) What costs are due to the "foreignness" of the bauxite investment in Jamaica? What would be the costs of the investment if it were locally owned?

b) What difference would it make to the Jamaican economy if the bauxite investment were undertaken by a United States corporation that invests in Jamaica but produces and markets only in the United States, instead of having the bauxite investment undertaken by an MNC that produces and markets in many countries? In other words, exactly how do the benefits and costs of the foreign investment differ because the foreign investment is undertaken by an MNC?

4. a) If the government of Jamaica wanted to maximize the net social benefit from bauxite investment, should it follow the recommendations in the following quotation?

"The future contribution of the bauxite based industry to the economy depends in large measure on whether a national policy for the industry is worked out or whether its fortunes continue to depend on the private needs of the companies which are involved in it. . . . National policy would be better served with a slower rate of depletion, with processing being pushed at least to the stage of aluminium smelting and with at least a majority share owned by the public sector—payment for existing assets being made out of future profits. The present balance of bargaining power is such that success in achieving these objectives might require a unified approach on the part of all Caribbean producers." [Owen Jefferson, *The Post-War Economic Development of Jamaica* (1972), p. 168.]

b) Would you advise the government to employ a decision analyst who would calculate the expected present values of the benefit and cost streams of alternative policies? What difficulties would the decision analyst face?

c) Do you think it is instructive to analyze Jamaica's development strategy as a problem of maximizing the return on an "exhaustible comparative advantage"—that is, as a problem of transforming a stock of mineral wealth into a more broadly structured economy composed of another set of long-term productive assets?

5. Considerable attention has been given to the Foreign Private Investment Code drawn up by the Andean Group (Bolivia, Chile, Colombia, Ecuador, Peru). Decision 24 of this code (adopted in 1970) is the first application of a forced divestment scheme, requiring foreign firms to sell equity to local interests, so as to transform them into joint ventures with 51 per cent local ownership within 15 to 20 years.

a) Do you think the central issue over the division of returns from a foreign investment is whether 100 per cent foreign ownership of an MNC is to be allowed, or a joint venture is to be required? Or are the real issues of MNC-behavior other than those over the division of ownership?

b) Would you argue that a "fade out" provision should be applied to the foreign bauxite firms in Jamaica?

6. a) Could the United States government adopt any policies to encourage more production of alumina in Jamaica instead of in the United States? Should it?

b) Should the United States government be concerned with the terms and the "fairness" of American foreign investment in Jamaica?

c) The principal instrumentality by which the United States government seeks to stimulate private investment in the developing countries is the Overseas Private Investment Corporation (OPIC) which offers investment insurance against three forms of risk associated with foreign investment: inconvertibility of foreign currency into dollars; expropriation; and war, revolution, or insurrection. The investment covered must be new investment, but it may be in the form of loans or equity.

Reviewing the operations of OPIC, the Subcommittee on Foreign Economic Policy of the Committee on Foreign Affairs conducted hearings in 1973. At these hearings, the President of the Reynolds Metals Company said:

"In 1970 the decision was made to expand the Alpart plant, requiring an estimated investment of $81,000,000. This decision . . . was made on the basis of the availability of OPIC insurance. In 1967, Reynolds completed the enlargement of its bauxite mining facilities in Jamaica, including the construction of a 6.3-mile-long conveyor belt to bring bauxite from the mines to the sea for shipment. The decision to go ahead on this project was dependent upon Reynolds obtaining OPIC insurance.

"It is clear that the insurance made it possible for my company to expand its facilities for a production of economical bauxite to meet the growing demand for aluminum in the

United States and that it has also contributed substantially to the industrial development of Jamaica." [Testimony of R. S. Reynolds, Jr., July 18, 1973.]

Do you think that there should be a risk insurance program such as that provided by OPIC? Should it insure investments by the large MNCs, or only smaller businesses?

7. A study of mineral exporting industries by the Organization of the Petroleum Exporting Countries (OPEC) concludes that "a) minerals are depletable resources; b) exports of raw materials are largely from developing to developed countries; c) mineral exploration, development, production, processing or marketing have, until very recently, been carried out mostly by foreign private concerns belonging to the developed countries; d) surplus productive capacity, or availability, has existed in a number of mineral exporting countries; e) the economic gap between the developing and the developed countries has generally been rising; f) minerals constitute a major source of foreign exchange earnings in a number of the developing countries concerned; g) export prices of minerals have been generally weakening in real terms, and/or have been subject to wide fluctuations; h) developing countries do not always have for their primary goods, exported in processed forms, free unimpeded access to markets in developed countries.

"The need for an integrated international commodity policy amongst exporters of primary products, as suggested by UNCTAD's Secretariat, is deeply felt in some developing countries. . . . The idea for an integrated international commodity policy can, in fact, be defended by reference to the findings of this study and to the above-mentioned characteristics common to countries exporting minerals, or other primary commodities . . .

"If developing countries exporting minerals and other raw materials are faced in their commercial dealings with big industrial powers and their giant corporations possessing vast know-how, economic resources and bargaining force, it is natural to expect them to get together with a view to exchanging information for their mutual benefit, to form producers' associations of the OPEC-CIPEC (copper-producing countries) type . . . and ultimately to agree on an integrated international commodity policy or a common approach vis-à-vis the developed industrial world and their business agents." [OPEC, *A Comparative Analysis of Selected Mineral Exporting Countries*, Bulletin No. 3 (July 1970), pp. 13–14.]

a) Do you think the oil analogy is valid for bauxite, and that it is possible to create "an OPEC for aluminum"?

b) Do you think that a wide range of Third World metal-producing countries have sizable potential for strategic market power? By what measures could the supplying countries exercise this market power? Under what conditions would they want to exercise their maximum leverage?

c) What exactly is meant by "an integrated international commodity policy"? What is its economic rationale? Its institutional mechanism? Its enforcement procedure?

8. In March 1974 it was announced that Jamaica had actually been selected as headquarters of a newly formed inter-governmental association of bauxite-producing countries—to be known as the International Bauxite Association. Member countries were to be Australia, Guyana, Guinea, Yugoslavia, Sierra Leone, and Jamaica.

Do you think the formation of the International Bauxite Association will have any significant effect on Jamaica's bargaining position vis-à-vis the MNCs?

9. In April 1974 a special session of the United Nations General Assembly on raw materials and development was held. Several speakers representing the group of 96 less-developed countries that called the special session urged cartel-type associations, modeled on the Organization of Petroleum Exporting Countries, for producers of bauxite, copper, iron ore, and other raw materials. In his opening address to the special session, Secretary General Waldheim stated that the main theme of the session was "to secure the optimum use of the world's natural resources with the basic objective of securing better conditions of social justice throughout the world."

Just what specific proposals would you recommend to secure this objective?

10. It has been suggested that some international authority should be established and empowered to regulate the MNCs (see for example, C. P. Kindleberger, *American Business Abroad* (1969), pp. 206–7.)

Do you think it would be possible to draft a code of conduct, with substantive content, that would be acceptable to both host country and MNC? Could there be some less rigid form of international mediation, such as an information-gathering agency that would provide a more informed basis for country-company bargaining? Or are there also problems in establishing such an agency?

D. READINGS

Beckford, George, *Persistent Poverty* (1972).

Bergsten, C. Fred, "The Threat from the Third World," *Foreign Policy* (Summer 1973).

Caves, R. E. "International Corporations: The Industrial Economics of Foreign Investment," *Economica* (1971).

Cohen, Benjamin I., *The Question of Imperialism: The Political Economy of Dominance and Dependence* (1973).

Dunning, J. H. (ed.), *International Investment* (1972).

Girvan, Norman, *The Caribbean Bauxite Industry* (1967).

———, *Foreign Capital and Economic Underdevelopment in Jamaica*, (1972).

———, "Making the Rules of the Game: Company-Country Agreements in the Bauxite Industry," *Social and Economic Studies* (December 1971).

———, "Multinational Corporations and Dependent Underdevelopment in Mineral-Export Economies," *Social and Economic Studies* (December 1970).

———, and Owen Jefferson, *Readings in the Political Economy of the Caribbean* (1971).

——— (ed.), *Dependence and Underdevelopment in the New World and the Old*, special issue of *Social and Economic Studies* (March 1973).

Hirschman, A. O., *How To Divest in Latin America and Why*, Princeton Essays in International Finance, No. 76 (November 1969).

Huggins, H. D., *Aluminium in Changing Communities* (1965).

International Bank for Reconstruction and Development, *Past and Prospective Trends in the World Aluminum Industry* (May 31, 1968), Report No. EC-163.

Jefferson, Owen, *The Post-War Economic Development of Jamaica* (1972).

Johnson, H. G., "The Multinational Corporation as a Development Agent," *Columbia Journal of World Business* (May–June 1970).

Killick, Tony, "The Benefits of Foreign Direct Investment and Its Alternatives: An Empirical Exploration," *Journal of Development Studies* (January 1973).

Kindleberger, C. P. (ed.), *The International Corporation* (1970).

Macdougall, G. D. A., "The Benefits and Costs of Private Investment from Abroad: A Theoretical Approach," *Economic Record* (1960).

Manley, Michael, "Overcoming Insularity in Jamaica," *Foreign Affairs* (October 1970).

——, *The Politics of Change: A Jamaican Testament* (1974).

Mikesell, R. F., *Foreign Investment in Petroleum and Mineral Industries* (1971).

Organisation for Economic Co-operation and Development, *Problems and Prospects of the Primary Aluminium Industry* (1973).

Parry, T. G., "The International Firm and National Economic Policy," *Economic Journal* (September 1973).

Seers, Dudley, "Big Companies and Small Countries," *Kyklos* (1963).

——, "The Mechanism of an Open Petroleum Economy," *Social and Economic Studies* (June 1964).

Streeten, Paul P., "Obstacles to Private Foreign Investment in LDCs," *Columbia Journal of World Business* (May–June 1972).

Sunkel, Osvaldo, "Big Business and 'Dependencia': A Latin American View," *Foreign Affairs* (April 1972).

——, "The Pattern of Latin American Dependence," in V. L. Urquidi and Rosemary Thorp (eds.), *Latin America in the International Economy* (1973).

Turner, Louis, *Multinational Companies and the Third World* (1973).

United Nations, *Multinational Corporations in World Development* (1973).

——, Studies in Economics of Industry 2: Pre-Investment Data for the Aluminum Industry, ST/CID/9 (1966).

Problem III
Export Substitution: Tariff Preferences for Development

A. THE CONTEXT

Reforms in trade relations between rich and poor countries have been increasingly urged since the meeting of UNCTAD I (Geneva, 1964) when the "Group of 77" poor countries demanded a "new trade policy." The outstanding feature of this new policy is the advocacy of tariff preferences to be extended by developed countries in favor of imports of semi-manufactures and manufactured goods from the LDCs into the developed countries. Confronted with the need for expanding trade opportunities, the LDCs have sought to promote nontraditional exports—not only through better market access, but even more significantly through preferential treatment.

1. A NEW TARIFF POLICY

The LDCs at UNCTAD I proposed a generalized, nonreciprocal system of preferences in favor of all LDCs. The United States, however, expressed its opposition to preferences "in principle," and the proposal received no action. Latin American countries continued to press for preferences on their industrial exports to the United States. Finally in 1967, in his Punta del Este speech, President Johnson stated that his administration was prepared to explore the possibility of establishing a generalized scheme of preferences.

Two other groups were also examining preferences. An OECD study group became the major representative of the developed countries. The position of this group is summarized below (pp. 217–20). The Group of 77 was represented by the Algiers Charter, also summarized below (pp. 215–17). While these two negotiating groups differed on the details of a proposed general system of preferences, nonetheless they were able to agree at UNCTAD II (New Delhi, 1968) on the desirability of a general system of preferences; there was unanimous approval of a solution committing the participating countries to implement a general system of preferences. After UNCTAD II, however, the drawing up of detailed proposals by a special committee of UNCTAD and the special group of OECD became protracted as considerable disagreement arose over the distribution of benefits and "burdens" of different preferential schemes.

The distribution of benefits among LDCs and the distribution of "burdens" among the developed countries will depend on the detailed mechanism of particular preferential schemes: the countries included, product coverage, duration of the scheme, method of securing preferential margins, depth of the tariff cuts effecting the preferences, whether preferences must be granted under a single system or through individual parallel schemes, compensation for removal of existing special preferences, safeguard mechanisms, treatment of the least developed among the LDCs, and the status of reverse preferences.

The Special Committee on Preferences of UNCTAD finally considered the revised preference offers submitted by the OECD countries and adopted "agreed conclusions" on generalized preferences at a meeting in 1970. The Trade and Development Board of UNCTAD then approved the recommendations and decisions of the Special Committee. Thus, a generalized system of preferences (GSP) has been brought to the stage of implementation after a period of nearly seven years of discussion and negotiation.

This achievement has been widely hailed as marking a profound and fundamental departure from most-favored-nation treatment. As expressed by the chairman of the Special Committee on Preferences: "We are breaking new ground. Nothing like this has even been attempted before." Beyond doubt, this constituted in many ways, in the words of the Secretary-General of UNCTAD, "a far-reaching and unprecedented undertaking. Never before, to my knowledge, has there been such a concentration of concerted efforts in favor of the developing countries in the field of trade." [1]

2. LIMITS OF IMPORT SUBSTITUTION

The rationale of preferences should be considered in the general context of trade and development. UNCTAD I represented a turning-point in trade policy by recognizing the defects of the previously pursued policy of import substitution and by now placing greater emphasis on export promotion—especially the encouragement of new, non-traditional exports.

Raúl Prebisch, the Secretary-General of UNCTAD, stressed in his report to UNCTAD I "the absolute necessity of building up trade in industrial exports," and pointed out a number of defects with the previous policy of import substitution. Prebisch stated that

> . . . the experience of the countries—especially the Latin American countries—which were . . . becoming industrialized in water-tight compartments is of particular interest . . . because it illustrates the problems that the other developing countries may have to face if, for lack of external markets, they too are forced to look inwards in their industrial development. The former countries are now confronted with the following consequences of their industrial development: (a) the simple and relatively easy phase of import substitution has reached, or is reaching its limit in the countries where industrialization has made most of its progress. As this happens, the need arises for technically complex and difficult substitution activities which usually require great capital intensity and very large markets if a reasonable degree of economic viability is to be attained. Thus there are limits to import substitution in the developing countries

1. R. Krishna Murti, "The Agreement on Preferences," *Journal of World Trade Law* (January–February 1971), pp. 45–46.

which cannot be exceeded without a frequent and considerable waste of capital . . .

(b) The relative smallness of national markets, in addition to other adverse factors, has often made the cost of industries excessive and necessitated recourse to very high protective tariffs; the latter in turn has had unfavorable effects on the industrial structure because it has encouraged the establishment of small uneconomical plants, weakened the incentive to introduce modern techniques, and slowed down the rise in productivity. Thus a real vicious circle has been created as regards exports of manufactured goods. These exports encounter great difficulties because internal costs are high, and internal costs are high because, among other reasons, the exports which would enlarge the markets are lacking. Had it been possible to develop industrial exports, the process of industrialization would have been more economical for it would have made possible the international division of labor in manufacturing.

(c) Usually industrialization has not been the result of a program but has been dictated by adverse external circumstances which made it necessary to restrict or ban imports; these measures have been applied especially to nonessential imports that can be dispensed with or postponed. Thus home production of these goods has been encouraged, absorbing scarce production resources, often regardless of cost . . .

(d) This substitution in respect of nonessential or non-urgently needed goods has led those developing countries which are most advanced in the process of industrialization to concentrate, so far as their imports are concerned, on essential goods, particularly those required by productive activities. Hence, any sizable drop in the earnings of primary exports can not be offset as easily as in former times by compressing imports, because nowadays the margin of such imports that can be eliminated without slowing the pace of internal economic activity and employment is much narrower.

(e) Finally, excessive protectionism has generally insulated the national markets from external competition, weakening and even destroying the incentive necessary for improving the quality of output and lowering costs under the private enterprise system. It has thus tended to stifle the initiative of enterprises as regards both the internal market and exports.

The development of industrial exports, in addition to counteracting the potential trade gap, will make it possible gradually to increase the advantages of industrialization by correcting its defects.[2]

From a number of empirical studies, many economists have also demonstrated that, in contrast to the idealized results of a rational import-substitution strategy, the actual results of inward-looking policies have frequently been perverse.[3] The foreign exchange constraint has actually intensified; prices have become more distorted; unemployment has increased; and the degree of inequality has become greater.

Instead of applying rational principles to the selection of import-replacement industries, many countries have simply shut off imports in an ad hoc response to a balance-of-payments crisis or in the naïve belief that it is the easiest route to industrialization. Only too often the ironic result has been that the more a country's development plan has concentrated its investment resources on protected import-substituting industries, and the more protection these industries received, the greater has been the requirement for foreign capital inflow to meet plan targets, and the more intense has been the balance-of-payments constraint facing the economy.[4] In many cases the import-substitution strategy has not been import-saving. Imports of fuel, industrial materials, capital goods, and even foodstuffs have had to increase, so that the ratio of imports to national income has even risen in many countries. At the same time, the widespread protection has not been effective in allowing import-substitute industries to attain a level of efficient production that would allow them to enter export markets. The

2. Raúl Prebisch, *Towards a New Trade Policy for Development*, Report by the Secretary-General of UNCTAD (1964), pp. 21–22.

3. I. M. D. Little, T. Scitovsky, M. Scott, *Industry and Trade in Some Developing Countries* (1970); Santiago Macario, "Protectionism and Industrialization in Latin America," *Economic Bulletin for Latin America* (March 1964); Stephen Lewis, Jr., *Pakistan: Industrialization and Trade Policy* (1970); Albert Hirschman, "The Political Economy of Import Substitution," *Quarterly Journal of Economics* (February 1968); Werner Baer, "Import Substitution Industrialization in Latin America: Experiences and Interpretations," *Latin American Research Review* (Spring 1972).

4. Stephen Lewis, Jr., "The Effects of Protection on the Growth Rate and on the Need for External Assistance," Research Memorandum No. 49, Center for Development Economics, Williams College (November 1972).

basic shortcoming of the broad-scale type of indiscriminate protection has been that it has led to an extensive range of consumer-goods industries producing small quantities of a large variety of goods for the home market. There has not been the intensive specialization that is the essential condition for the development of an export industry. Nor has the import-substitution strategy led to any generalized industrialization process: the import-substitute industries have remained for the most part enclaves, alien to the rest of the domestic economy—almost reminiscent of the old pattern of foreign investment.

The syndrome of import-substitution policies often resulted in a set of price distortions. The rate of interest in the urban industrial sector has been kept artificially low; wages for unskilled labor have been too high, given the labor surplus; agricultural prices have been undervalued; and the domestic currency has been overvalued in terms of foreign exchange. Price distortions have contributed to financial repression and trade distortion which have had the effects of misallocating resources, biasing production to capital-intensive techniques, and imposing an implicit levy or "negative" protection on agriculture and exports.[5] Although the protected import-substitution industry may be profitable in terms of local currency, the cost in domestic resources of saving foreign exchange may be excessive. When valued at world prices, there have been many cases in which the domestic value added in the import-replacement industry has been negative—that is, the value of the industry's tradable output, at world prices, is less than the value of its tradable inputs, at world prices.[6]

With the increasing concern about the amount of unemployment and degree of inequality in developing countries, economists have recognized that the industrialization process based on import-substitution has been unable to absorb the unemployed and underemployed. Instead, unemployment rates have increased as the rural underemployed and the disguised unemployed have migrated to the urban manufacturing sector

5. For a more comprehensive analysis of these results, see E. S. Shaw, *Financial Deepening in Economic Development* (1973); R. I. McKinnon, *Money and Capital* (1973).

6. See references in note 3, above.

in the hopes of securing a wage-paying job, but for a variety of reasons the result has simply been an increase in open unemployment in the urban sector.[7] In many countries, the problems of unemployment and inequality have been inseparable from the import-substitution strategy: protectionism and licensing have increased economic rents; low interest rates and an overvalued exchange rate have favored upper income levels; and the subsidization of the urban manufacturing sector has redistributed income from the rural to the urban population and also from wages to profits.[8]

Recognizing their disappointing experiences with import-substitution strategy, many countries now seek to promote manufactured exports in order to relax their foreign exchange constraint and provide a base for industrialization with greater employment opportunities. For if, on the one side, the experience of import-substitution industrialization has been disappointing, on the other side, there remains pessimism with respect to exports of primary products. Whether with good reason or not, it is widely believed that the demand for primary products is sluggish, receipts from primary exports are unstable, and the terms of trade for primary producers tend to deteriorate. It is now commonly thought that the widening trade gap can be narrowed only by creating and taking advantage of new opportunities for exporting manufactured goods.

In simplistic terms, the routes to industrialization are by expansion of the home market (a policy of import substitution with industrialization proceeding from the "top down"); or by processing of primary products for export (industrialization from the "bottom up"); or by the export of semi-manufactures and manufactures.

Export substitution—the promotion of nontraditional exports—may take various forms: (1) processed "resource-based" primary products (such as vegetable oils, foodstuffs); (2) mature labor-intensive final products (such as textiles, footwear, leather goods); (3) newer "labor-intensive" processes, compo-

---

7. See G. M. Meier, "Development without Employment," *Banca Nazionale del Lavoro Quarterly Review* (September 1969); International Labour Office, *Towards Full Employment, A Programme for Colombia* (1970).

8. See references in note 3, above.

nents, and assembly in vertically integrated international firms (such as electronic components, engineering products, automobile parts, office machinery parts).

To promote the first two categories of exports, the policy emphasis is on greater market access through tariff liberalization, removal of escalation in the importing countries' tariff structures, and reduction of nontariff barriers. To realize the potential of the latter two categories, however, the emphasis is much more on tariff preferences. The quest has been for the granting of general preferences by the developed countries to the LDCs on manufactures and semi-manufactures without requiring preferences in return.[9]

3. THE STATISTICAL RECORD

Until now the export of manufactures has been highly concentrated among a few countries and a few products. With its exports of manufactures valued at close to $2 billion in 1971, Hong Kong is the largest LDC-exporter of manufactured goods, but Pakistan and the Republic of Korea achieved the highest average annual increase in the growth of manufactures during the 1960's. In 1971, thirteen countries accounted for two-thirds of the exports of manufactures from the LDCs to the developed countries. Table I indicates the major LDC-exporters of manufactures in 1971, and Table II shows the changes in exports according to product groups.

Among the first exports from developing countries are textiles, clothing, leather products, and footwear. These are still the most important exports for each of the leading exporting countries. The major exporters in the 1960s were those countries which could acquire a comparative advantage through low labor costs and a favorable resource base. But by the mid-1960s, the development of electronic and electrical compo-

9. Only to a minor extent has there been interest in regional preferential systems among the LDCs themselves by which they would be allowed to discriminate in favor of one another without having to enter into a full-fledged customs union or free trade area, comprising substantially all the commerce of the member nations (as required by Article XXIV of GATT with respect to preferential trading arrangements). This is probably because regional preferences among the developing countries would neither raise the supply of foreign exchange from the more developed countries nor offer the possibility of providing "aid" to the LDCs.

Table I. Leading Developing Country Exporters of Manufactures to Twenty-one Developed Market Economy Countries, 1962, 1970, and 1971

Exporting country or territory	Value of exports (million dollars)		Cumulative percentage	Annual average percentage increase	
	1962	1971	1971	1962–70	1970–71
1. Hong Kong	414.1	1961.2	15.5	19.8	11.8
2. Venezuela	539.6	772.8	21.7	3.8	6.6
3. Yugoslavia	200.6	718.9	27.4	15.7	11.9
4. Republic of Korea	7.5	681.2	32.8	70.4	28.2
5. Mexico	189.5	642.4	37.9	14.3	16.6
6. Chile	359.7	590.5	42.5	11.0	−28.6
7. Zambia	309.3	531.3	46.7	14.5	−41.9
8. India	368.4	529.9	50.9	3.7	7.4
9. Netherland Antilles	460.7	497.3	54.9	1.8	− 6.8
10. Brazil	86.7	430.8	58.3	18.2	30.1
11. Zaire	213.1	401.1	61.5	14.8	−37.3
12. Malaysia	209.6	333.8	64.1	5.9	0.9
13. Singapore	49.2	316.0	66.6	19.7	52.2
14. Trinidad and Tobago	161.0	299.8	69.0	8.0	0.8
15. Iran	110.9	272.7	71.2	8.2	31.0

SOURCE: UNCTAD, Committee on Manufactures, *Trade in Manufactures of Developing Countries: 1972 Review*, TD/B/C.2/124, p. 35.

nents, chemicals, and equipment had introduced a phase of more sophisticated industrial exports, representing the movement of multinational enterprises to LDC locations and the combination of the international mobility of capital, technology, high skills and market access with the availability of lower cost labor in the LDCs. Beyond the traditional earlier industrial exports such as clothing and textiles, the products now being exported to developed countries include electrical appliances, telecommunications equipment, machine tools, office machines, cameras, optical equipment, aircraft parts, musical instruments, vehicles, and steel products.

A more comprehensive view of the developing countries' export record is given in the following survey.

Table II. Imports by Product Group of Manufactures by Twenty-one Developed Market Economy Countries (DMEC) from Developing Countries (DC) and the World, 1962, 1970, and 1971

Product group	Imports from DC (million dollars) 1962	Imports from DC (million dollars) 1971	Annual average percentage change 1962-1970 DC	Annual average percentage change 1962-1970 World	Annual average percentage change 1970-1971 DC	Annual average percentage change 1970-1971 World	DC percentage share 1962	DC percentage share 1971	Product share in total DMEC imports from DC 1962	Product share in total DMEC imports from DC 1971
Food products	408.9	850.3	8.4	7.9	9.3	10.7	16.0	16.4	7.7	6.7
Drink and tobacco products	305.1	101.0	-4.5	8.0	-51.9	10.8	27.4	4.4	5.8	0.8
Wood products and furniture	251.7	664.6	11.8	10.3	7.9	14.0	11.2	11.8	4.8	5.3
Rubber products	5.8	27.8	21.5	13.7	1.2	17.6	0.9	1.3	0.1	0.2
Leather and footwear	96.1	396.8	15.7	14.4	28.9	20.5	12.2	14.2	1.8	3.1
Textiles	551.7	1174.2	7.8	9.4	17.2	16.5	13.1	11.7	10.4	9.3
Clothing	233.0	1453.2	21.4	18.1	32.0	21.8	18.3	24.7	4.4	11.5
Chemicals	223.2	510.3	9.4	14.2	11.2	9.4	4.5	3.3	4.2	4.0
Pulp paper and board	16.2	44.5	12.9	9.2	4.5	2.6	0.5	0.7	0.3	0.4
Nonmetallic mineral products	23.9	72.0	12.6	11.9	16.4	10.8	2.2	2.4	0.5	0.6
Iron and steel	49.7	277.7	24.9	13.3	-5.5	1.2	1.3	2.6	0.9	2.2
Worked non-ferrous metals	28.4	140.5	24.2	15.3	-12.5	-6.6	3.0	5.1	0.5	1.1
Road motor vehicles	9.9	42.7	12.0	20.3	74.6	26.9	0.3	0.2	0.2	0.3
Other engineering and metal products	92.5	1010.6	31.0	13.9	26.0	12.1	0.6	1.9	1.7	8.0
Miscellaneous light manufactures	124.3	755.2	26.5	16.0	-7.4	12.1	5.2	8.6	2.3	6.0
Petroleum products	1582.2	2693.3	5.3	7.5	12.5	17.0	48.2	39.4	29.9	21.3
Unworked non-ferrous metals	1285.1	2402.4	12.7	13.6	-28.0	-20.7	46.7	39.8	24.3	19.0
TOTAL MANUFACTURES	5287.6	12617.3	11.3	13.3	1.5	11.2	9.5	7.5	100.0	100.0

SOURCE: Same as Table I. Note that DC (Developing Countries) in this Table refers to less-developed countries.

EXPORTS OF MANUFACTURES FROM DEVELOPING COUNTRIES*

The value of world exports of manufactures rose from $75 billion in 1962 to $190 billion in 1970. Exports of manufactures from developing countries rose more than three-fold from $3.1 billion in 1962 to $9.6 billion in 1970 in current prices, representing an impressive growth rate of 15.2 per cent per annum for the 1962–1970 period, compared with the rate of 12.3 per cent for total world exports of manufactures [see Table III]. The developing countries' share in world exports of manufactures therefore rose from 4.1 per cent in 1962 to 5.1 per cent in 1970. In 1970, the latest year for which data are available, expansion of developing countries' exports of manufactures slowed down to 12.9 per cent which was lower than the rate of 14.9 per cent for total world exports of manufactures. Hence, developing countries' share actually fell slightly in 1970.

Of total exports of manufactures from developing countries in 1970, $5.8 billion went to developed market economy countries, $2.9 billion to other developing countries, and $0.8 billion to socialist countries of Eastern Europe and Asia. Between 1962 and 1970 the relative importance of the three classes of countries changed significantly as markets for developing countries' exports of manufactures. In total exports of manufactures of developing countries, the share of the developed market economy countries rose from 53 per cent in 1962 to 60 per cent in 1970; that of exports to other developing countries fell from 41 per cent to 30 per cent; and the share of the socialist countries of Eastern Europe and Asia rose from 6 per cent to 8 per cent.

During the period 1962 to 1970 exports of manufactures from developing countries to developed market economy countries increased faster in the second half of the period than in the first. But the overall export performance of developing countries was adversely affected by the deceleration of their exports of manufactures to other developing countries and to the socialist countries of Eastern Europe and Asia in the period 1966 to 1970 [see Table III].

The share of manufactures in total merchandise exports of developing countries increased significantly during the period under consideration. This share rose from 11 per cent in 1962 to 18 per cent in 1970. In fact their exports of manufactures grew almost twice as fast as their total exports during this period. Hence, the diversification of developing countries' exports achieved during the First United Nations Development Decade was not negligible. But the share of manufactures in developing countries' total exports in 1970 was still low compared with the corresponding share of 72 per cent

* UNCTAD, Committee on Manufactures, *Trade in Manufactures of Developing Countries: 1972 Review*, TD/B/C.2/124, p. 1–4. The coverage of manufactures is limited to SITC sections 5 to 8 less division 68 (non-ferrous metals).

Table III. Network of World Trade in Manufactures (SITC 5 to 8 less 68)
(1962, 1966, and 1970)
(Billion US dollars, f.o.b.)

Exports from \ Exports to	Developed market economy countries	Developing countries	Socialist countries of Eastern Europe and Asia	World
DEVELOPED MARKET ECONOMY COUNTRIES				
1962	41.4	16.3	2.1	62.0
1966	68.8	22.2	3.5	95.3
1970	118.5	33.6	5.9	159.8
DEVELOPING COUNTRIES				
1962	1.6	1.3	0.2	3.1
1966	3.0	2.0	0.6	5.6
1970	5.8	2.9	0.8	9.6
SOCIALIST COUNTRIES OF EASTERN EUROPE AND ASIA				
1962	0.9	1.5	7.4	9.9
1966	1.5	2.5	9.3	13.3
1970	2.4	3.2	13.3	19.1
WORLD				
1962	44.0	19.2	9.6	75.1
1966	73.5	26.8	13.2	114.5
1970	127.4	40.1	20.0	189.7

SOURCES: United Nations, *Monthly Bulletin of Statistics*, various issues; UNCTAD, *Handbook of International Trade and Development Statistics, 1972.*

for the developed market economy countries and 58 per cent for the socialist countries of Eastern Europe and Asia.

Among the broad groups of manufactures, developing countries' exports grew most rapidly in clothing (23 per cent a year from $540 million in 1966 to $1.25 billion in 1970), much faster than world exports in clothing, capturing one-fifth of the world market by 1970. Exports of iron and steel from developing countries grew rapidly and much faster than world exports in iron and steel. Developing countries also did well in exports of machinery and transport equipment, the value of which rose from $413 million in 1962 to $1.5 billion in 1970 at an annual rate of 17.5 per cent compared with 13.2 per cent for world exports of this product group. However, in 1970 developing countries' exports accounted for only 1.7 per cent of world exports of this product group.

Exports of miscellaneous manufactures (SITC 6 and 8 less 65 and 68) which include clothing and iron and steel make up the bulk of exports of manufactures from developing countries (57 per cent in 1970). The value of these exports rose from $1.4 billion in 1962 to $5.5 billion in 1970 at an annual rate of 16.4 per cent compared with 11.9 per cent for world exports of miscellaneous manufactures. As a result developing countries' share rose from 5.2 per cent in 1962 to 8.3 per cent in 1970.

The two major product groups in which exports from developing countries grew relatively slowly were textiles and chemicals. Developing countries' exports of chemicals increased at 12.7 per cent a year between 1962 and 1970, which is lower than the growth of their exports of all manufactures, but about the same rate as that of world exports of chemicals. In 1962 exports of textiles from developing countries were worth almost $1 billion, or close to one-third of their exports of manufactures in that year, but these exports grew slowly at 8.0 per cent a year, preventing developing countries from achieving a higher rate of expansion in total exports of manufactures.

Several conclusions emerge from the recent record of trade in manufactures. It is clear that the absolute level of manufactured exports from the LDCs is still low and is concentrated in a relatively few countries and commodities. Nonetheless, it is striking that the growth rate of manufactured exports from the LDCs has been rapid. An increasing number of developing countries have been able to expand their exports over a widening range of manufactures. Some thirty developing countries have started to move beyond the traditional pattern of specialization in primary exports and have become significant exporters of manufactured goods. The range of manufactured exports has widened, reflecting growing skills, experience, and the mobility of capital and operation of multinational corporations.

If policy reforms are undertaken by developed and less developed countries alike, the export potential in manufactures can become substantially higher than the 10 to 15 per cent per annum growth rate which has been used for most trade projections for the decade of the 1970's. Trade in manufactures is the most rapidly growing sector of the world economy, and if the total exports of manufactures from developing countries now only equals the yearly increase in world trade in manufactures, this can be interpreted as indicative of the high export potential. Many a developing country could meet its foreign exchange requirements if it could capture but a small fraction of the annual incremental expansion in world trade in manufactures.

One careful study concludes:

> The experience of the 1960s suggests that semi-industrialized countries have a significant comparative advantage in a wide range of products in which they can combine relatively low labor costs, that is relatively low wages but high skills, with modern technology, management and commercial practice. Existing tariff levels can not keep out textiles, clothing, footwear, electrical products and steel; a wide variety of new products, ranging from optical instruments to hydro-electric generators are now coming into the same category. Developed countries, working on the assumption that developing country exports are going to continue to be simple, labor intensive consumer goods are likely to find themselves—indeed are already finding themselves—totally unprepared for such new directions in international trade in manufactures.[10]

New directions in international trade can even be interpreted as signifying the beginnings of a new international industrial revolution. The increasing rate of diffusion of technology, transportation and communication developments, and new forms of transnational enterprise are becoming increasingly effective technical elements of a new international division of labor. The new forms of transnational enterprise are especially significant: multinational enterprise, world-wide sourcing, and international subcontracting. These technical elements allow the internationalization of production and marketing, making it technically possible for the developing countries to move on to the export of semi-manufactures and manufactures. In a sense, Japan's domestic model of capital-stretching by farming out and subcontracting to small-size, labor-intensive industry can be followed on an international scale. The instructive Japanese model of utilizing labor-intensive processes and component specialization, along with larger-scale, capital-intensive production when necessary, might now be replicated world-wide. Indeed, now that its

10. H. B. Chenery and H. Hughes, "The International Division of Labor: The Case of Industry," in *Towards a New World Economy,* Papers and Proceedings of the Fifth European Conference of the Society for International Development (1972), p. 96.

comparative advantage has moved on to higher-skill, capital-intensive products, Japan is setting another international example in the migration of its own labor-intensive industries to other countries in Asia that have a labor surplus.

But while all this is technically possible, its success depends on support by more appropriate policy measures. The policy elements of the new international industrial revolution must ensure that the potentially beneficial effects of the technical elements are actually realized and that their detrimental effects on the developing countries are limited. To do this, priority must be given to new measures of trade policy coupled with attention to more appropriate forms of transferring foreign knowledge. Tariff preferences may be highly significant in enabling the preference-receiving countries to take advantage of labor-intensive methods of processing, assembly, and component manufacture for export within vertically integrated international industries, with the resultant benefits of relaxing their foreign exchange constraint and also improving their employment prospects. But while the road to greater investment in LDCs and a new era of industrial competitiveness may be paved with preferences,[11] the power of the multinational enterprise may also be its limitation—if it exploits its proprietary knowledge by receiving an excessive return, inhibits the development of more appropriate knowledge, or is the source of external diseconomies in the host countries.

4. THE VALUE OF PREFERENCES

Much of the LDCs' case for general preferences rests on their grievances against the trade policies of the developed countries and the mechanism of bargaining for tariff reductions under GATT. The average ad valorem tariff rate on the developed countries' imports of manufactures may not appear excessively high, but it is argued that this does not truly reflect the high incidence of the developed countries' tariff barriers on imports from the LDCs. Some of the highest tariff rates are on imports of labor-intensive and technologically simple con-

11. H. G. Johnson, "LDC Investment: The Road Is Paved with Preferences," *Columbia Journal of World Business* (January–February 1968).

sumer goods which may have the greatest production potential for the LDCs. Even more significant is the complaint that the escalation of tariff rates in the industrial countries according to the degree of processing is especially discouraging to the export of processed goods from the developing countries. There is considerable justification to this grievance: empirical studies do show that effective rates of protection on value added in the developed countries are much higher than the nominal tariff rates on commodities.[12]

Nontariff restrictions—witness the use of quantitative restrictions, internal taxes and revenue duties, practices of customs administration, and "agreements to avoid market disruption" such as in the case of textile quotas [13]—also inhibit the developing countries' exports of manufactures. Finally, it is observed that if a developing country were to resort to export subsidies instead of seeking the alternative of preferences, the advanced country would then impose countervailing duties nullifying the export subsidy.

If the tariff structures and nontariff restrictions of the advanced countries thwart export promotion, so too—it is argued—have the negotiations under GATT failed to liberalize trade to the benefit of the developing countries. It is claimed that equal tariff treatment under the principle of nondiscrimination has really meant preferred tariff treatment for the advanced industrial nations. This is because the negotiations for tariff reductions have depended upon the willingness of the principal-supplier nations to enter into such negotiations; the commodities for which there has been trade liberalization have been those predominantly supplied by the industrial countries; and while trade has expanded among the developed countries, the most-favored-nation extension of these trade concessions has meant little to the LDCs. By their choice of the items for reciprocal tariff reduction, the advanced countries have actually been able to practice indirect discrimination against the LDCs, notwithstanding the most-favored-na-

---

12. See Bela Balassa, "Tariff Protection in Industrial Countries: An Evaluation," *Journal of Political Economy* (December 1965), pp. 573–94.

13. G. M. Meier, *Problems of Trade Policy* (1973), Problem II.

tion principle.[14] A departure from the most-favored-nation
principle is therefore urged to allow preferred treatment and
reverse discrimination in favor of exports from developing
countries.

This type of compensatory discrimination is justified by
some in UNCTAD with the claim that preferences would pro-
tect infant industries. Since infant industry protection is now
allowed by GATT and widely practiced by the developing
countries, it is argued that it should be extended to world
markets instead of being limited to only the domestic market.
In essence, the case for preferences becomes an argument in
favor of "internationalizing" protection—a logical extension of
the infant industry justification for favorable treatment.

This may have a certain logical appeal, but its implications
should be clearly understood. Although the case for infant industry protection depends essentially on external economies,
it is difficult to comprehend the relevance of this when the externalities arise in the preference-receiving country but the
governmental assistance is to be provided by the preference-
granting country. Moreover, whereas national protection of an
infant industry entails the subsidization of domestic producers
by domestic consumers, the preference-giving country would
subsidize industrial imports from the LDCs by transferring income from the consumers of the preference-giving country to
producers in the preference-receiving country—and that is
quite a different matter. Complex procedural and administrative problems are also involved if preferences are to be
granted only to the products of industries that are selected as
having the greatest infant-industry potentialities. If a system of
common preference rates were instituted, this would apply to
even those industries that do not need the large size of world
markets to realize economies of scale and a competitive position. It is also question-begging to assert that preferences need
be only temporary: if the external economies are reversible or

14. The "linear" approach of the Kennedy Round reduced the relevance of this criticism, although the exceptions list and the "tariff disparities" procedure still allowed
some indirect discrimination; G. M. Meier, *Problems of Trade Policy* (1973), Problem I.

the exporting industries do not become truly competitive, the preferences would have to be permanent.

Perhaps the strongest argument in favor of preferences is that it may allow foreign aid to be increased in the disguised form of trade policy. If trade preferences would enable the exporters of the developing countries to charge the higher domestic price of the importing country instead of the lower world market price, the effect would be to transfer resources from the richer to the poorer countries as under aid. If preferences allow LDC-export prices to rise, then there is a transfer of some of the custom revenue or rents to domestic factors under protection to the LDC-producer whose price now exceeds costs. But instead of government-to-government aid, this would constitute consumer-to-producer aid. Consumers in the preference-granting country would pay the full domestic price to producers who export from the preference-receiving countries, instead of paying as previously part of the price-cum-tariff to themselves as beneficiaries of their government's tariff proceeds.

Increased trade will not be equivalent to aid, however, if the preference-receiving country is enabled to export more, but only at the same prices as prevailed before. In this situation, the LDC would realize only the "normal" gains from trade— that is, the ability to import goods that are worth more than the goods that could have been produced at home with the resources used to produce the additional exports. Insofar as import-replacement policies are excessively costly, this gain could be considerable; but it still could never be so great as to equal the value of the additional export proceeds if these were received as a free grant.

Given the experience of the high cost of import substitution, export promotion is now also supported on grounds that the domestic resource cost of earning foreign exchange is less than the domestic resource cost of saving foreign exchange through import substitution. Some empirical studies of the factor requirements of industrial exports and imports indicate that if capital and foreign exchange are true constraints and labor is not, the value of exports that could be produced with a given use of scarce factors is greater than the value of imports that could be replaced.[15]

Moreover, exports can be expected to be more favorable to employment-generation than can import substitution. Where labor is abundant, it will be relatively inexpensive, and products that are labor-intensive in production will be most competitive under preferences. With the exogenous demand of the world market being potentially unlimited, the scope for generating employment through exports is greater than in the narrower domestic market of import substitution. The composition of demand on world markets also tends to be more employment-generating than does the local demand for middle- and high-income consumer goods.

The following materials indicate some of the difficult technical, procedural, and political questions that have arisen in settling upon any one of the large number of alternative preference schemes that have been advocated.

B. THE ISSUES

5. THE PLEA FOR PREFERENCES

Ever since the first session of UNCTAD there has been continual discussion and negotiation on the granting of special tariff treatment for developing countries. Although the variety of proposals that have been debated differ in details, they all reflect the underlying philosophy first enunciated at UNCTAD I.

THE QUESTION OF PREFERENCES *

The case for preferential treatment for exports of developing countries is that it would help the industries of developing countries to overcome the difficulties that they encounter in export markets because of their high initial costs. It is a temporary measure which, by opening up larger markets to

* Report of the Secretary-General of UNCTAD (Raúl Prebisch), *Towards a New Trade Policy for Development*, United Nations (1964), pp. 65–70.

15. John Sheahan, "Trade and Employment: Industrial Exports as Compared to Import Substitution in Mexico," Center for Development Economics, Williams College (December 1971).

the industries of developing countries, would enable them to lower their costs and thus compete on world markets without the need for continuing preference.

The case is thus a logical extension of the infant industry argument. It is not a matter of controversy among economists that national protection of infant industries is justifiable wherever such industries have a long-run prospect of reaching a high level of efficiency.

In order to be efficient, those industries must have access to wider markets; otherwise they may not be able to break out of the vicious circle of low output and high costs. Such markets must be sought in the developed countries as well as in other developing countries. But if infant industries need protection in the domestic market because of high costs, they obviously need even more protection in foreign markets, whether developed or developing, in the form of preferential treatment. It is for this reason that the following two suggestions have been made: (a) developing countries should give preference to imports from other developing countries in their own markets; (b) developed countries should give preference to imports from developing countries in their own markets.

The two suggestions raise somewhat different issues. The main features of the first have already been outlined, and the following discussion will concentrate on the second.

GATT sanctioned the continuation of preferential arrangements in force at the time the Agreement was signed, but prohibited new arrangements of this sort except where they represented a stage in the setting up of customs unions or free-trade areas.

The reason for the prohibition was, and still is, the belief that countries ought to treat one another equally in their foreign trade and not grant advantages to some countries that they are not prepared to extend to others. But however valid the most-favoured-nation principle may be in regulating trade relations among equals, it is not a suitable concept for trade involving countries of vastly unequal economic strength. The acceptance by the Meeting of Ministers of GATT in May 1963 of non-reciprocal tariff concessions to developing countries was a valuable first step in recognizing the need for special encouragement to the trade of these countries. Adoption of the principle of preferential treatment for the trade of developing countries is the logical next step. . . .

The introduction of a new system of preferences would involve the mutual adjustment of various conflicting interests among the developing countries on the one hand, and between the developing and the industrial countries, on the other. There may be a temptation to try and take account of any difficulties that arise in reaching such adjustment by introducing complicating devices and refinements into the scheme so as to cater to particular preoccupations. Certain of these devices and refinements could indeed prove to be indispensable, but the general proposition should be borne in mind that the greater the complication of the scheme, the less chance it has of being accepted or found workable.

The first question for consideration is: which countries should grant preferences? The hope and expectation, as already noted, is that all developed countries would agree to grant preferences to all developing countries. While it may be doubted whether the scheme could be effectively implemented unless all major developed countries agreed to participate, unanimity would not be essential. The scheme might enter into force when an important group of countries indicated their willingness to participate.

So far as the participation of the socialist countries in the concession of preferences is concerned, as indicated elsewhere, tariffs do not have the same meaning in these countries as in private-enterprise economies. Nevertheless, whenever tariffs are imposed, free entry should be assured to imports from developing countries. At the same time, the socialist countries should favour imports from developing countries in their foreign trade plans, and their State trading agencies should give effect to such preferences in their purchasing arrangements.

The implementation of all such measures could be evaluated in the light of actual performance, and would be one of the subjects for annual review within the new organizational scheme of trade and development that might be suggested by the Conference.

The selection of countries to benefit from preferences is somewhat more difficult. No single criterion has been found satisfactory in identifying those countries which should be regarded as qualifying for preferential treatment. Such factors as per capita income, the size of the country, the share of agriculture and industry in total employment and output, and the impact of the primary export sector on the growth of the economy should be considered. If these factors are taken into account, it is relatively easy to decide which are and which have ceased to be developing countries in most cases. There is, nevertheless, a small group of borderline cases at the top of the per capita income range and it is not an easy matter to establish the cut-off point among them.

The problem is, perhaps, not too important from the standpoint of the industrial countries, because imports of manufactures from the developing countries are not likely to be a matter of overwhelming consequence for them in any case, as we have seen. But they are for some developing countries which may fear that they will not be able to benefit from preferences if they have to compete with other more advanced members of the developing group. The problem of which developing countries should be included in the scheme is thus closely linked to the problem of gradation or differentiation of preferences which will be examined below.

Selection of General Preferences and Their Duration

Most of the discussion of preferences thus far has proceeded on the assumption that they should be granted on a selective basis for particular products. The main consideration underlying this approach appears to be the desire to exclude products which would raise domestic problems for the developed countries, notably those produced in relatively weak or stagnant sectors of the economy of these countries. There may also be a desire to direct the efforts of developing countries towards industries offering substantial growth potential and the prospect of viability within a reasonable number of years, making it possible to discontinue the preferences.

These two considerations appear reasonable enough, but if they are examined more closely, serious disadvantages may be observed.

First and foremost, the experience of GATT and of other bodies has shown that a system of selective negotiations, product by product, raises great difficulties. Naturally enough, each industry which considers itself threatened by foreign competition is liable to adopt a severely defensive attitude and seek to maintain the *status quo*. This very understandable attitude does not find its logical counterbalance in the industries which may increase their exports to the developing countries as the foreign-exchange earnings of the latter advance, since these advantages are still problematical and therefore do not provide a tangible incentive for the adoption of preferences. Nor is it to be expected that an industry that felt itself affected by imports would examine this matter from the viewpoint of the economy as a whole and not for its own particular situation.

If, moreover, the preferences to be granted by all developed countries are to be standard in terms of commodity coverage, the ultimate list of products qualifying for preference is likely to be the lowest common denominator of all national lists; since any industry regarded as vulnerable in any one country is likely to have its way with the general list of all countries.

From the standpoint of the developing countries, moreover, it is difficult to imagine how a suitable selection of industries for preferential treatment could be made. It would surely be better to leave scope for the initiative of enterprises to seek out the best opportunities, subject, of course, to measures of guidance and assistance, in which Governments should have a very important role, as will be seen later. One wonders what degree of success might have attended efforts, in any of the countries that are now industrialized, to draw up a precise pattern of possible industrial exports in advance when they were at the earliest stage of development. It is hardly likely that an effective selection could now be made, from the whole range of industry, of all those particular branches which might prove to be successful in particular developing countries in the long run.

Thus the danger is that a selective list of products qualifying for preference may turn out to be unduly restricted and drawn up much more with an eye to static considerations, than to the dynamic possibilities of a new international division of labour. For this reason, a better and simpler approach would be for preferential treatment to be granted in principle to all imports from the developing countries, subject only to certain specified exclusions, as well as certain safeguards, as indicated below.

Much of the discussion that has taken place so far has been related to preferential treatment for semi-finished and finished manufactures only. Acceptance of this limitation would raise a number of difficulties in defining the scope of these products, calling for expert study and recommendation.

Expert study would also be required of the problem of defining the origin of products manufactured or semi-manufactured from imported materials or components. Neither these nor any other difficulties seem to be of major consequence, and they should not prevent the Conference from adopting a decision in principle in favour of preferences. Indeed, this decision in principle is necessary in order to provide, through common agreement of Governments, a framework within which the technicians will be required to work out practical details.

A small margin of preference is not likely to provide adequate incentives for establishing new export industries in developing countries. If a new system of preferences is worth introducing at all, the margins of preference should provide incentives that are clearly adequate in relation to the magnitude of the problem.

Since many or most of the tariffs applied to manufactures by the industrial countries are relatively low, and are expected to fall even further as a result of the Kennedy round, the optimum solution would be to grant free entry to imports from developing countries. For the members of EEC and EFTA this would simply mean granting to the developing countries treatment not less favourable than they are prepared to give one another.

Since the new preferential system is intended as an encouragement to infant industries, it will be evident that some provision must be made for the elimination of preferences once the industries are firmly established. In general, preferences should be introduced for a period of no less than ten years with respect to any given industry in any developing country. At the end of the ten-year period, preferences would be withdrawn unless it could be shown, to the satisfaction of an appropriate international authority, that special circumstances warranted their continuation. The ten-year period would be reckoned from the time of the initial granting of preferences to exports of a particular industry in a given country even though this would mean that plants established subsequently in the same country would not benefit from the full period of preference.

The fact that preferential treatment for any one industry in a developing country would normally come to an end after ten years would have two advantages. For one thing, it would compel the entrepreneurs concerned to concentrate on making the industry fully competitive by the time the shelter of preferences was withdrawn. A second advantage would result from the fact that infant industries, established shortly after the inception of the scheme in countries that are still at an early stage of development, would count their ten-year period of preference from the time such preference was first applied to any industry subject to this régime. This means that such industries would enjoy preferential treatment not merely in relation to the industries of developed countries but also in relation to those of the more advanced developing countries, once the respective industries of the latter countries were no longer entitled to preferences.

The duration of preferences should probably not be fixed at less than ten years. Sufficient time must be allowed for their incentives to take effect and for significant results to be achieved in export markets. In the conditions obtaining in developing countries, a short-term scheme of preferences would scarcely be better than no scheme at all.

Thus the duration of preferences raises an issue similar to that involved in the margin of preference, namely, that there is a minimum scale and duration below which the incentive provided would be inadequate. It would not be worth facing all the political and other difficulties entailed in a new departure from the most-favoured-nation principle simply for the sake of token margins of preference on a few selected products for a very limited period, amounting to little more *in toto* than a gesture in the face of the immense problems of the trade gap.

The joint Declaration of the 77 Developing Countries at the conclusion of UNCTAD I recognized the urgent need for diversifying and expanding exports of manufactures and semi-manufactures from developing countries, and recommended that the Secretary-General of the United Nations convene a committee of governmental representatives to examine further the question of tariff preferences. Convened the following year, the committee outlined some specific elements of a preferential system: all developed countries should grant, for all manufactures and semi-manufactures toward all developing countries, duty-free preferential access to their markets without limitation on volume; the developing countries recognized, however, that the duration of the preferences should be limited in time and that it should be possible, under certain conditions, for the developed countries to exclude products from the benefits of the system and to apply safeguard clauses; on the other hand, the system should take into account the special needs of the least developed countries and provide, for those developing countries that already enjoy preferences in developed countries, advantages at least equivalent to those which are now enjoyed so that these existing preferences can be suspended.

6. SUBSTANTIVE PROVISIONS

Many different views on privileged treatment for exports from LDCs were presented at UNCTAD II (New Delhi, 1968). At a ministerial meeting of the Group of 77 in 1967 the Charter of Algiers had been adopted. Among other steps suggested in a program of action to be taken by UNCTAD II, this Charter recommended the following.

PRINCIPLES FOR A GENERAL SYSTEM OF PREFERENCES *

The following principles should be adopted in order to implement a general system of preferences. They should be accepted simultaneously as complementary and indivisible measures.

1. At UNCTAD II there should be negotiations which should lead to the conclusion of an agreement on a general system of tariff preferences on a non-discriminatory and non-reciprocal basis. The agreement should provide for unrestricted and duty-free access to the markets of all developed countries for all manufactures and semi-manufactures from all developing countries.

2. Without prejudice to the general provisions contained in paragraph 1 above, the escape clause actions as envisaged below may be taken; in particular special treatment may be granted by developed countries to the less developed among the developing countries.

3. The manufactures and semi-manufactures covered by the preferential system should include all processed and semi-processed primary products of all developing countries.

4. All developed countries should grant such preferences to all developing countries.

5. The form of the escape clause action, the objective criteria which should govern the application of escape clause action by developed countries and the procedures that should be followed in such cases must be agreed upon internationally. Such action must however be temporary in nature and be subject to international consultation, approval and review.

6. The preferential system must be conceived in such a way as to make it possible for the least advanced among developing countries to share in its benefits. Accordingly any time limits of the system should be flexible so that countries at present in very incipient stages of development will also be able to reap its advantages. Escape clause actions limiting or excluding particular exports should not apply to the less competitive products from less advanced countries. Specific commitments should be taken for technical and financial assistance in the establishment of export oriented industries in least advanced countries, with a view to markets both in the developed world and in other developing countries.

7. The new system of general preferences should ensure at least equivalent advantages to developing countries enjoying preferences in certain developed countries to enable them to suspend their existing preferences on manufactures and semi-manufactures. From the beginning, provisions

* *Charter of Algiers*, Ministerial Meeting of the Group of 77, MM 77/I/20, 30 October 1967, pp. 16–17.

should be incorporated in the system of general preferences, for the developed countries to redress any adverse situation which may arise for these developing countries as a consequence of the institution of the general system of preferences.

8. In order to achieve the objective of the general preferential system the arrangement should last long enough to enable all developing countries to benefit from it. Initially the arrangement should last for 20 years and should be reviewed towards the end of this initial period. In any event the preferential treatment should not thereafter be abruptly terminated.

9. In order that the general system of preferences should make an adequate contribution to the balance of payments of the developing countries, the developed countries should not reduce their aid to them or nullify or impair the benefits of preferences through other measures.

10. Suitable machinery within UNCTAD should be established to supervise and ensure the effective implementation of a general system of preferences in accordance with the foregoing paragraphs.

Representing the more developed countries, a group within the Organisation for Economic Co-operation and Development (OECD) reached broad agreement in a Report by the Special Group on Trade with Developing Countries. This report was also submitted to UNCTAD II.

OECD REPORT*

The Special Group recommend that member Governments of the OECD support a statement on the following lines to be presented to the developing countries at the second session of the United Nations Conference on Trade and Development. The United States member of the Group stated that in his view it would be necessary for this statement to include, in addition, the point made by him at the end of part one of this report.

(1) Temporary advantages in the form of generalized arrangements for special tariff treatment for developing countries in the markets of developed countries can assist the developing countries to increase their export earnings and so contribute to an acceleration in their rates of economic growth.

(2) The potential benefits for developing countries will be maximized by the largest possible participation of developed countries in arrangements for the grant of such special tariff treatment.

* Report by the Special Group on Trade with Developing Countries of the Organisation for Economic Co-operation and Development, Document TD/56, 29 January 1968.

(3) Such new arrangements should aim to accord broadly equivalent opportunities in all developed countries to all developing countries.

(4) The arrangements should be designed so as to result in an equitable distribution among the developed countries of increased import opportunities to their markets, and should take into account the effects on the exports of third countries.

(5) Any new arrangements for the grant of special tariff treatment cannot be put into effect without the support of the developing countries, and their views should be taken into account in the formulation of any such arrangements.

(6) The grant of temporary tariff advantages to developing countries would not constitute a binding commitment and should not in any way impede the reduction of tariffs on a most-favoured-nation (m.f.n.) basis, whether unilaterally or following an international tariff negotiation.

Discussions among member Governments of the OECD have led to a broad measure of agreement on a number of key elements which might be included in arrangements for the grant of special tariff treatment.

A—Beneficiary Countries

Special tariff treatment should be given to the exports of any country, territory or area claiming developing status. This formula would get over the difficulty which would otherwise arise of reaching international agreement on objective criteria to determine relative stages of development.

Individual developed countries might, however, decline to accord special tariff treatment to a particular country claiming developing status on grounds which they hold to be compelling. Such *ab initio* exclusion of a particular country would not be based on competitive considerations (which would have to be dealt with by the procedures discussed under sections C and G below).

It is to be expected that no country will claim developing status unless there are *bona fide* grounds for it to do so; and that such a claim would be relinquished if those grounds ceased to exist.

B—Product Coverage

Special tariff treatment should apply in principle to all manufactured and semi-manufactured products. Other products could be included on a case-by-case basis.

C—Exceptions

It is probable that developed countries will find it necessary to exclude from the outset from the benefit of the special tariff treatment a limited number of products in respect of which developing countries are already competitive.

D—Rules of Origin

The grant of special tariff treatment will require the application of rules of origin to determine the conditions under which imports shall qualify for admission at special rates of duty. It will be necessary to determine how best to achieve the objectives of ensuring that the rules are in accordance with the intentions of the new arrangements and of providing broadly equivalent new import opportunities into each developed market.

E—Duration

The special tariff treatment should be temporary and degressive. Margins of preferences would not be guaranteed. The initial arrangements should be for a period of ten years with provision for a major review before the end of this period to determine whether the special tariff treatment should be continued, modified or abolished. It is obvious that developed countries may wish before the ten-year period has elapsed to consider the feasibility of a further international negotiation to reduce tariffs on an m.f.n. basis. If they do so and the negotiations were successful, an element of degressivity would automatically be introduced into the arrangements for developing countries.

F—Depth of Cuts

The improved access for developing countries may take the form of duty-free treatment or substantial reductions below m.f.n. rates.

G—Safeguards and Adjustments

Any scheme of special tariff treatment must inevitably include some safeguard or adjustment arrangements to avoid the risks of dislocation of industry and labour.

Safeguards may be either related to the possibility of withdrawal or modification of special tariff treatment when imports of particular products reach certain limits (defined in advance by reference to domestic production, consumption or imports), or they can be related to determination by the developed country concerned of the causing or the threat of injury from such imports.

These questions call for examination with a view to agreement among developed countries. It will be for the countries according special tariff treatment to ensure that safeguards and adjustments are applied in a manner consonant with the principle of equitable sharing of improved access and taking account of the effects of the arrangements on the exports of third countries.

H—Preferences Received by Some Developing Countries in the Markets of Some Developed Countries

It is recognized that many countries would see as an important objective of the new arrangements a movement in the direction of equality of treatment for the exports of all developing countries in developed country markets. At the same time, developing countries at present receiving preferences in some such markets would expect the arrangements to provide them with increased export opportunities to compensate for their sharing of their present advantages.

I—Action by Countries with Centrally-Planned Economies

Both in order to maximize benefits for the developing countries and to provide for equitable distribution of appropriate measures among developed countries, the grant of special tariff treatment by developed countries with market economies should be matched by arrangements by countries with centrally-planned economies which would similarly increase the opportunities for the export to them of products from developing countries.

J—Action by Developing Countries

The arrangements should not involve the grant of reciprocal advantages by developing countries for the exports of developed countries. They should, however, be the occasion for developing countries to broaden market opportunities among themselves on a regional basis. They should also be of assistance to the developing countries in their efforts to accelerate improvement in the conditions of employment and the standards of living of their people. It would help if these countries agreed to take measures to encourage foreign investment as an additional spur to industrialization.

The United States member stated that, in his view, a key element in any arrangements for the grant of special tariff treatment is the phasing out, as rapidly as possible, of existing preferences extended by some developing countries to some developed countries.

At the conclusion of UNCTAD II, the Conference adopted resolution 21 (II), in which the Conference recognized "the unanimous agreement in favor of the early establishment of a mutually acceptable system of generalized nonreciprocal and nondiscriminatory preferences which would be beneficial to the developing countries," and "the need for further intensive work to formulate such a system." The objective of such a system that would be in favor of the developing countries, including special measures favoring the least advanced among them, should be to increase their exports, promote their industrialization, and accelerate their rate of economic growth. To this end, the Conference established a Special Committee on Preferences to carry out the necessary consultations and to draw up a final report to the Trade and Development Board of UNCTAD.

The Special Committee met in four sessions over the course of the next two years. As a basis for the series of consultations between the prospective preference-giving and preference-receiving countries, a number of substantive areas were identified for negotiation. These included: product coverage and extent of preferences; safeguard mechanisms; duration of the system; special measures for the least advanced countries; existing and reverse preferences; institutional arrangements; and measures which the socialist countries of Eastern Europe might adopt.

In its final report, the Special Committee set forth its Agreed Conclusions.

AGREED CONCLUSIONS
OF THE SPECIAL COMMITTEE ON PREFERENCES*

The Special Committee on Preferences:

1. Recalls that in its resolution 21 (II), the United Nations Conference on Trade and Development at its second session recognized the unanimous agreement in favour of the early establishment of a mutually acceptable system of generalized, non-reciprocal, non-discriminatory preferences which would be beneficial to the developing countries.

2. Further recalls the agreement that the objectives of the generalized, non-reciprocal, non-discriminatory system of preferences in favour of the developing countries, including special measures in favour of the least developed among the developing countries, should be: (1) to increase their export earnings; (b) to promote their industrialization; and (c) to accelerate their rates of economic growth.

3. Welcomes with appreciation the revised submissions by the developed market-economy countries.

These submissions represent an important success in the efforts and endeavours in UNCTAD in order to put a generalized system of preferences into operation and an important element in the fulfilment of the aims and objectives of Conference resolution 21 (II) mentioned above and in the international strategy for development in the 1970s.

4. Welcomes with appreciation the joint declaration of several socialist countries of Eastern Europe, as supplemented and clarified in their individual statements, which constitute a useful and positive contribution in the light of the objectives of Conference resolution 21 (II).

5. Notes the expectations of developing countries regarding the generalized system of preferences as expressed in the relevant parts of the Charter of Algiers.

6. Notes the observations, suggestions, and requests made by the devel-

---

* Official Records of the Trade and Development Board, Tenth Session, Supplement No. 6A, 1970, pp. 3–6.

oping countries on the submissions of the developed market-economy countries during the consultations which have taken place in the Special Committee, and in particular those contained in the report on its fourth session; and notes also that some of the suggestions and requests have been taken into account in the revised submission.

7. Notes also the explanations given by the prospective preference-giving countries on their submissions and their statements that they will, as far as possible, take into account the observations, suggestions and requests of the developing countries, including those of the least developed among them.

8. Considers that efforts for further improvements should be pursued in a dynamic context in the light of the objectives of Conference resolution 21 (II).

9. Recognizes that these preferential arrangements are mutually acceptable and represent a co-operative effort which has resulted from the detailed and intensive consultations between the developed and developing countries which have taken place in UNCTAD. This co-operation will continue to be reflected in the consultations which will take place in the future in connexion with the periodic reviews of the system and its operation.

10. Notes the determination of the prospective preference-giving countries to seek as rapidly as possible the necessary legislative or other sanction with the aim of implementing the preferential arrangements as early as possible in 1971.

11. Recommends that the Trade and Development Board at its fourth special session adopt the report of the Special Committee on its fourth session, take note of these Conclusions, approve the institutional arrangements proposed in section VIIII and take a decision on the appropriate UNCTAD body referred to in that section.

II. Reverse Preferences and Special Preferences

1. The Special Committee notes that, consistent with Conference resolution 21 (II), there is agreement with the objective that in principle all developing countries should participate as beneficiaries from the outset and that the attainment of this objective, in relation to the question of reverse preferences, which remains to be resolved, will require further consultations between the parties directly concerned. These consultations should be pursued as a matter of urgency with a view to finding solutions before the implementation of the schemes. The Secretary-General of UNCTAD will assist in these consultations with the agreement of the Governments concerned.

2. Developing countries which will be sharing their existing tariff advantages in some developed countries as the result of the introduction of the generalized system of preferences will expect the new access in other developed countries to provide export opportunities at least to compensate them.

3. As a result of the periodic reviews in UNCTAD and of bilateral or multilateral consultations between the countries concerned, those countries granting tariff advantages will, when reviewing the operation of the generalized system of preferences, give careful consideration to the extent to which the developing countries enjoying tariff advantages have benefited over-all from the system.

III. Safeguard Mechanisms

1. All proposed individual schemes of preferences provide for certain safeguard mechanisms (for example, *a priori* limitation or escape-clause type measures) so as to retain some degree of control by preference-giving countries over the trade which might be generated by the new tariff advantages. The preference-giving countries reserve the right to make changes in the detailed application as in the scope of their measures, and in particular, if deemed necessary, to limit or withdraw entirely of partly some of the tariff advantages granted. The preference-giving countries, however, declare that such measures would remain exceptional and would be decided on only after taking due account in so far as their legal provisions permit of the aims of the generalized system of preferences and the general interests of the developing countries, and in particular the interests of the least developed among the developing countries.

2. Preference-giving countries will offer opportunities for appropriate consultations to beneficiary countries, in particular to those having a substantial trade interest in the product concerned, in connexion with the use of safeguard measures; where prior consultations are not possible, preference-giving countries will undertake for the purpose above to inform all beneficiary countries, through the Secretary-General of UNCTAD, with a minimum of delay, of the action taken. Safeguard measures taken should be reviewed from time to time by the preference-giving country concerned with the aim of relaxing or eliminating them as quickly as possible.

3. Certain preference-giving countries provide for a mechanism including an *a priori* limitation formula under which quantitative ceilings will be placed on preferential imports. Some of these countries might, nevertheless, have recourse also to escape type measures, for those products which are not covered by *a priori* limitation formulae.

4. For those countries which do not envisage *a priori* limitations, escape-type measures are the main safeguards at their disposal.

IV. Beneficiaries

1. The Special Committee noted the individual submissions of the preference-giving countries on this subject and the joint position of the countries members of the Organisation for Economic Co-operation and Development.

2. The spokesman on behalf of the developing countries members of the Group of 77 made a statement on the question of beneficiaries.

V. Special Measures in Favour of the Least Developed
among the Developing Countries

1. In implementing Conference resolution 21 (II), and as provided therein, the special need for improving the economic situation of the least developed among the developing countries is recognized. It is important that these countries should benefit to the fullest extent possible from the generalized system of preferences. In this context, the provisions of Conference resolution 24 (II) should be borne in mind.

2. The preference-giving countries will consider, as far as possible, on a case-by-case basis, the inclusion in the generalized system of preferences of products of export interest mainly to the least developed among the developing countries, and as appropriate, greater tariff reductions on such products.

3. The preference-giving countries declare that escape clause measures would remain exceptional and would be decided on only after due account has been taken, in so far as their legal provisions permit, of the interests of the least developed among the developing countries.

4. During the annual review of the operation of the generalized system of preferences, special attention should be given by the institutional machinery to the effects of the system on the volume of exports and export earnings of the least developed countries and in regard to other objectives of Conference resolution 21 (II). This machinery should further investigate and consult on the special measures in favour of those countries within the generalized system as provided in Conference resolution 21 (II).

5. The Special Committee recommends to the Trade and Development Board that it suggest to each of its main committees that, taking into account the imminent implementation of a generalized system of preferences, priority attention should be given to measures in the field of competence of these committees that would be related or complementary to the generalized system of preferences, especially measures which would enable the least developed among the developing countries to participate fully in that system.

6. Besides those mentioned above, other additional measures have been suggested with a view to enabling developing countries and specially the least developed among them to derive additional benefits from the generalized system of preferences. The international efforts in this field should give priority to:

(a) The identification of products for which the generalized system of preferences opens up new or improved export possibilities for the least developed countries;

(b) Market studies for such products;

(c) Assistance to the improvement of export and export-promotion services or the establishment of such new services where appropriate.

7. The Special Committee invites the Trade and Development Board to call the attention of other appropriate international organizations to the im-

portance of taking measures related to the generalized system of preferences. Such measures might include, as appropriate, financial and technical assistance for the establishment and development of industries likely to further the exports of products included in the generalized system of preferences, as well as financial assistance for pre-investment studies for such industries.

VI. Duration

The initial duration of the generalized system of preferences will be ten years. A comprehensive review will be held some time before the end of the ten-year period to determine, in the light of the objectives of Conference resolution 21 (II), whether the preferential system should be continued beyond that period.

VII. Rules of Origin

1. It is agreed that the rules of origin should facilitate the achievement of the objectives of Conference resolution 21 (II) on the generalized system of preferences, in this connexion, to ensure effectively for the beneficiary countries the advantages of preferential treatment for those exports which will qualify therefor; to help to ensure equivalence in conditions of access to the markets of the preference-giving countries, and to avoid distortion of trade.

2. Satisfactory functioning of the rules of origin will be greatly helped if it is possible to establish close and confident collaboration between the competent authorities of the donor and beneficiary countries, particularly concerning documentation and control. It is agreed that such co-operation should be assured bilaterally and as appropriate through the institutional arrangements as provided for in the relevant part of these conclusions.

3. It is recognized that it is desirable to have rules of origin as uniform as possible and as simple to administer as practicable. The Working Group on Rules of Origin had, at a technical level, formulated preliminary texts on a number of important aspects of the rules of origin. However, in regard to the basic element, for any rules of origin, namely the criterion for substantial transformation, the Group did not at this stage arrive at common views.

4. In view of the importance which the Special Committee attaches to putting into effect the generalized system of preferences as rapidly as possible, it might be necessary to apply, at the outset, origin rules which are different in certain aspects. This would not preclude further efforts to achieve, as far as possible, more harmonization at a later stage.

5. In view of the substantial progress made in drawing up common solutions on matters such as a standard form of origin certificate and agreed rules and undertakings as to verifications, sanctions, and mutual co-operation, the administrative difficulties from the use of different systems of origin at the initial stage will be minimized.

6. The Group should conclude as soon as possible its examination of all technical aspects of the rules of origin for the generalized system of prefer-

ences, with a view to agreeing on as many common elements in the rules of origin as possible at this stage. Such technical aspects include harmonization of the different elements used in the determination of substantial transformation among preference-giving countries applying the same criteria in this respect and the questions of cumulative treatment of beneficiary countries and treatment of developed country content. In this connexion the Working Group should also examine possible solutions to specific problems of the least developed among the developing countries. To avoid any delays and to facilitate the implementation of the generalized system of preferences, the Group's conclusions including agreed texts on rules of origin should be remitted directly both to the prospective preference-giving countries and prospective beneficiaries to faciliate appropriate domestic action. The secretariat of UNCTAD should be invited to compile and distribute to Governments of member States an integrated text on rules of origin that will be applied by the preference-giving countries for the purpose of the generalized system of preferences.

VIII. Institutional Arrangements

1. The Special Committee on Preferences agrees that there should be appropriate machinery within UNCTAD to deal with the questions relating to the implementation of Conference resolution 21 (II) and bearing in mind Conference resolution 24 (II). The [appropriate UNCTAD body] should have the following terms of reference:

(a) It will review:

(i) The effects of the generalized system of preferences on exports and export earnings, industrialization and the rates of economic growth of the beneficiary countries including the least developed among the developing countries and in so doing will consider *inter alia* questions related to product coverage, exception lists, depths of cut, working of safeguard mechanisms (including ceilings and escape clauses) and rules of origin;

(ii) The effects of the generalized system of preferences on the process of industrialization as well as on the volume of exports and export earnings of the least developed among the developing countries, and review and study the special measures in favour of those countries within the generalized system as provided for in Conference resolution 21 (II);

(iii) Especially the effects on the export earnings of developing countries from the sharing of their existing tariff advantages with the rest of the developing countries as a result of the generalized system of preferences, in particular in order to avoid that these countries might be adversely affected;

(iv) Complementary efforts made by developing countries to utilize as fully as possible the benefits from the potential trade advantages created by the grant of special tariff treatment;

(v) Other problems related to the operation of the system;

(b) It will review questions related to measures taken by the socialist countries of Eastern Europe with a view to contributing to the attainment of the objectives of Conference resolution 21 (II);

(c) The above-mentioned functions would appropriately be carried out by means of:

(i) An annual review and analysis of the functioning of the system;

(ii) A triennial review to assess the benefits of the system for the beneficiary countries and the possibilities of improvement of the system and of its operation;

(iii) A comprehensive review towards the end of the initial period of the system, to determine, in the light of the objectives of Conference resolution 21 (II), whether the preferential system should be continued beyond that period.

2. All these periodic reviews would also provide opportunity for multilateral or bilateral consultations between preference-giving countries and beneficiary countries on the system as initially applied, on the modalities of its application and on subsequent changes. These reviews will provide opportunity for consultations between developed market-economy countries and developing countries with respect to possible improvements in the system and between the socialist countries of Eastern Europe and the developing countries with a view to the early and effective implementation of measures by the former, as set forth in their joint declaration, designed to contribute to the attainment of the objectives of Conference resolution 21 (II).

3. The Special Committee on Preferences considers that there may also be a need for consultations of an *ad hoc* character on specific aspects of the system that require urgent consideration. Such consultations could be arranged in agreement with interested Governments of member States and with the assistance when desired of the Secretary-General of UNCTAD.

IX. Legal Status

1. The Special Committee recognizes that no country intends to invoke its rights to most-favoured-nation treatment with a view to obtaining, in whole or in part, the preferential treatment granted to developing countries in accordance with Conference resolution 21 (II) and that the contracting parties to the General Agreement on Tariffs and Trade intend to seek the required waiver or waivers as soon as possible.

2. The Special Committee takes note of the statement made by the preference-giving countries that the legal status of the tariff preferences to be accorded to the beneficiary countries by each preference-giving country individually will be governed by the following considerations:

(a) The tariff preferences are temporary in nature;

(b) Their grant does not constitute a binding commitment and, in particular, it does not in any way prevent:

(i) their subsequent withdrawal in whole or in part; or

(ii) the subsequent reduction of tariffs on a most-favoured nation basis, whether unilaterally or following international tariff negotiations;

(c) Their grant is conditional upon the necessary waiver or waivers in respect of existing international obligations, in particular in the General Agreement on Tariffs and Trade.

7. REVIEW OF SCHEMES OF GENERALIZED PREFERENCES

In agreeing to the generalized system of preferences (GSP) outlined by the Special Committee in UNCTAD, the prospective preference-giving countries indicated that they would put into effect as early as possible a scheme of preferential treatment. In 1971 the Contracting Parties of GATT agreed to waive the m.f.n. (most favored nation) nondiscrimination provisions of Article I of the General Agreement in order to allow developed contracting parties to accord favorable treatment to developing countries.

No single preferential system, however, has yet been agreed upon by all countries. Instead of a common world-wide scheme, a number of different systems have been adopted by individual countries or groups of countries such as the European Economic Community. Several country arrangements have been put into effect, but the United States by the end of 1973 had not yet implemented a preferential agreement, although it had participated in international discussions of special tariff treatment.

STATUS OF IMPLEMENTATION OF THE SCHEMES *

The following developed market economy countries implemented their respective schemes of generalized preferences between 1 July 1971 and 1 April 1972: Austria, EEC (Belgium, Luxembourg, the Federal Republic of Germany, France, Italy, and the Netherlands), Ireland, Japan, New Zealand, the Nordic countries (Denmark, Finland, Norway and Sweden), Switzerland and the United Kingdom. Canada and the United States of America take part as preference-giving countries, but have not yet implemented their schemes. In view of the importance of these two markets for developing countries, the early implementation of their respective schemes would contribute significantly to the achievement of the objectives of the GSP.

Among the socialist countries of Eastern Europe having a customs tariff, the following also implemented their respective schemes of generalized preferences early in 1972: Bulgaria, Czechoslovakia and Hungary. The USSR has been granting preferential treatment to developing countries

---

* UNCTAD, *General Report on the Implementation of the Generalized System of Preferences*, TD/B/C.3/9, 9 March 1973, pp. 2, 4–5, 7, 11–14.

since 1965. Poland, which does not have a customs tariff, has introduced special measures of a preferential nature designed to expand imports from developing countries. Special measures of this kind have also been taken by Bulgaria, Czechoslovakia and the USSR, in accordance with the joint declaration made by those countries and Hungary and Poland at the second part of the fourth session of the Special Committee on Preferences.

Australia has been applying a system of tariff preferences for developing countries since 1966 on selected manufactures and semi-manufactures and handicraft products. . . .

Product Coverage

In general, the schemes cover only selected agricultural and fishery products. . . . [I]mports of these products under generalized preferences account for only a minor share of the total dutiable imports of agricultural and fishery products from the beneficiaries by preference-giving market economy countries. The precise product coverage also varies from one scheme to another. Most of the agricultural products of current export interest to a large number of developing countries are excluded from the schemes, and their inclusion would substantially increase the immediate benefits accruing to the developing countries, in particular to the least developed among them.

In general, the schemes all cover manufactures and semi-manufactures in BTN chapters 25–99, with the notable exceptions of textiles, leather and petroleum products. They also cover all primary commodities in BTN chapters 25–99, except that the scheme of New Zealand extends such treatment only to selected primary commodities and that of EEC excludes all primary commodities, as well as base metals up to the stage of ingots. While the number of products in BTN chapters 25–99 in the various schemes for which preferential treatment is not accorded is relatively small, the trade involved is substantial, averaging 62 per cent of 1970 preference-giving countries' imports of all such dutiable products from the beneficiaries. . . . Furthermore, they are products which are often subject to high tariff and non-tariff barriers. Since the products involved are of major export interest to the developing countries, the importance of extending preferential treatment to these products cannot be over-emphasized.

Depth of Tariff Cut

With regard to agricultural products in BTN chapters 1–24, Finland, Norway and Sweden apply duty-free treatment to products covered by their respective schemes. The United Kingdom accords similar treatment, except for a few items. The other preference-giving countries, namely Austria, Denmark, EEC, Japan, New Zealand and Switzerland, apply various degrees of tariff cuts.

In view of the generally high tariff protection accorded agricultural products, the preferential tariff margins are significant on most products for which GSP duty-free treatment applies. However, in the case of EEC, the largest import market, the margins amount to only about 4 percentage points.

With regard to products in BTN chapters 25–99 covered by their respective schemes, EEC, Denmark, Finland, Norway, Sweden and the United Kingdom apply duty-free treatment. So does Japan, except for certain products on which a 50 per cent reduction of the mfn rate is applied. Austria and Switzerland apply a linear 30 per cent reduction of the mfn duties, Ireland a reduction of one-third, and New Zealand varying rates of reduction, depending on the product. Owing to the progressive increase in the rate of mfn duty as the degree of processing of products in BTN chapters 25–99 increases, the preferential margins are relatively high on finished goods covered by the schemes and are smaller on semi-manufactures and raw materials. In the case of preference-giving countries providing for preferential duty-free entry, the margins correspond to the mfn rates of duty.

Safeguard Measures

All schemes of preferences provide for safeguard mechanisms so as to retain some degree of control by preference-giving countries over the trade which might be generated by the new tariff advantages. Certain guiding principles in applying these safeguards are set out in section III of the Agreed Conclusions of the Special Committee on Preferences.

The safeguard provisions of the schemes applied by developed market economy countries can be classified into two broad categories: *a priori* limitations and the application of escape clauses. EEC and Japan apply an *a priori* limitation formula with respect to products in BTN chapters 25–99. The escape clause is applied by the other preference-giving countries with respect to all preferential imports and by EEC and Japan with respect to products in BTN chapters 1–24. . . .

Eligibility for Preferential Treatment

To qualify for preferential treatment goods must satisfy the direct consignment rule and comply with the origin criteria specified by the importing preference-giving country.

In general, goods are considered to have originated in a preference-receiving country if they have been produced in that country either wholly or by substantial transformation from materials and/or components imported or of undetermined origin.

All preference-giving market economy countries which have implemented their schemes, except New Zealand, base their origin requirements on the process criterion. In this case the transformation must be such as to lead to the exported goods being classified under a BTN heading other than that relating to any of the imported materials and/or components used in production. In addition, special rules have been prescribed for certain classes of goods in lists of qualifying and non-qualifying processes. These lists of processes, and differences among them in the various schemes, have been analysed in the comparative study mentioned above. . . .

General Trade Flows

The periods in which the schemes implemented so far have been in operation are too short to draw many conclusions about the benefits actually accruing to the developing countries. However, some idea of the probable benefits can be obtained through a consideration of the trade in 1970 which would have been covered by the various schemes, had they been in operation in that year.

These 1970 trade flows include all those preference-giving market economy countries which have implemented their schemes and for which computer-tape data were available to the UNCTAD secretariat in sufficient detail. For these countries combined, almost two-thirds ($15 billion out of $24 billion) of imports from the beneficiaries were admitted free of duty under mfn tariff treatment. Of the remaining $9 billion, imports of agricultural and fishery products account for 43 per cent ($3.9 billion); with minor exceptions (about $200 million) these products are not included in the schemes. There remained only $5.1 billion, or 21 per cent of total imports from the beneficiaries, of dutiable industrial products, including raw materials (BTN chapters 25–99).

Even though in principle all of these industrial products qualify for preferential treatment under the existing schemes, there are a certain number of exceptions. For example, EEC excludes all industrial raw materials accounting for just over one-third of their dutiable imports of products (in BTN chapters 25–99) from the beneficiaries. The other preference-giving countries, with the sole exception of Denmark, exclude various items (mainly petroleum, textile and leather goods). For Japan, EEC and the United Kingdom such exclusions accounted in 1970 for 78 per cent, 38 per cent, and 11 per cent respectively of their dutiable products (BTN chapters 25–99) imported from the beneficiaries. Of the remaining preference-giving market economy countries only in Sweden is a substantial share (70 per cent in 1970) of dutiable imports of such products from beneficiaries excluded.

These imports excluded from preferential treatment can be summarized as follows:

	Imports from beneficiaries ($ billion)	*Share of total (per cent)*
All products	24.0	100
less Duty-free under mfn	15.0	63
less Dutiable agricultural and fishery products not covered by the schemes	3.7	15
less Dutiable industrial products not covered by the schemes	3.2	13
equals Products covered by the schemes	2.1	9

Thus, in the final analysis only $2.1 billion of imports by the preference-giving countries from the beneficiaries, or roughly one-fourth of their total dutiable imports from the beneficiaries, would have qualified for generalized preferences if the schemes had been in operation in 1970.

The operation and effects of generalized preferences granted by the EEC are reviewed in greater detail in the following.

THE EEC'S SCHEME *

The EEC, which lent support to the idea of preferences in favour of developing countries from the start, was the first among preference-giving countries to implement a scheme with effect from 1 July 1971. The scheme is valid for a ten-year period and is administered through Community regulations and decisions on an annual basis. Preferential treatment was initially valid until the end of 1971 and was extended, with certain modifications, to the end of 1972.

It is useful to recall the essential elements of this scheme. Duty-free treatment applies to industrial manufactures and semi-manufactures in chapters 25–99 of the Brussels Tariff Nomenclature (BTN). Industrial raw materials and metals up to the stage of ingot within these chapters are excluded from such a treatment. However, imports of products covered by the scheme are subject to a *priori* limitations in the form of ceilings or tariff quotas.

Preferential treatment is also applied to selected processed and semi-processed agricultural products within BTN chapters 1 to 24. The reduction of duties on these products amounts to about 4 percentage points of the most-favoured-nation (mfn) rates. Preferential imports of these products are not subject to a *priori* limitation but to the normal type of safeguard in the form of an escape clause.

These preferences are granted to developing countries members of the group of "77" as well as to the overseas territories of countries members of the EEC and of third countries. However, with respect to cotton textiles, preferential treatment is subject to certain conditions. Furthermore, dependent countries and territories do not enjoy preferential treatment with respect to textiles and footwear. Beneficiaries under the scheme also include those to which the Community grants preferences under other tariff régimes. Since these special preferences bestow greater benefits, the countries concerned have not been taken into account in this study of the trade implications of the scheme.

In view of the recent date of the scheme and of the time-lag which occurs before the relevant trade statistics become available, it is not possible to attempt to give a precise evaluation of the effects of the scheme on imports

* UNCTAD Secretariat, *Operation and Effects of Generalized Preferences Granted by the European Economic Community*, TD/B/C.5/3, 11 January 1973, pp. 1–7.

from beneficiaries. However, an indication of the trade coverage of the EEC scheme was derived from the detailed information available concerning the Community's imports from actual beneficiaries in 1970.

Total EEC imports from actual beneficiaries in that year amounted to $12.3 billion, of which $8.6 billion or 70 per cent of the total were admitted duty-free under mfn treatment. The remaining $3.7 billion of imports were dutiable. Of these dutiable imports, some $871 million, or 23 per cent, would have been covered by the scheme had it been in effect in 1970. Of the total imports of dutiable agricultural products in BTN chapters 1–24, amounting to $2.4 billion, some $44 million would have been covered by the scheme. Hence, the scheme would have benefited less than 2 per cent of total imports of agricultural products, which constitute two-thirds of EEC dutiable imports from actual beneficiaries. Furthermore, of the total dutiable imports of products in BTN chapters 25–99 amounting to $1.3 billion, some $827 million, or 64 per cent of the total, would have been covered by the scheme. The remaining $500 million of dutiable imports consist of industrial raw materials excluded from generalized preferences, cotton textiles in respect of which all but seven developing countries did not receive preferential treatment in 1971 and 1972, and textiles and footwear in respect of which overseas territories do not enjoy preferential treatment.

Since the *a priori* limitations have a determining effect on imports of products covered by the scheme, much of the analysis in this study deals with the implications of these limitations for the prospects for expanded trade.

The preferential tariffs granted by the Community under such a system are expected to provide incentives for importers in the EEC to turn increasingly to the developing countries as sources of supplies. The incentives for such switching continue to operate so long as the tariff preferences are applied to expanded imports. This last point is especially relevant in that the EEC scheme places *a priori* limitations on preferential imports of manufactures and semi-manufactures. Imports in excess of these limitations face mfn duties and, thus, the tariff preferences disappear, as do the incentives to switch sources of imports.

In administering its system of *a priori* limitations the EEC has designated products as either sensitive or non-sensitive, depending upon the expected impact of preferential imports on the domestic market. The non-sensitive products are subject to *a priori* limitations in the form of Community ceilings applied product by product. Since preferential imports of these products are not expected seriously to disrupt the domestic markets, preferential trade is generally not monitored closely. There is, however, a set of products within this category (designated as semi-sensitive) which have been chosen for special surveillance. So far as these products are concerned preferential imports are unlikely to exceed the ceilings in total. Moreover, the product by product administration means that any unutilized portion of the ceiling for one product will not be transferred to another and, consequently, it is expected that preferential trade will amount to something less than the aggregated value of the ceilings. It is, however, possible that preferential imports for individual semisensitive products may exceed the ceiling.

In addition to imposing the ceiling limitations, the EEC scheme provides that no single beneficiary will qualify for preferential treatment as regards trade in excess of 50 per cent of the ceiling for any product. The reason for this "maximum amount" limitation is the desire to reserve a part of the ceiling figure applicable to any one product for the less competitive developing countries. However, the effect of this provision in 1971 and 1972 often was simply to limit preferential treatment to EEC imports from major suppliers, little benefit accruing to the minor or less competitive beneficiary countries. As a consequence, preferential trade, which is already limited to something less than the aggregated value of the ceilings, is further reduced.

The products designated as "sensitive" are subject to *a priori* limitations in the form of Community tariff quotas and also to maximum amount limitations. In addition, these sensitive products are subject to a system of allocation under which the Community's tariff quota is subdivided among the member States according to an "arbitrary" fixed formula which bears little relationship to the pattern of EEC imports from the developing countries. Since there is no reserve quota, or other means of re-allocating the unutilized portion of the quotas of individual member States, preferential trade is almost certainly constrained to something less than the value of the Community tariff quota for each product. Thus, the lack of a reserve quota will lead to an under-utilization of the tariff quotas provided under the scheme.

In order to gain some insight into the impact of these various limitations on preferential trade, a product by product examination of trade flows covered by the scheme was conducted. This examination showed that less than one-third of the beneficiaries' trade in sensitive products with the EEC was likely to receive preferential treatment under the scheme. Equally important, the preferential trade fell short of the aggregated value of the tariff quotas by over 50 per cent. The picture for semi-sensitive products differed slightly, as 60 per cent of actual trade received preferential treatment under the scheme. However, trade to the value of over $28 million received mfn treatment even though $60 million of the value of the ceilings went unutilized. If the trade in all products covered by the system of *a priori* limitations (sensitive, semi-sensitive and strictly non-sensitive) is taken together, it is seen that only $430 million of roughly $800 million (54 per cent) of the trade in 1970 would have qualified for preferential treatment had the scheme been in operation in that year. Since the trade of actual beneficiaries with the EEC in these products has been growing at a rate of 20 per cent annually, it is expected that the share of their trade which will have received preferential treatment in 1972 will be found to be noticeably smaller than the 54 per cent indicated above.

The analysis indicates that the *a priori* limitations as presently applied are inadequate to cover the existing trade flows, let alone to provide for an expansion of the developing countries' trade under preferential treatment.

Moreover, the additional restrictions on preferential trade (product by product administration of the ceilings and tariff quotas, maximum amount limitations and the allocation provision for sensitive products) have had the result that much less trade is receiving GSP treatment than was provided for under the scheme. The analysis of the 1972 scheme also demonstrates that the supplementary amount provision for increasing the ceilings or tariff quotas is inadequate to provide for an expansion of the trade of beneficiaries.

The above examination assumes that all 1970 trade flows under the scheme meet the requirements of the rules of origin. Early evidence indicates, however, that the rules of origin will disqualify some trade from preferential treatment under the scheme. Unfortunately, there appears to be no reliable method of quantifying this excluded trade. What can be mentioned, though, is that the countries most likely to be adversely affected by the origin requirements are the developing countries which depend upon imported components in order to produce the types of manufactured and semi-manufactured products that qualify for preferential treatment.

The analysis also makes an assessment of the benefits which accrue to the developing countries. The expected increase in demand for developing countries' exports should stimulate the creation of new export capacity either through the mobilization of domestic resources or of foreign capital, thus leading to the accomplishment of the threefold GSP objectives mentioned above. However, the limitations placed on preferential trade under the EEC scheme present serious impediments to the achievement of these objectives. In the first place, more than half of the trade of the beneficiaries would be affected by the reimposition of the Common Customs Tariff (CCT) at some time during the year and, in the majority of cases, before the preceding year's level of trade has been reached. The re-establishment of the CCT eliminates the incentives created by the tariff preference for the remainder of the year. Consequently, as regards the products affected, importers will have no incentive to expand their rate of importation substantially beyond the rate prevailing in the previous year. Such an expansion requires that the preferential tariffs apply at the margin, i.e., for expanded trade.

A second problem created by the system of *a priori* limitations arises because in many cases the EEC importers do not know when the CCT will be reimposed and, therefore, cannot know in advance whether or not their imports will qualify for preferential treatment. This uncertainty is further aggravated in that EEC importers often do not know if the contracted goods satisfy the requirements specified in the Rules of Origin. Because of this uncertainty and because imports are contracted much in advance of the actual receipt of the goods, many EEC importers will probably be unwilling to contract with exporters in beneficiary countries at prices which reflect preferential tariff rates. The reason is the possibility that the tariff status of the goods might change from preferred to mfn during the time-lag between the date of the contract and the actual receipt of the goods. On the other hand, the tariff preference does provide implicit incentives, as often as preferential treatment is received. In such cases, the EEC importer stands to earn a wind-fall profit. Since the possibility of such a profit only exists when goods originate in a beneficiary country, importers are likely to take advantage of every opportunity to switch from non-beneficiary countries to beneficiary countries as the source of their imports at mfn prices. Such implicit benefits are literally impossible to quantify but are certain to bring some favourable effects to the beneficiary countries. But it is not unlikely that a very considerable share if not the bulk of the tariff revenues foregone by the EEC will accrue to EEC importers.

The final problem involves the stimulus of preferential tariff treatment for the expansion of export capacity. Since preferential treatment under the GSP affects primarily manufactured and semi-manufactured products, an increase in exports generally requires the creation of new productive capacity, including the expansion of existing capacity. Such increases further require the mobilization and/or re-allocation of domestic capital resources or of foreign capital. These investment decisions generally involve substantial sums of money which must be committed over a period of time, whereas profits accrue only after a certain time-lag. Consequently, any investment decisions concerning products covered by the scheme must take into account the restrictions placed on preferential trade and, in all probability, will discount preferential treatment for sensitive and most semi-sensitive products. Generally, it might be expected that investment decisions regarding the strictly non-sensitive products could be influenced by the preference accorded under the scheme. However, since thirty strictly non-sensitive products under the 1971 scheme were re-designated as sensitive or semi-sensitive under the 1972 scheme, investors face a definite degree of uncertainty even for non-sensitive products, especially because investment decisions are long-run decisions and do not succeed or fail on the basis of special tariff treatment during one or two years. This does not mean that investors will shy away from investing in products covered by the scheme. Rather, the conclusion is that the preferential treatment will largely be ignored when such investment decisions are under consideration.

There is, however, one very important exception to this expectation; namely, the case of multinational corporations which import manufactured or semi-manufactured products from their own plants in beneficiary countries into the EEC. The multinational corporation is both the exporter and the importer. Since it performs the importer function, it is in a perfect position to receive the tariff revenues forgone by the EEC member States as a result of the preference. The multinational corporations, which currently assemble many manufactured products in the developing countries, can obtain preferential treatment under the scheme provided that they enhance the degree of processing sufficiently to make the assembled products eligible for treatment as goods originating in a beneficiary country. Consequently, these corporations have an incentive to invest in production capacity in the beneficiary countries which will produce enough of the assembled components in order that the final exported product qualifies for preferential tariff treatment. The division of the corporation which is located in EEC member countries thereby will save the mfn duty previously paid on these imports. Hence there is a second implicit benefit; a benefit which cannot be quantified but is almost certain to accrue to the beneficiary countries. Admittedly, this situation requires further evaluation in its various aspects.

From the above analysis it appears therefore that the preferential advantages under the EEC scheme in its present form are rather limited and are not likely to provide much scope for the fulfilment of its declared objectives. In drawing up the preferential arrangements, however, the preference-giving countries had agreed that "efforts for further improvements of the GSP should be pursued in a dynamic context in the light of Conference resolution 21 (II)." Thus the EEC, like the other preference-giving countries, was fully aware of the limitations of the scheme which was to be initially applied and had recognized the need for improvement in the light of experience.

It would appear that the operation of the scheme, although the period has been short, convinced the Community of the necessity for substantial efforts for its improvement. This resolve was fully reflected in the Summit meeting held in Paris in October 1972 at which the Heads of State or of Government of the countries of the enlarged Community expressed the conviction that the Community must respond even more than in the past to the expectations of all developing countries. More specifically they invited the Institutions of the Community and member States to adopt progressively an overall policy comprising, *inter alia,* "the improvement of generalized preferences with the aim of achieving a steady increase in imports of manufactures from the developing countries. In this connexion the Community Institutions will study from the beginning of 1973 the conditions which will permit the achievement of a substantial growth target."

It should be added that on the same occasion the President of the Commission of the European Communities urged the summit to take a decision, *inter alia,* on "improvement of the scheme of generalized preferences with the aim of achieving an annual increase of about 15 per cent in the Community's imports of manufactures from the developing countries."

To the extent that this study can contribute to the efforts of the Community to improve its scheme, the following measures which need to be taken in this respect may be spelt out:

i. Extension of product coverage to processed and semi-processed agricultural products with deeper tariff cuts and, in so far as full duty-free treatment is not accorded, elimination of the element of protection on processing;

ii. Extension of coverage of products in BTN chapters 25–99 to include dutiable industrial raw materials and base metals;

iii. Liberal application of the system of *a priori* limitations and revision of the method of calculating ceilings and tariff quotas. First, for the calculation of ceilings or tariff quotas, products should be defined at a high level of aggregation, and at least, at the level of four-digit BTN tariff heading. Secondly, the reference year for the calculation of the basic amount needs to be much closer to the year to which the ceiling or tariff quota applies. Thirdly, the supplementary amount should be so computed as to result in a ceiling or tariff quota that is higher than current imports for each product. Fourthly, where the ceilings or tariff quotas are expressed in value terms account needs to be taken of the increase in import prices which occurred between the reference year(s) chosen for calculation of the ceilings or tariff quotas and the year of operation of the scheme. Fifthly, the maximum amount limitation would need to be revised to avoid non-utilization of the ceiling figure or the tariff quota.

iv. Liberalization of the system of tariff quotas and of the procedures for its administration. In this connexion, the tariff quota should be so administered as to avoid uncertainty regarding the entitlement to preferential treatment on the part of both importer and exporter. Moreover, in the allocation of the tariff quotas among member States, the establishment of a reserve quota would seem necessary to avoid sterilization of part of the tariff quota.

In the Trade Reform Bill before Congress in 1974, the administration requested authority to grant generalized tariff preferences to the developing countries. The administration's proposal provided for duty-free entry of articles, principally manufactured products, designated by the President. Beneficiary countries would be determined by the President following criteria established in the new trade legislation. The amount of preferential treatment would be determined by a "competitive formula" which would allow special tariff treatment up to the point when a developing country becomes so competitive that it is supplying 50 per cent of the total value of United States imports of an article or $25 million worth of that article. Relevant sections from this bill, as introduced in the House of Representatives follow.

TITLE VI—GENERALIZED SYSTEM OF PREFERENCES *

Sec. 601. Purposes.—The purpose of this title is to promote the general welfare, foreign policy and security of the United States by enabling the United States to participate with other developed countries in granting generalized tariff preferences to exports of manufactured and semimanufactured products and of selected other products from developing countries.

* H.R. 6767, 93rd Congress, 1st Session (April 10, 1973).

The Congress finds that the welfare and security of the United States are enhanced by efforts to further the economic development of the developing countries, and that such development may be assisted by providing increased access to markets in the developed countries, including the United States, for exports from developing countries.

Sec. 602. Authority To Extend Preferences.—Notwithstanding the provisions of section 407 of this Act, the President may designate any article as an eligible article, may provide duty-free treatment for any eligible article from any beneficiary developing country designated under section 604, and may modify or supplement any such action consistent with the provisions of this title. In taking any such action, the President shall have due regard for—

1. the purpose of this title;
2. the anticipated impact of such action on United States producers of like or directly competitive products; and
3. the extent to which other major developed countries are undertaking a comparable effort to assist beneficiary developing countries by granting preferences with respect to imports of products of such countries.

Sec. 604. Beneficiary Developing Country.—(a) Subject to the provisions of subsection (b), the President may designate any country a beneficiary developing country, taking into account—

1. the purpose of this title;
2. any expression by such country of its desire to be so designated;
3. the level of economic development of such country, including its per capita gross national product, the living standards of its inhabitants, and any other economic factors which he deems appropriate;
4. whether or not the other major developed countries are extending generalized preferential tariff treatment to such country; and
5. whether or not such country has nationalized, expropriated, or seized ownership or control of property owned by a United States citizen, or any corporation, partnership, or association not less than 50 per centum beneficially owned by citizens of the United States without provision for the payment of prompt, adequate, and effective compensation.

(b) The President shall not designate any country a beneficiary developing country—

1. the products of which are not receiving most-favored-nation treatment by reason of general headnote 3(e) to the Tariff Schedules of the United States; or
2. which accords preferential treatment to the products of a developed country other than the United States, unless the President has received assurances satisfactory to him that such preferential treatment will be eliminated before January 1, 1976.

Sec. 605. Limitations on Preferential Treatment.—(a) The President may modify, withdraw, suspend, or limit the application of the preferential treatment accorded under section 602 with respect to any article or with respect to any country: *Provided,* That no rate of duty shall be established in respect of any article pursuant to this section other than the rate which would apply in the absence of this title. In taking any such action, the President shall consider the factors set forth in sections 602 and 604 (a) of this title.

(b) The President shall withdraw or suspend the designation of a country as a beneficiary developing country if, subsequent to such designation—

1. the products of such country are excluded from the benefit of most-favored-nation treatment by reason of general headnote 3(e) to the Tariff Schedules of the United States; or

2. he determines that such country has not eliminated or will not eliminate preferential treatment accorded by it to the products of a developed country other than the United States before January 1, 1976.

(c) Whenever the President determines that a country has supplied 50 per centum by value of the total imports of an eligible article into the United States, or has supplied a quantity of such article to the United States having a value of more than $25,000,000, on an annual basis over a representative period, that country shall not be considered a beneficiary developing country in respect of such article, unless the President determines that it is in the national interest to designate, or to continue the designation of such country as a beneficiary developing country in respect of such article. . . .

Sec. 607. Effective Period of Preferences.—No preferential treatment under this title shall remain in effect for a period in excess of ten years after the effective date of the grant of such preferential treatment or after December 31, 1984, whichever is the earlier.

8. EFFICACY OF PREFERENCES

The foregoing section included some critical evaluation of the limitations of preferential schemes in practice. The potential efficacy of preferential treatment, however, should be examined more generally. Preferences will be more effective in expanding an LDC's exports to the extent that a larger portion of the LDC's export products come within the scope of the GSP, the margin of preferential treatment is greater, the ceiling limitations in the importing countries are less restrictive, and the longer is the period of special treatment. The developing economy will also have to be adept in reforming policies to take advantage of the opportunities offered by the GSP.

Until now, LDC exports have been mainly agricultural or duty-free under most-favored-nation treatment—and hence outside the scope of GSP treatment on dutiable manufactures and semi-manufactures. The future effect can be greater if the preference-granting countries do not exclude products of export-interest to the LDCs, and if the LDCs reorient their trade pattern toward more exports on which preferences are granted. The expansion of GSP trade would become especially significant if it included processed agricultural products, textiles subject to the Long-Term Cotton Arrangement, and other manufactures and semi-manufactures currently subject to quantitative restrictions in developed countries. The preferences will also be more effective, the higher are the nonpreferential tariffs on competing imports from other developed countries.

If preferential treatment is really to become of consequence, the preference-granting countries will undoubtedly have to undertake an adjustment assistance program to deal with the labor-displacement from imports, instead of invoking ceiling limitations, or subjecting imports to the m.f.n. duties beyond certain quotas. In order that an escape clause not be invoked so readily as to nullify the value of a preferential scheme, the UNCTAD secretariat has presented the following suggestions for developing economic criteria for an escape action: [16]

> a. It must be recognized that one of the main objectives of the extension of preferences is to facilitate imports from developing countries. The mere fact that this is realized provides no justification for withdrawing or restricting the preferences. The escape-clause action should relate solely to eventual injury from actual, rather than hypothetical, imports. The impact of imports can only be judged fairly after they have occurred, and their competitive effect has been demonstrated.
>
> b. If domestic producers are shown to be in difficulty, it must be demonstrated that the operative cause lies in the excessive preferred imports themselves and not in other factors, such as non-preferred imports, lagging domestic technology, rigidity of marketing and competitive patterns in the domestic industry, or other factors for which the preferred imports are not responsible.
>
> c. The seriousness of injury should not be judged by artificial segregation of products unrelated to the practical organization of an industry. To lose sales of one product, while business is booming in other products, hardly presents a sit-

16. UNCTAD, *Study on Criteria for Invoking the Escape Clause in a General System of Preferences for Exports of Manufactures and Semi-Manufactures from Developing Countries*, TD/19/Supp. 1 (11 January 1968), pp. 76–77.

uation in which a domestic producer can be considered to be suffering injury.

d. In a world economy becoming more and more interrelated, developed countries should not insist on retaining non-competitive and inefficient industries. Countries must recognize that there is an economic point at which it is not worth preserving at any cost domestic production of this kind. Where this is the case, it should be recognized that the difficulties encountered are attributable to the law of comparative advantage, rather than to the generous admission of imports.

e. International consultation, including where feasible international approval, should be instituted to give effective safeguard against erosion of acquired preferences by unjustifiable resort to escape-clause actions. This procedure would equally safeguard the interests of the importing and exporting countries, and would help overcome the lack or imperfect definition of quantifiable criteria for resort to escape actions. Finally, it would help maintain an equitable distribution among the developed countries of increased import opportunities to their markets as a result of preferences.

f. As far as the national procedure is concerned for applying the escape clause, the open investigation method, including a public hearing, could also contribute to the stability of concessions granted under a general system of preferences, if under such procedure the interests of developing countries were taken into account on an equal footing with those of domestic producers.

g. Where it is determined that escape action is justifiable, there remains the formulation of a proper measure of relief. Here, international good faith dictates balancing the economic interests of domestic producers against the economic interests of producers in developing countries who may have instituted or expanded production in reliance upon preferential access to the particular market. Escape-clause relief should not require the complete withdrawal of a preference. An intermediate rate of duty, or a tariff quota, might suffice to give fair protection to the domestic producers and still provide a reasonable opportunity to the foreign suppliers who counted on the preference.

h. The relief afforded by an escape clause to domestic producers should be temporary and should not be designed to create a permanent exception to the tariff preferences, but rather to afford a breathing spell for these producers, to enable them to carry out adjustment measures, with or without governmental assistance, and to make them better able to

cope with import competition. When the domestic producers do not take effective action to cope with foreign competition promptly, the escape-clause relief should be withdrawn. The best method of insuring such a domestic
response is to afford escape-clause relief only for a limited
fixed period, and to make it clear that extensions would only
be granted for progressively shorter periods which would finally taper-off, based on a showing of major progress toward
making relief unnecessary.

i. Developed countries should consider, both at the national and international level, adjustment assistance measures to help domestic industries which experience difficulties because of increased imports from developing countries
resulting from the grant of preferences to move out of such
production lines. To the extent that this assistance is offered
to mitigate the eventual adverse effects of safeguard actions
on exports of developing countries, it would greatly ease the
fears that the existence of an escape clause endangers the
substance of tariff preferences.

If preference-granting countries will have to do more to
make preferences more effective, so too will the developing
countries have to adopt industrial policy and planning measures specifically designed to increase output with an export
potential. The high tariffs and quantitative restrictions on imports have raised the cost of export production, and overvalued
exchange rates have hindered export expansion. To take advantage of the opportunities presented by preferences, the
LDCs may have to pursue domestic policies of disinflation,
devaluation, or liberalization of import duties when these are
implicitly taxing exports. The government may also have to
support the early operations of new exporting firms with marketing assistance, export credits, and other measures designed
to overcome the exporter's risk aversion.

Relative to the problem of efficacy are complex questions
of equity that are raised by any preferential scheme. Uniform
preferences might act inequitably in imposing the burden of
subsidizing imports on only a few of the developed countries
and in conferring the benefits of expanding exports on only a
few LDCs. While exports will tend to be concentrated in the
preference-granting countries with the highest duties, these
countries are not necessarily those that have the greatest abil-

ity to pay the subsidy entailed in granting preferences. To overcome the inequality in the impact of imports, it would be necessary either to depart from uniform-percentage preferences—thus permitting the higher duty countries to give smaller preference margins—or to allow the higher duty country to impose some type of import quota.

On the burden side, the distributional impact of a preferential arrangement will clearly differ from that under explicit aid. The question of "burden" to the preference-granting countries is, however, in itself ambiguous. Should the aid component of preferences be considered as a "burden"? Is it a burden if preferences result in the replacement of uncompetitive domestic production that was previously protected but is now replaced by cheaper imports? How should the burden be assessed if the imports from the LDC displace imports from another developed country?

On the benefit side, the gains from preferences may accrue only to those few LDCs that already account for the bulk of manufactured exports from developing countries and in those countries that are more readily capable of attaining a competitive cost advantage. If the result of preferences is to be similar to aid, then preferences should not exclude the most competitive industries. If, however, it is to be for the objective of industrialization, then special concessions ought to be offered the least competitive industries. If the benefits of preferences were to be more evenly distributed among the developing countries, it would be necessary to give preferences on selected products to selected countries in order to distinguish among countries and industries according to their relative degree of development and competitive need. But this would open the negotiations on preferences to many political influences and special interests.

Insofar as private foreign investment is likely to be induced by preferences, the question of the distribution of gains and losses among countries should also be related to some of the issues raised in Problem II regarding the role of multinational corporations and private overseas investment. The multinational corporations have great capacity to take advantage of preferences in order to extend their practices of world-wide sourcing, international subcontracting, and decomposing production activities and internationalizing the production of components and intermediate parts. Granted an effective preferential scheme, it might not be too much of an exaggeration to envisage a new international industrial revolution based on the combination of the multinational enterprise, the transfer of technology and high skills to the surplus labor in the LDCs, and the favorable treatment of exports of labor-intensive manufactures from the LDCs.

A test of the extent to which countries will cooperate in improving their preference schemes will be seen in the outcome of the round of comprehensive multilateral trade negotiations that began in 1974 within the framework of GATT. These trade negotiations will be of great importance in determining some answers to the questions that this Problem has raised about the value of preferences.

C. QUESTIONS

1. It has been said that "there is real danger that the type of preference system which the industrialized countries can accept will meet neither the economic nor the political requirements of the situation. . . . The potential for some improvement of the LDCs' export earnings is real; but the danger of an adverse effect on international trade relations is no less real. The challenge confronting the industrialized nations lies in their willingness and ability to make the hard choices necessary for agreement on a system of preferences which will represent an improvement rather than a deterioration of the present situation." [W. Michael Blumenthal, "A World of Preferences," *Foreign Affairs*, April 1970, p. 553.]

a) What would you consider the major characteristics of such a system to be? How does this system compare with the generalized system of preferences adopted by UNCTAD? By the EEC? Japan?

b) What exactly is the "burden" that preferences impose upon the importing country? Is this equivalent to the granting of aid? Has there been excessive concern with the problem of "burden sharing" in devising a preference scheme?

c) Can a preferential scheme be of less value than no

scheme if its implementation is geared to the most protective-minded of the "donor countries" and if there are automatic protective devices?

2. a) What is the purpose of the principle of nondiscrimination—the most-favored-nation principle—in GATT [Article I]?

b) Despite this principle, has the actual course of tariff negotiations meant preferred tariff treatment for the advanced industrial nations?

c) Do you think that the granting of special tariff treatment might so undermine the m.f.n. principle that the risks outweigh the possible advantages for developing countries?

3. a) In a preference scheme, how should the initial list of beneficiary countries be established? Should it then be modified over time?

b) What special provisions, if any, would you recommend be granted to the least developed of the developing countries?

c) What are the arguments for limiting the duration of a preferential system? Is there any reason why an initial period of 10 years' duration is more appropriate than any other time period?

d) What are the special problems created by reverse preferences? Should they be abolished?

e) What are the special problems related to preferences for primary products?

4. Under what conditions would you recommend that an escape clause or "adjustment procedure" device be invoked to limit the impact of preferential imports on producers in developed countries?

5. A major question of a generalized system of preferences is how the benefits and losses will be distributed. What can economic theory contribute to illuminating this question?

6. What are some of the empirical problems involved in attempting to determine the quantitative significance of a preference scheme on the export earnings of a developing country?

7. A "negative" tariff, analogous to a negative income tax, has sometimes been proposed—e.g., a subsidy on imports from LDCs greater than the tariff on these imports. Would this be more effective than preferences, insofar as the subsidy would give preference over local producers as well as over rival exporters from another developed country?

8. Consider the duty-free quota provision of the EEC's preference scheme.

a) If the duty-free quota "bites"—i.e., if actual imports exceed the amount of imports on which there is no tariff—is there any incentive for the developing countries to expand their exports and their investment in exports to the EEC at any rate faster than they would have done if there had been no generalized preferences at all?

b) Are the chief beneficiaries of a duty-free quota likely to be the developing country suppliers or the importers? Why?

9. Even if a uniform preferential scheme can not be negotiated for all nations, would it be useful to try and reach international agreement on at least some common criteria for the individual schemes—such as, the determination of beneficiary countries, or safeguard measures, or duration? On what features of a preference scheme do you think it is most important to secure harmonization?

10. The promotion of labor-intensive processes and component manufacturing in LDCs by multinational enterprises has been called "shallow development" because "the type of labor utilized represents generally the weakest and less organized part of the labor class, thus limiting possibilities for increasing labor returns. . . . [And there is] absence of marketing know-how effects for the host country since the goods traded are within the captive markets of affiliates. Final product promotion is handled abroad by the foreign centers of decision making." [Constantine V. Vaitsos, "Employment Effects of Foreign Direct Investments in Developing Countries," New Delhi Conference on Technology and Employment, March 1973 (mimeographed), pp. 29–30.]

a) Do you agree with this designation of "shallowness" for this type of development?

b) In what ways may export substitution influence the course of a country's development differently from import substitution?

c) How would the contribution of export of manufactures from Jamaica differ from the contribution of a resource-based export such as bauxite?

d) Do you think Jamaica's bargaining power over foreign investment in manufacturing components would be less than it is over foreign investment in bauxite?

11. If import substitution has been oversubsidized in many LDCs, is it also possible to oversubsidize export substitution? Consider whether it is possible for the opportunity cost of capital and other inputs to the host country to exceed the measured value added.

12. The shift in emphasis from import-substitution to export-substitution as the major trade strategy in development requires a parallel policy shift from policy measures applied by the individual LDC to international cooperation. Has there been sufficient international cooperation? If not, what have been the limitations or difficulties?

D. READINGS

Cohen, B. I., and D. G. Sisler, "Exports of Developing Countries in the 1960s," *Review of Economics and Statistics* (November 1971).

Cooper, Richard N., "The European Community's System of Generalized Tariff Preferences," *Journal of Development Studies* (July 1972).

Helleiner, G. K., "Manufactured Exports from Less Developed Countries and Multinational Firms," *Economic Journal* (March 1973).

Hughes, Helen (ed.), *Prospects for Partnership: Industrialization and Trade Policies in the 1970's* (1973).

Johnson, H. G. (ed.), *Trade Strategy for Rich and Poor Nations* (1971).

————, "LDC Investment: The Road Is Paved with Preferences," *Columbia Journal of World Business* (January 1968).

————, "Trade Preferences and Developing Countries," *Lloyds Bank Review* (April 1966).

————, *Economic Policies Toward Less Developed Countries* (1967).

Larry, Hal B., *Imports of Manufactures from Less Developed Countries* (1968).

Leontiades, James, "International Sourcing in the LDCs," *Columbia Journal of World Business* (September 1971).

Macraw, Douglas, "The Future of International Business," *The Economist* (January 22, 1972).

Murray, T., "How Helpful Is the Generalised System of Preferences to Developing Countries?" *Economic Journal* (June 1973).

UNCTAD, *Incentives for Industrial Exports* (1970).

————, *Measures for the Expansion and Diversification of Exports of Manufactures* (12 February 1971).

Wall, David, "Problems with Preferences," *International Affairs* (1970).

————, *The Third World Challenge: Preferences for Development* (1968).

Watanabe, Susumu, "International Subcontracting, Employment and Skill Promotion," *International Labour Review* (May 1972).